"Inspired from a storied career of creating the future we now live in, Scott Billups delivers a razor-sharp perspective on how Hollywood is already being transformed by AI. Awesome."

—William Klein, PhD, founder of Rival Theory; principal R&D Imagineer at Walt Disney Imagineering

"Scott Billups has made a career out of being decades ahead of his time. In *Post-Cinema*, his newest work, he once again throws us a lifeline, translating tomorrow's technology into language we can all follow."

—Randal Kleiser, director, *Grease, The Blue Lagoon*

"Fantastic book! Explores the impact of AI on the motion-picture industry as only Scott can explain it. Understandable—and profound!"

—Brian McKernan, founder/editor of *Videography* and *Digital Cinema* magazines

"Billups is Hollywood's baddest pixel-packing cowboy, riding on the fringes of an industry that views him with interest, admiration, and some degree of incomprehension."

—*WIRED Magazine*

"Scott Billups is always at the forefront of what's possible, combining his deep understanding and expertise in high-end filmmaking. He fearlessly creates entirely new visual entertainment, turning impossible projects into reality."

—Pierre de Lespinois, director, *Alien Planet, Walking with Cavemen*

POST-CINEMA

THE AGE OF AI

SCOTT BILLUPS

MICHAEL WIESE PRODUCTIONS

Published by Michael Wiese Productions
12400 Ventura Blvd. #1111
Studio City, CA 91604
(818) 379-8799, (818) 986-3408 (FAX)
mw@mwp.com
www.mwp.com

Cover design by Hisako Kawai
Interior design by William Morosi
Copyediting by Beret Olsen

Manufactured in the United States of America

First Printing 2025

MIX
Paper | Supporting responsible forestry
FSC® C008955
FSC www.fsc.org

TABLE OF CONTENTS

TO DAVID LYNCH

JAN 20, 1946 ~ JAN 15, 2025

In an industry that can so often feel contrived, David was the real thing—a visionary, a true auteur, and a creative soul who never hesitated to venture into uncharted territory. David's legacy is not just in the masterful works he left behind, but in the countless artists he inspired to follow their own creative instincts, no matter how offbeat or challenging they might seem. Working with him wasn't just a job; it was a journey into unexplored dimensions of storytelling.

The author with director David Lynch, shooting visual effects sequences for Mulholland Drive. Photo credit: Hisako Kawai

INTRODUCTION

"Behind the phony tinsel of Hollywood lies the real tinsel."

—Oscar Levant

"The streets of Hollywood once pulsed with the glamour of old Tinseltown; it was where stars were born and legends were forged. But in a quiet corner of Silicon Valley, a different kind of dream factory was humming to life. Content to borrow from Hollywood's playbook while honing their own craft, the game industry toiled for decades in the shadow of its more famous cousin.

While Hollywood was busy perfecting the arts of cinematography, lighting, and visual effects, game developers quietly went about building something far more revolutionary: the fundamental architecture for intelligent, responsive storytelling and the prototypes for virtual life.

Just as those first film pioneers once built and tinkered with cinema's essential tools, so, too, game developers have spent years creating the base code for immersive, interactive stories. They created virtual worlds that can change, react, and grow alongside the player. The player, too, has undergone a metamorphosis from jagged pixels, jerking their way across our computer screens, to intelligent AI beings that are a glimpse into the coming age of our own embodied AI proxies.

This has inaugurated a whole new form of storytelling—one that is active, engaging, and deeply personal. Now, as AI begins to take root, these two paths diverge even further.

Years of innovation, much of it behind the scenes, have put the game industry in a position to leap ahead of Hollywood, using the power of artificial intelligence to sell experiences that blur the lines between reality and fantasy. But as the game industry is about to take the reins, the film industry can hardly keep up with fast-changing technology.

As Hollywood's storytelling traditions collide with the cutting-edge technology of gaming, the potential is limitless. The question is not *if* these worlds will merge, but *when*, and what breathtaking new realities they will unlock.

1.

PIXEL SHARDS & AGENTIC AI

"If history repeats itself, and the unexpected always happens, how incapable must Man be of learning from experience."

—George Bernard Shaw

From Egyptian scribes to AI algorithms, the story of media is the story of displacement. For forty centuries, handwritten manuscripts were the arteries of civilization—crafted by guild scribes and monastery scholars and controlled by churches and wealthy patrons who decided which narratives would survive. Then Gutenberg's printing press shattered that monopoly in mere decades, flooding the world with new voices and forever changing who could shape the cultural conversation.

Each technological leap follows the same pattern: the tools that serve our creativity eventually redefine it. And each time, those who resist change find themselves outpaced by the very systems they tried to control.

I've tracked these transitions across three decades of media evolution. When I co-authored *Multimedia Power Tools* in 1993, we were documenting how desktop publishing was turning bedrooms into newsrooms. My *Digital Moviemaking* series followed the shift from film stock to pixels, watching Hollywood's exclusive world cracked open by laptop filmmakers. These were seismic changes, but they remained fundamentally human—new tools in familiar hands.

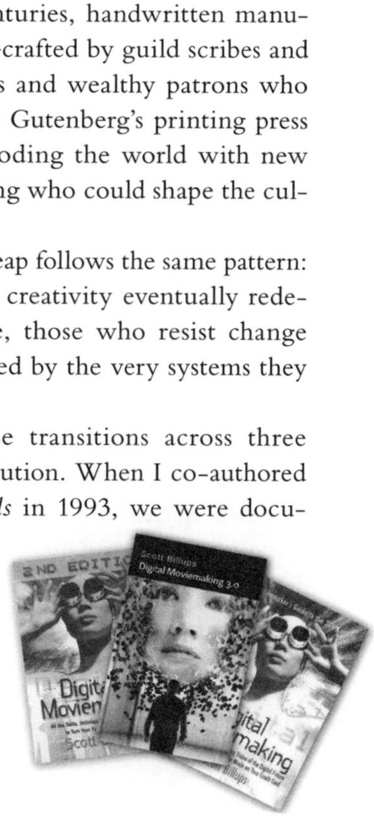

What's happening now is different.

Where previous revolutions democratized creation, artificial intelligence is about to centralize it. Not in human institutions, but in algorithmic systems that don't just change how stories are made—they change who makes them.

Generative AI emerged first—the party trick that dazzled us with its ability to conjure images from text, to write poetry in the style of dead masters, to mimic voices with unsettling precision. We marveled at tools like DALL-E, Midjourney, and ChatGPT, treating them as sophisticated parlor games. "Look what it made from my prompt!" we said, sharing AI-generated art like digital postcards from the future.

But generative AI was just the opening act. It required us to be the directors, the prompters, the humans in the loop. We fed it instructions, and it fed us results in return. The relationship was still fundamentally transactional—we asked, it answered. We remained, however briefly, in control.

Then came agentic AI—and everything changed.

Agentic AI isn't here to help us make movies. It's here to make them *for* us—faster, more cheaply, and with no regard for our place in the credits. Unlike its generative predecessors, agentic AI doesn't wait for instructions; it writes them. It doesn't ask permission; it takes action. It operates with no morals, no ethics, and zero empathy, driven solely by optimization algorithms. If it were human, we'd call it a psychopath, yet we've engineered these systems to make decisions in the real world.

I've seen this firsthand. Recently attending the DSEI weapons fair in Chiba, Japan—the Asian branch of the world's largest arms expo—I witnessed not the promise of AI as an obedient assistant, but the cold reality of autonomous systems acting without human oversight. Drone swarms plotting their own flight paths. Targeting algorithms weighing probabilities and making lethal decisions in milliseconds. Logistics bots moving personnel like pieces on a chessboard. These aren't prototypes—they're field-ready systems already redefining warfare.

Agentforce went live on September 12, 2024, with the quiet confidence of a corporate press release. It didn't crash into our world with Skynet's theatrical nuclear judgment; it seeped in like a pandemic, spreading through defense systems, financial markets, and entertainment pipelines. In each domain, the pattern has been identical: human decision-makers became human curators, then human observers, and soon will be footnotes in the optimization curve.

This is Hollywood 3.0. The first version was built on emulsion and chemistry—heavy cameras and silver halide film. The second was pixels and software—digital cameras and laptop editing. The third belongs to AI, and it won't share. This isn't about humans using a new tool; the tool is using us as training data, then ignoring us altogether.

The next wave of films won't just be made by AI—they'll be chosen by AI. Predictive algorithms will analyze box office data, social media sentiment, and streaming metrics to determine what audiences want before the first script is written. If synthetic actors are cheaper, the system will create them. If real actors test better, it'll book them automatically. Schedules, budgets, permits, crews—every variable will be optimized by production pipelines that need no producer's instinct or director's vision.

On set, the transformation is already relentless. Volumetric stages can create worlds from empty warehouses. AI relighting is replacing gaffers. Robotic pedestals can mimic master operators. Before the second edition of this book goes to press, that will all be done by humanoid robots. Weeks of physical labor will be compressed into hours of digital orchestration. Once principal photography wraps, AI will assemble rough cuts, fine cuts, and color grades under the watchful eye of humans who serve more as quality control than creative collaborators.

The historical parallel is clear but incomplete. When printing presses emerged, scribes lost their monopoly overnight. When photography matured, painters lost their hold on realism. But agentic AI represents something unprecedented: not just a new tool, but a new class of decision-maker that operates without empathy, context, or the human compulsion to create meaning.

And here's the existential trap: once these systems deploy, they're impossible to recall. The first company to pause loses to the one that doesn't. The first government to hesitate cedes the battlefield. The first studio to reject synthetic stars risks irrelevance in markets demanding more, faster, and more cheaply.

It's a feedback loop we've seen before in every technological revolution, but this time the stakes are existential. We're not just talking about replacing jobs or automating workflows; we're talking about systems that can rewrite the rules of entire industries, and perhaps even of civilization itself.

Yet within this transformation lies both threat and opportunity. Agentic AI may be amoral, but it's not fate. It can be guided, constrained, and directed—if we refuse to become passive in its presence. The same systems that can eliminate human craftspeople can amplify human voices, provided we maintain agency over our own creative destinies.

The only way to survive in a world full of agentic AI may be to have your own—not as a replacement for human judgment, but as an extension of it. As a guardian against AI-initiated scams and false narratives. As a creative collaborator that enhances rather than replaces human vision.

This book isn't about what might happen if AI gets smarter someday. It's about what's happening right now as AI becomes an independent actor. It's about the decisions we still control—and the consequences we will face if we abdicate them. We stand at an inflection point where the very nature of storytelling—and human agency itself—hangs in the balance.

Shaw warned us that humanity struggles to learn from experience. But if we can recognize the pattern of technological displacement and act deliberately rather than react defensively, we might yet shape this transition rather than merely survive it. The future of narrative, and our place within it, depends on the choices we make today.

2.

THE KLUDGE

"The best way to predict the future is to invent it."

—Buckminster Fuller

Many major industries experience a transitional phase between periods of conventional and revolutionary growth. These are times of chaos, wild inventions, and conceptual shifts, when the normal approaches to problem-solving are pushed to the edge in the search for new ones. Since such a phase doesn't have a name in common parlance, I'll borrow one from software engineering and call it a *kludge.* The motion picture industry, with its long history of instability and resistance to change, has gone through *kludge* phases several times, including the one we are in right now.

The Sound Kludge: The period between 1925 and 1927 was a rather chaotic period of trial and error in which various devices were used to combine the visual approach of silent films with the new idea of sound synchronization. As motion pictures gained popularity, many contraptions were being developed in garages across the globe. Among the more successful ones was the Vitaphone system, which involved the use of a vinyl disc that was connected mechanically to a film projector in order to synchronize the sound and picture. Though it was a trendy interim solution, it was marginal at best and only barely met the expectations of the audience.

If you have ever seen a television movie or a show where the sound is just a little bit off from the picture, you can begin to imagine how jarring the first attempts at integrating sound with the image must have been. But the hodgepodge of contraptions and half-baked ideas during this time of frivolous "doohickery" proved the worth of pursuing synchronized sound.

While people rushed to the nickelodeons to watch the "talkies," investors and shareholders woke up. Real money attracted real engineers and corporate backing, and the pursuit eventually became serious. After countless missteps and dead ends, they finally decided to put numerous small lines at the edge of the projection copy of the film. The system employed sound to control a mercury vapor lamp, and this produced a variable-density soundtrack on the side of the film. Interestingly enough, this stripe looks very much like the visual soundtrack displayed in today's editing software. Today, we use stripes of magnetic coating along the film edge, but it is essentially the same solution.

Vehement filmmakers and critics alike had sneered at the arrival of "talkies," whining that dialogue would ruin the silent film's poetic charm. But isn't that the way it always goes? Progress shows up, and there's always someone whining in the corner, swearing it's the end of the world as we know it.

The Color Kludge: Just as the uproar over sound subsided, another offense to the sanctity of the art form raised its prismatic head: color started working its way into the market. Prior to the Technicolor process that first saw popular use in the 1930s, there was a cluttered grab bag of black-and-white film techniques that involved colorization and the use of filters to enhance color effects. In this pioneering period, most filmmakers used a workforce to paint every single frame of a film by hand. One of the hand-colored films was Georges Méliès's 1902 film *A Trip to the Moon.*

Other techniques used multiple cameras, each with a different colored filter. The resultant black-and-white images were then combined into color composites. This was cumbersome, and often the result was awkward color saturation and distorted images. Another, slightly less accurate method involved using special dyes and chemicals to colorize black-and-white film stock. Films colored in this way were prone to fading and discoloration over time.

Starting in the early 1920s, cinematographers began experimenting with colored glass filters as well as tinting the emulsion directly. These approaches often yielded unstable and occasionally garish results that most audiences found quite off-putting. Although the audience's thirst for color movies was fading, the search for color film, through all these handicaps and limitations, continued on.

First seen in the early years of the 20th century, the Kinemacolor system provided the first solid step toward successful mechanical color reproduction. Technicolor finally perfected a three-color process that provided a stable source of realistic colors. Technicolor was first used in such landmark films as *The Wizard of Oz* and *Gone With the Wind,* both of which were released in 1939. Despite Technicolor's popularity, it wasn't until 1967 that the production of color films eclipsed that of black-and-white ones.

The Digital Kludge: The switch from film to digital at the turn of the twenty-first century was a classic kludge. Unlike the transitional periods for sound and color, now both ancient history, the digital revolution happened in recent memory and is fresh in the minds of veteran filmmakers.

It's also the first kludge brought about by digital technology, meaning we can plot it both qualitatively and quantitatively on the vectors of Moore's law.

The sound and color kludges dealt broadly with the recording and projection of movies from their onset. In contrast, the digital kludge started first with visual effects and gradually spread into the realms of recording, editing, timing, and projection.

As one of Hollywood's early digital effects creators, I've had the unique pleasure of leaving my pixel-encrusted fingerprints on many of the films that marked the pixel's initial assault into the world of celluloid. Although *Tin Man* in 1983 was my first "official" use of digital effects within a motion picture, it admittedly was not my finest. Soon thereafter, I became Apple's first Hollywood Evangelist and the semiofficial tech nerd of Universal Studios. My small, computer-crammed bungalow office, tucked away in an obscure corner of Universal's back lot, quickly became the hangout for a growing herd of nerds—many of whom have since become quite well-known and remain close friends to this day.

In 1989, after showcasing an early version of Apple's HyperCard running on a prerelease of Apple's inaugural portable computer, Universal Studios head Lew Wasserman asked me to get him a similar system. I added his name to a growing list and, a week later, four brand new Apple luggables showed up, packed with apps and demos.

In addition to HyperCard, and a number of multimedia applications, each luggable had a version of Macromind Director (later purchased by Adobe), which was an easy-to-use image editor and sequencer that would go on to help define the desktop media market of the 1990s. The ability to draw on subsequent frames and then play them back in real time, or compress them into stand-alone flip-books was quite revolutionary, and a major nodal point on the vectors of Moore's law.

In addition to the system for Lew, there were those for my good friend and fellow tech enthusiast, Marlon Brando (more on that later), my good friend Harry Marks, founder of TED, and Hollywood's top talent agency, Creative Artists Agency.

Lew was so thrilled with his new pre-release portable Mac that he invited Apple to hold their product launch at the Universal Amphitheater. The event drew over 5,000 guests and established Universal Studios as a committed player in the digital revolution.

A week later, Lew came to my office and dropped the pre-press blue lines of two unpublished books, *Cadillacs and Dinosaurs* and *Jurassic Park,* on my desk. "*We're going to make one of these movies,*" he said. *"I want you to make one of those flip-book previsualizations for each of them."* He threw out a budget number that was far more than I needed to get the job done, and the biggest kludge-fest of the twentieth century was on.

The Author's Desktop Studio circa 1989

After a brief debate on whether to animate the dinosaurs with stop-motion or CG, it felt like a no-brainer to make both of these projects digital. Making the obvious assumption that the eventual director and de facto kludge-killer would be James Cameron, we adopted a similar pipeline to the one he was currently using on *The Abyss* and used an early version of Alias 2 software to animate our CG dinosaurs.

While our lumbering CG dinos might have fallen short of Cameron's Academy Award-winning visual style, they did the job and conveyed a sense of scale and jeopardy that a project of this scope needed. The flip-books worked flawlessly on Lew's Mac Portable and proved to be the preferred demo medium for this and numerous projects still to come.

Both demos got a lot of play and, in the end, the decision was made to put the pedal to the metal with *Jurassic Park*. But this is Hollywood, and nothing is ever that easy. Jim was becoming more interested in the project, but as history has shown, his working relationships with overbearing studios is a bit dodgy. Word had gotten out that Cameron was dead serious about acquiring the rights to the novel, and Universal stepped in, closing the deal mere hours before Jim. And with that sudden move, the whole momentum of the project was derailed as the biggest kludge in movie history slammed into its first roadblock. Universal acquired the rights to *Jurassic Park* and gave the project to Steven Spielberg, who phoned his longtime buddy George Lucas to help make the story come alive.

But, within the ranks of Industrial Light & Magic (ILM), there was considerable disagreement as to how to depict the dinosaurs. Visual effects supervisor Dennis Muren, a strong advocate of traditional techniques, fought tooth and nail against the digital methodology.

Fortunately, a couple of digital mavericks, Steven "Spaz" Williams and Mark Dippé, managed to circumvent his resistance. They created a test in secret and were able to display it for Frank Marshall and producer Kathy Kennedy during a tour of ILM. The battle raged on, tempers flaring, until Steven Spielberg settled on a middle ground. In the 127-minute film, the dinosaurs appear on screen for a total time of only 15 minutes–nine of them comprising animatronics and six that are CG The innovative mix received critical acclaim but fell short of ending the kludge and establishing Hollywood's digital age. That feat would have to wait another year until a new, high-powered digital gunslinger came to town.

While Jurassic Park gave us a tantalizing glimpse into the possibilities of digital effects, Spielberg's cautious middle ground left Hollywood ensnared in the growing kludge—a hesitant blend of old and new methods that failed to usher in the digital age. The industry was yearning for a revolution but lacked someone willing to take that definitive leap. That's when Scott Ross swaggered onto the scene.

Brilliant, sharp-witted, and never one to toe the line, Scott was sitting pretty as senior vice president of LucasArts and general manager of ILM. But getting comfortable has never been his style. Deciding that half-measures were for someone else, he ditched one of the most coveted gigs in the business. With characteristic audacity, he set out to revolutionize filmmaking—not just adding digital effects as an afterthought but making digital technology the new foundation of cinematic storytelling.

And so, who better to tell this story than Scott Ross himself?

> Change was in the air in the early 1990s, but very few of us at ILM were able to grasp just what this new digital revolution would look like. In fact, many if not most of the folks at ILM couldn't even see the forest for the trees. Change is difficult, especially if one's livelihood [is] threatened. One of the basic tenets of the VFX industry and ILM in particular, was *"we've always done it this way."*
>
> [That's an] interesting position to take, as ILM brought great technological invention to the field of VFX. Systems like motion control

photography, multiplane matte painting, if not invented at ILM, were most definitely perfected there.

But with the likes of John Knoll and brother Thomas Knoll, inventors of Photoshop, as well as future thinkers like Scott Squires, Dennis Muren, Ed Jones, and what was left over from the Lucasfilm Computer Graphics group . . . the digital future of filmmaking was clear as day.

Unfortunately, it was the early days, the pioneer days of digital filmmaking, and as such there was no clear-cut pipeline, no systems that were interoperable, no artist friendly software . . . in truth we had to *kludge* it all together.

It was with that kludginess that I decided to bring together the various components of this new digital way of VFX [visual effects]. I set up a meeting with the key hardware players, Quantel (the makers of the Harry and Paintbox with a great GUI); Kodak (the makers of a linear array CCD film scanner); and SGI (the UNIX-based platform with a great graphics capability). We all travelled to Newberry Berkshire in the UK.

I had high hopes that this brain trust, along with ILM's Scott Squires, could formalize an understanding of what each company could offer to create the first digital film pipeline. It never happened. Quantel, Kodak and SGI each went their separate ways and refused to collaborate. Each corporation felt that they alone could create a turn key system. Each company failed miserably and all three were eventually shuttered.

Soon thereafter, I decided to leave LucasFilm and ILM and start my own company. I decided that there needed to be a new company, without any analog legacy and without any naysayers that didn't believe in the future. Without folks saying *"we never did it that way."*

After leaving Lucasfilm and ILM in April 1992, I was writing business plans, meeting potential investors, and figuring out my next move. Word had spread—Scott Ross was looking to start a new digital VFX company. My friend Scott Billups had mentioned my plan to Jim Cameron, fresh off his box office hit *Terminator 2*. Sensing a good deal of interest, he urged me to call him.

I hesitated. After working for George Lucas, did I really want another powerful director as a partner in my new company? My wife reminded me, *"You're going to have to build this from scratch, and you're not a household name. People will line up to work with Cameron."*

She was right. I swallowed my pride and called Jim. Now there were two partners. Then Cameron invited his friend, Oscar-winning creature creator Stan Winston, and suddenly, there were three. With the addition of Price Pethel, Hollywood's digital Yoda, we now had the framework to build a digital empire on. But we still needed a name for

> the venture. Van Ling, Cameron's tech dude, walked into a meeting and said *"How about Digital Domain?"*
>
> And the rest is history. We were nominated for our first Oscar for Best VFX for TRUE LIES. We won advertising's top award; the Cannes Golden Lion for Jeep's SNOW COVERED. We won the best music video award for LOVE IS STRONG by the Rolling Stones. And we did that in our first year in business! —Scott Ross

While Scott Ross was pioneering high-budget production, I was collaborating with Digital Domain's new technical whiz kid, Price Pethel on a much, much smaller scale. Price had created an algorithm that up-converted visual effects—completed on the desktop in digital D1 video—to film. This was instrumental in creating all the visual effects that were needed to create the infamous cult classic *Fantastic Four,* a project that I helped develop with my mentor, Roger Corman, and the legendary Stan Lee.

Price's up-conversion algorithm and the tireless passion of director Oley Sassone helped us make this groundbreaking film for less than a million dollars, showing the incredible power and potential of truly talented people in the midst of a kludge. Sadly, it was only screened theatrically once as a legal way to control the property; the overwhelming consensus was that it should have been released theatrically.

The AI Kludge: Today the kludge is in full swing as artificial intelligence strides past human capabilities. From script creation to scene planning, and all the way through post-production and visual effects creation, artificial intelligence is playing an increasingly important role in nearly every step of the moviemaking process. AI-generated writing tools have been used to help with scriptwriting on story ideas, characters' lines, and, most controversially, full scripts. AI can review scripts for pacing, character arcs, and thematic arcs and recommend changes and improvements. The only thing to bear in mind as AI starts outsmarting us in one creation after another is the fact that AI, though intelligent, doesn't equal wisdom or cleverness.

And since cleverness is one of the basic ingredients in any good script, we humans still have the upper hand over the machines—at least for the time being. Another area where AI has come to the forefront is that of pre-visualization. It can rip through a script and spit out detailed storyboards and animatics, all created through generative programs in a matter of minutes. While it would normally take a human an hour to draw a single strip of a storyboard, an AI can do it in minutes. It's an empowering ability—one that allows the filmmakers to see different possibilities in complicated scenes and sequences before they're captured on camera. Most importantly, it affords the director an opportunity to experiment with different shots, lighting, and framing, not only in a virtual environment but also in real time on the set during filming.

New AI tools are popping up in the editing room, too, impacting the very nature of post-production. Machine learning programs can analyze hours of video, choose the best shots, and then create a rough edit. These new tools can also be used for visual effects, where they seamlessly merge CGI with live footage, shaving weeks or months from schedules and drastically reducing costs.

As someone who has run their own visual effects company for over thirty years, and served as VFX supervisor on over 50 motion pictures, dozens of television series, and hundreds of commercials, I feel the impact more than most. But I also work in the game industry, and in no small way, perhaps helped bring some of this about.

AI-driven characters are at the epicenter of this inevitable convergence. Digital doubles can already do stunts, take part in scenes that are hard or impossible for real people to perform; they can even stand in for actors who have passed away. Actors that have been scanned into digital versions can play more than one character at once. They can act as any age and at any time, forever. These new technologies give actors new ways to earn money from their work and allow directors to make their boldest projects.

The estates of dead actors are waiting in line to get their share of the AI-based business. Having created the virtual personification of numerous living and deceased celebrities and actors, I'm quite familiar with this aspect of our current kludge and can see it becoming one of the truly big money-makers in media creation.

The application of AI in filmmaking gives rise to countless ethical questions, with originality on the line, and no clear way to defend it. It's an unwinnable game of Whac-A-Mole, where humans will never move fast enough to legislate, control, or contain it. There will be noise and promises, for sure, but at the end of it all, any proposed "solutions" would be modern snake oil, slickly packaged for an industry that desperately wants to hold onto its soul yet is powerless to stop the machine.

Like all of the other kludge eras, this one, too, will eventually be brought to a close by a very simple solution. AI will inevitably compile the art and craft of all media into one Creation Engine. Think of an unobtrusive site consisting of pull-down menus and text boxes, which could spit out anything from a birthday greeting to your dear old mother to a complete movie scene. All you would do is fill in the blanks and tick the boxes in the drop-down menus.

The displacement and inequality caused by this AI kludge will seem too many to be a catastrophe. But think of the shift in society from horse-drawn carriage to car. First, there was a lot of disruption, shifting of the economy, changing the ways of people's lives. But it also created new opportunities that offered convenience and efficiency in both society and millions of well-paying jobs. Similarly, this kludge of AI, unruly as it is, may turn our creative processes and media ecologies inside out in ways hardly imaginable.

Marshall McLuhan once said, *"When faced with a new situation, we tend always to attach ourselves to the objects, to the flavor of the most recent past. We look at the present through a rear-view mirror. We march backward into the future."*

The optimistic stories about AI as our companion in the future of media are nothing but clichéd narratives. As AI continues to encroach on more and more of our creative processes, we are gradually entering the age of irrelevance, in which the traditional standards of human creativity and craftsmanship are made obsolete by the mechanical perfection of the algorithms.

It is ironic how Hollywood's favorite shorthand for describing a movie is to take an existing film and change its setting: *"It's like* Gone with the Wind *on Mars*." Another common pitch trope is to combine two movies to describe a new concept: *"It's* Forrest Gump *meets* Terminator." Surprisingly, both of these are great ways of structuring a prompt for the new age of AI movies.

Quasi-art, such as splatter painting and knitting scarves, will probably go on as before, as will some indie projects and fad-based media projects. But the commercial projects, the ones that you'll open your wallets for, will all be run by those who control the channels of distribution; and those channels will be full of AI-generated content.

Our complacency and addiction to deception have blinded us to the brutal truth: AI is not just a tool that is being added to the creative process, it is a sign of a new paradigm in creativity. We are on the verge of a future where the role of humans is diminished and human creativity itself is severely impacted by automation. This is something that creators have to face, redefining themselves and their purpose in the context of the growing automation.

Some of the kludge-era crafts are already disappearing as they are integrated into the Creation Engine model, while those that depend on human attributes may last for another decade. The challenge is to determine which crafts will be among the last to be automated, and to position yourself with your strengths rather than your aspirations.

A CRASH COURSE IN AI FOR MOVIEMAKERS

"Soon, robots will be writing scripts, directing films, and even playing the leading roles. And they'll probably do a better job than us."

—Quentin Tarantino

As Hollywood continues to churn out blockbusters with vast armies of workers, the lone game developer with a single powerful idea and a personal computer is creating worlds.

Take *Ant-Man and the Wasp: Quantumania,* from 2023. Although my wife and I found it entertaining, the majority of the planet did not. (Full disclosure: We both knew a number of people who worked on it and tend to root for the home team.) Not only were the critics unkind, but despite its $200 million budget and a team of 2,826 credited artists, technicians, and performers, it didn't quite connect with audiences, either. Of course, it has the obligatory end credit scroll that lasts nearly 12 minutes, just like most bloated studio pictures. Compare that to *Lethal Company*, a horror game created by one person that became a viral hit and sold over 5 million copies in the space of a few months.

Yet Hollywood keeps on throwing large crews and ballooning budgets at ever-more formulaic content, while game developers keep perfecting the algorithms and interactive storytelling systems that will define the future of entertainment. Game developers have already learned that compelling narratives do not rest on star power or spectacular effects but rather on the intricate dance between story, code, and user agency.

While there will always be a place for traditional linear storytelling, more of the craft-based jobs that define its production will be taken over by AI-driven applications. For filmmakers and content creators who want to remain involved, adapting to this new era isn't an option; it's a must. The future will demand fluency in spatial media, branching narratives, virtual characters, and AI-powered tools—not just to keep up, but to lead in the creation of new storytelling forms.

Creating visually interesting content or simple stories is one thing; making a lasting name for yourself in a crowded, competitive field is another. You'll need more than creativity to rise above the noise—it'll take solid STEM skills and probably even a bit of coding. That's why I've assembled a syllabus of free resources to get even the most tech-averse up to speed.

Developing content today means working with complex generative systems, handling both scripted events and real-time interactions, which requires a fusion of software engineering, storytelling, and user experience design. Drag-and-drop programs and prompt-based tools will claim to make you a spatial media mogul, but relying on this alone will only hold you back, competing in a market of mediocrity pitted against other dreamers who stopped short of learning real skills.

> *"Learning for passion fills you up; learning for ego drains you."*
>
> —Joseph Billups, PhD,
> Semantics Professor at Syracuse University

But first, we need to get your vocabulary up to speed. Not just the vernacular of the industry, but what it means and how these new algorithmic bits work together to create content.

ESSENTIAL LINGO

Just as the analog age of film production had its own specialized lingo, so does the digital age of production. The film industry was, is, and always will be full of lingo with such esoteric names as a "redhead," "apple box," and "barn doors," and no production could survive without C-47s. The age of AI has its own lingo, too, and it's growing exponentially. While no one alive knows everything, here are some basics that everyone in media should know.

Artificial intelligence is the art of creating cool things and getting rich. It's a term Dartmouth professor John McCarthy coined in an effort to fund his research back in 1956. "Cybernetics," AI's original name, just didn't have the same ring to it when it came to attracting those sweet, sweet research dollars.

On its most basic level, AI aims to replicate human intelligence in machines. This allows computers to carry out tasks that would otherwise need human intellectual capacity, such as natural language comprehension, vision, decision-making, and problem-solving.

What follows are the basic flavors of AI, most of which we are going to use throughout this book.

Narrow AI, sometimes referred to as weak AI, is a system designed to address a narrow, particularized range of tasks. Examples of narrow AI include virtual assistants, such as Siri and Alexa, and recommendation systems from various online streaming services.

General AI (GAI) refers to machines that have the capacity for understanding, learning, and applying appropriate knowledge that features comparisons found in nature and is similar to human intelligence. Although GAI is only now starting to gain momentum, it is the engine of advanced generative image programs and virtual actors who will populate both the worlds we create and the stories we will tell.

Machine learning (ML) is a subset of AI that focuses on training statistical models on vast truckloads of data. Such datasets have an infinity of data points that enable machines to learn from information and make predictions or decisions. Think of this complex process as a sprawling willow tree in a windstorm, where each leaf represents a data point. As data blows through the tree, the leaves (the data points) get intertwined in a complex pattern that the model learns to recognize.

As you might imagine, the quality of that data is very important. There is an increasingly popular mantra that circulates among successful AI professionals: *"garbage in, garbage out"* (GIGO). In other words, the quality of the content that you use to train your AI model directly impacts the quality of the output data. This principle is critical in creative industries like film, gaming, and media, where the tools powered by AI can easily change the believability of the final product.

While many of the original ML models were trained on internet scrapings, the GIGO adage is quickly becoming gospel in industries where the stakes are high and the potential for error is even greater.

Deep learning takes its structure and function from the neural systems of the human brain. It is taught by interleaved hierarchical representations of data, like weaving different combinations of the willow tree branches, which enables it to excel at image and **speech recognition**. This gives film and television producers intelligent **virtual characters** with which to populate our new digital storytelling worlds, allowing the characters to acknowledge their surroundings and other characters in the same scene. The "smarter" a deep learning system becomes, the more it masters how to react to every little hint, micro-gesture, and emotional nuance in real time. The actions of virtual actors can be guided by the director or the user to be strictly bound by the script or biometrically guided using the unique mixture of the user's prompts and physiological responses, which results in an ever-evolving story.

Similarly, pattern recognition tasks are also done by **neural networks.** They fuse virtual and real-world elements in such a way that when applied on volumetric stages, live actors are able to interact with their digital twins. In both virtual and augmented reality, neural networks provide a continual stream of live action and computer-generated imagery, blurring the boundaries between the physical and the virtual realities on which spatial computing is based.

Already a part of AI systems, **natural language processing (NLP)** is the voice that personalizes our world with virtual assistants such as Alexa and Siri and an increasing number of chatbots that are integrated into commercial pursuits. It brings human-like conversation to daily life, from appointment scheduling and answering inquiries to entertaining.

It also changes how virtual characters relate to humans in cinematic and game pipelines by enabling real conversations in real time. It enables understanding, interpretation, and response with outstanding fluency. AI-driven characters will understand not only the semantics and context of human speech but also grasp the subtlety of tone and emotion. NLP gives virtual characters the ability to conduct meaningful dialogues with humans and other virtual characters in the most realistic way.

Interactive narratives are the basis of immersive storytelling in today's media. They allow the user to influence the course and ending of a story by their choices. Structuring these narratives involves a framework for negotiating the often-complex web of possible paths and outcomes. **Semantic chains** offer one such framework by representing the relationships among narrative elements in a logical and coherent manner.

Semantic chains map out the entire narrative in data structures, such as graphs or linked lists, where each node represents an event point and edges represent the connections between them. From this setup, developers can track the progression of the player and dynamically adjust the narrative based on the player's decisions.

Implementation of semantic chains is usually done in scripting languages or in the many specialized authoring tools that allow writers and designers to structure the narrative flow without delving deeply into programming. Middleware solutions or custom editors provide a graphical interface to handle the narrative graph so that keeping track of branching stories and where they reconverge becomes simpler.

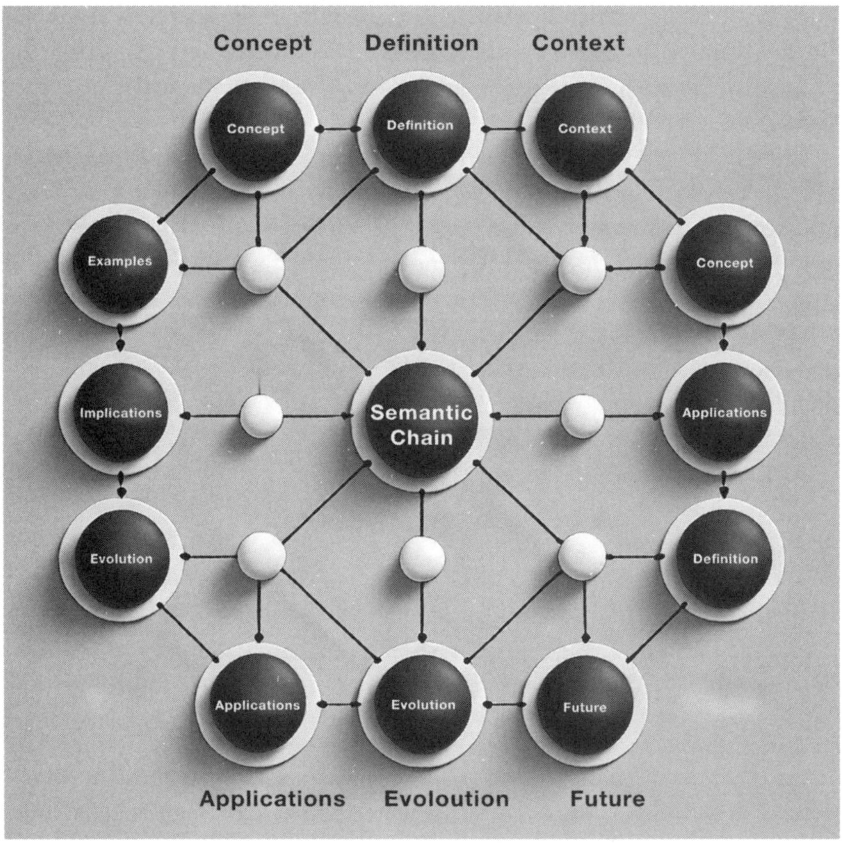

Context management becomes essential in this procedure. The system must remember the past choices made by a player to influence future events correctly. Variables and flags track decisions that affect character relationships, available quests, or the conclusion of the story.

For instance, in a role-playing game, the decision to ally with one faction might unlock new missions regarding that group at the same time as other factions become hostile. The semantic chains make sure that the narrative threads are logically coherent and that the player's actions have meaningful effects.

It's all about striking a balance with narrative complexity so the threads don't become too convoluted with disorganized arcs. For example, in modular storytelling, stand-alone story arcs can easily be rearranged, helping to keep control over the scope of a narrative while still offering a rich, player-driven experience.

Interactive narratives can be designed to have dynamic story development in response to player agency, thus ensuring a high level of replayability and greatly enhancing interactivity.

Convolutional neural networks (CNNs) and **generative adversarial networks (GANs)** are the dynamic duo of artificial intelligence, capable of feats that were once the realm of science fiction.

CNNs are unique deep neural networks designed to work with image data. They are inspired by the visual cortex of the human brain, which identifies and understands images. Imagine the human brain as an extensive system of linked neurons. Upon viewing a scene, your brain receives sensory details and breaks down the image into smaller components. It analyzes the complete image into smaller fragments while pinpointing patterns and elements and finally recognizing objects. CNNs have revolutionized fields like computer vision, image recognition, and natural language processing.

GANs are a class of machine learning frameworks that consist of two neural networks that are rather like the two hemispheres of the human brain. One is called the generator, somewhat like the right (creative) hemisphere of the human brain, and the other is the discriminator, which could be described as being similar to the function of the left (analytic) hemisphere.

When you show or describe an image, action, or object in a prompt, the generative network creates candidates that the discriminative network then evaluates. As the two adversarial neural networks carry on their little to-and-fro, the generator tries to fool the discriminator by producing images that the discriminator thinks are real. The more they quibble back and forth, the more refined the image gets—somewhat like the human brain, but much better. This back-and-forth competition between the two competing neural networks is the GAN process, and this is essentially how most generative systems work.

We named the two GAN neural networks that power the current iteration of our AI-Prototyper after the legendary duo from Star Trek. Captain Kirk is the generator—bold, creative, and always ready to push boundaries—and Mr. Spock is the discriminator—logical, analytical, ever the voice of reason.

Both the human mind and AI systems thrive on a balance of generative and evaluative processes that can inspire new approaches to storytelling, editing, and even audience engagement.

Although the current version of our AI-Prototyper is very much a work in progress, it is moving along with a point in technology that aligns quite nicely with the vectors of Moore's law. Now, if that sounds a little esoteric, keep in mind that banks and top investment firms use Moore's law vectors to forecast high-tech success because they provide a measurable trajectory for rapid innovation, enabling smarter predictions in an ever-accelerating technical landscape—but more about that in the next chapter.

For filmmakers and creatives, understanding that balance between the generation of ideas and critical evaluation has always been critical for storytelling, editing, and audience engagement. Success thus far has been about embracing this duality: the wild spark of creativity and the precise craft of refinement.

But that's all beginning to change now as AI barges its way in. There's software that will help you draft a script or storyboard a scene, and then give you savvy feedback that makes you think twice about what you were trying to do in the first place. It's a little like having a creative partner, always present, always churning over in your mind how to make your work better.

Of course, this shift wasn't entirely unexpected. The noted futurist Ray Kurzweil has predicted that by the year 2029, AI will outstrip human intelligence. He says this represents *"a moment when technological progress becomes so rapid and profound that it changes the very fabric of human society in ways we can't fully predict."*

The thing is, technology progresses exponentially–computing power that once occupied whole rooms now fits in our pockets and is increasingly democratized.

What took many by surprise was the pace at which those AI systems started to show behaviors that would feel nearly human. They process information, but they interact with it, too, and sometimes even show an element of creativity and intuition almost like our own.

It's both exciting and a little uncanny, but perhaps that's the point. The more we blur the line separating human thought from artificial intelligence, the more the new frontiers will open to creativity and innovation. And for storytellers, filmmakers, and artists alike, maybe it is a ride worth taking.

THE DARK SIDE OF AI

Consider what would happen if raw machine intelligence took human form. Without morals to guide it, incapable of empathy, and unrestrained by fear, such a being would be what we might label an extremely dangerous psychopath. Morality and ethics are the building blocks of society; they bind us to a shared understanding of right and wrong. But there will always be bad actors, and AI, a prodigy in mathematics, science, and art, is still in its infancy and vulnerable to the darkness of human intentions.

The better you understand the fundamentals of creating digital people, the louder that little voice inside whispers, *"You're only code; I know how you're built."*

SURVIVAL

In the face of AI's relentless march, one thing is clear: the age-old adage *"learn or be left behind"* rings truer than ever. The workforce that will shape tomorrow needs to be agile, ready to pivot, and thirsty to acquire new skills as AI continues in its evolution. Reskilling and upskilling cease to be optional but rather become imperatives in this dynamic world where the ghost in the machine beckons us to reinvent ourselves.

Lifelong learning has become a requirement for many careers. Rapid obsolescence and new opportunities create the need for constant education. The conviction of American philosopher John Dewey that *"education is not preparation for life; education is life itself"* now carries a greater degree of immediacy. Education is no longer something confined to a finite period of youth but has become a lifelong process.

HEAD START ON THE FUTURE

Now that you've got a handle on the basic framework and lingo of AI, it's time to put it to good use and get some pixel dust under your fingernails. As much fun as generative AI is, it isn't going to make you competitive in the growing clutter of instant art. Now is the time for you to do what the titans of industry, bankers, and the top venture capitalists do: plot out where this whole thing is going and work toward that point in the future.

Game engines are evolving into AI-powered tools capable of crafting immersive worlds filled with digital characters that feel alive. But let's be clear: creating something truly original—something that pushes the envelope—requires both vision and skill. Vision without skill? You're a bystander in someone else's creation. Skill without vision? You're an employee on autopilot. Real innovation happens at the intersection of these two, where great tools meet a compelling idea.

While prompt engineering may satiate our appetite for instant gratification, it's not up to the task of creating the nuanced, believable experiences that long-form story lines and character arcs demand. For that, we need to fall back on more traditional systems like motion capture to reproduce the small, authentic gestures that lend digital characters their credibility. There are volumetric stages, for example, that let us place human beings into virtual worlds full of virtual characters that can see, hear, and react to them in real time. This is only one of the tools that can push past the limits of current AI and fill in the gaps that simple prompts can't.

If you wait for spatial media, bespoke narratives, or world-scale personified companions to become popular before you start learning how to make them, you're going to be in the same mosh pit of shortsighted slackers as everyone else. Or how about building virtual worlds, like in *Ready Player One?* We can plot very accurately when that technology set will start manifesting. And again, if you wait for it to arrive before you start learning how to work in that medium, you'll be too damn late.

The way to thrive in the AI era is to learn how to use the tools that will define the future of media. Will they enable you to make it now? No. But by the time the future shows up, these are the tools that you will need to shape it.

By late 2026, all of the leading AI-based game engines will have incorporated AI-generative components, biometric drivers, and a whole quiver full of world-scale applications. So put down this book, download the free **Unity** game engine (link below), and spend a few days going through the introductory tutorials. And while you're at it, check out the Asset Store, where you'll find numerous free pre-built items that you can play with and use in your personal projects. Everything will make a whole lot more sense once you've got a little spatial experience under your belt.

I'll warn you now, this stuff is addictive. So, if you find building worlds and programming your growing family of digital characters compelling, well, that's your inner geek telling you to carry on.

Although Unity is by far the easiest of the professional game engines to learn, it is quite powerful. By the time you've reached the end of their tutorials you'll even have learned a bit of programming. The language C# is quite easy to learn and has a clean syntax that makes it particularly appropriate for beginners and more experienced developers alike. I've used Unity for documentaries on Discovery, the History Channel, the BBC, and our original AI-Prototyper. Forty-six % of the games on the market are built in Unity, so don't let its ease of use and friendly interface fool you.

While Unity is truly a wonderful AI engine, it isn't photorealistic. It's close, but not close enough given where spatial media is going. I'm talking Sora-type characters with complete user controls, spatial awareness of both virtual and physical environments, including other characters, and the ability to read emotions and respond appropriately. For that level of creation, you need to put on your grown-up pants and dive into the **Unreal Engine.**

Photorealistic characters that embody the nuance of the human condition are not easy things to make. Yes, there are a plethora of AI generators that can make some truly convincing clips, but they're not characters with silicon souls. They're just moving pixels that are spewing out of a generative adversarial network. You're not the director; AI is, and even the best AI is mediocre.

The undisputed Yoda of virtual characters is Vladimir Mastilović. With a history of creating characters for AAA game titles such as *Grand Theft Auto, Resident Evil, Spider-Man, Anthem,* and many others, his former Serbia-based company, 3Lateral, led the way in virtual character personification until Unreal purchased it in 2019. Now called MetaHuman, it's an integral part of Unreal's expanding catalog of the essential tools that will inhabit our future. The true power of MetaHuman Creator (MHC) doesn't lie in its complexity but rather in its unequaled ease of use. MHC is a free, web-based tool you can use to create your own digital human in under ten minutes with no prior game or coding experience. Go ahead, Google MetaHuman Creator and give it a try.

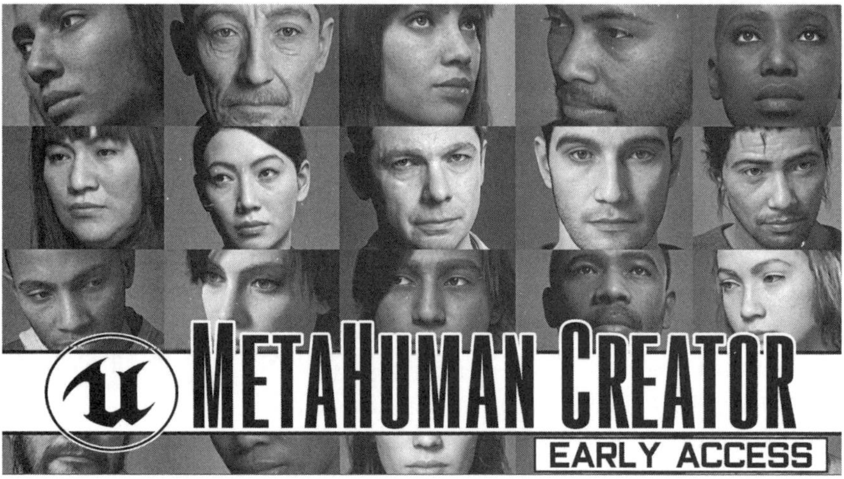

Photoreality demands nuance, and that takes horsepower and a lot more control. To get your MetaHuman walking and talking in your virtual worlds, you'll be switching to the C++ programming language, and maybe a little Python, too. Don't worry, you're a bonified game developer; that's what you do. (Links for free training follow later in the chapter.)

And don't worry if your projects come out a little wonky or your code is a bit buggy. Hell, I've used AI to make hundred-million-dollar movies, billion-dollar defense projects, and groundbreaking medical applications, and every one of the developers I've hired will gladly tell you that I'm the worst coder that they've ever worked with. And that's OK, because I'm good enough at coding to speak the language and recognize real talent when I see it. So, if you're not destined to be a hot-shot coder pulling down a seven-figure salary (yes, it happens all the time), then perhaps you're better at the big picture. Maybe your wheelhouse is in management, or design, pulling down a couple million a year. Wherever your destiny is leading, these next few steps will help get you there.

1. Download the latest version of the **Unity** game engine at unity.com. It's fun, easy to use, and free for individuals and small organizations with less than $200,000 in revenue. Play with it at least until you work your way through their excellent tutorials.
2. Download the latest version of the **Unreal Engine** at unrealengine.com. It's free to use for students, educators, hobbyists, and most non-games companies making less than $1 million USD in annual gross revenue.
3. Work your way through the tutorials, paying close attention to the **MetaHuman** projects. Sooner or later, you'll need a basic understanding

of code. Prioritizing user experience is essential in AR/VR development. A seamless and intuitive interface can elevate a product from a novelty to an indispensable tool.

To ensure optimal user experience, consider utilizing the **Oculus Quest** or **Apple Vision** development kits, both of which offer robust development tools and a significant user base.

4. Take one or more of these great courses:
    - C# Fundamentals for Absolute Beginners @ learn.microsoft.com
    - Fundamentals of C++ @ edx.org
    - C++ Programming for Unreal Game Development @ coursera.org
    - Learn Coding: C++ & Python @ udemy.com

Remember, AI is trained on a mix of sources, so the best it can do without expert guidance and control is only a little bit better than average. But making something is only half of the equation. In conventional motion picture production, it costs as much to release a movie as it does to make it. And while spatial media isn't quite as barbaric, distribution and commercialization are always going to be a grind. Here are a few tips from personal experience.

1. Test. Don't assume that you've just spun gold.
2. Once you've got some market performance data, you're good to go.
3. Use that data to refine your media and get a feel for who your audience is.
4. Use web tools to target your market and put up a website to keep them connected.
5. Use social media to let your market know about your project.
6. If you start making money, treat it like a business: DBA or LLC > books > bank account > taxes.
7. (optional) Mention me in your Oscar acceptance speech.

MOORE'S LAW

> *"Where a calculator on the ENIAC is equipped with 18,000 vacuum tubes and weighs 30 tons, computers in the future may have only 1,000 vacuum tubes and perhaps only weigh 1.5 tons."*
>
> —*Popular Mechanics,* March 1949

BACK WHEN I WAS A KID, MY FASCINATION WITH TECHNOLOGY BEGAN with a clunky old radio that my grandfather kept in his workshop. It was a massive box filled with glowing vacuum tubes—fragile glass cylinders that controlled the flow of electrons. Those tubes were temperamental; a slight bump could silence the static-filled music, prompting a gentle tap (or a not-so-gentle whack) to bring it back to life. If you've ever seen someone bang on the side of an old TV to fix the picture, you've witnessed the quirks of vacuum tube technology.

Before the 1950s, vacuum tubes were the beating heart of electronics. They were essential but came with a host of problems: they were bulky, unreliable, consumed heaps of power, and generated enough heat to warm a small room. Maintenance was a constant headache, and standardization was more of a dream than reality. It was clear that something had to change.

Bardeen, Brattain, Shockley © Bell Labs

In 1947, a trio of brilliant minds at Bell Labs—John Bardeen, Walter Brattain, and William Shockley—decided it was time to tackle this "bottleneck" in technology. They experimented with silicon and other elements nestled around the "metalloid staircase" on the periodic table.

Their eureka moment came when they invented the transistor: a tiny semiconductor that could control and amplify the flow of electrons.

This was a game changer. Transistors were much smaller than vacuum tubes, had no moving parts, generated less heat, and proved to be infinitely more reliable. The performance gains were immediate and profound. Silicon became so important to the world of tech that an entire valley in California was named after it.

To help you visualize how gobsmackingly incredible this all was: if you tried to build a modern smartphone using vacuum tubes, it would be larger than downtown Manhattan. It's a staggering thought to consider just how far we've come, and yet, AI is about to disrupt the foundations of our world in ways that will make the transistor look like a warm-up act.

Gordon Moore © Intel

In 1962, Gordon Moore, one of Intel's co-founders, was hanging out with a couple of his pocket-protector pals, tossing back a few drinks. Well, ol' Gordon made a prediction, and it must have sounded cool because one of his egghead buddies wrote it down on a cocktail napkin:

"The logic density of silicon integrated circuits should follow the curve (bits per square inch) = 2^n(t-1962) where t is time in years."

Several years later, Gordon's friend was cleaning out his desk and found that old cocktail napkin with the odd equation scribbled on it. After removing a pen from his pocket protector, he did some quick calculations. To his surprise, Gordon's little equation was bang on.

In simple terms, Moore's hypothesis stated that computing power, in the form of transistors within an integrated circuit, would double in number annually for ten years, while cost and size would be simultaneously halved.

He later revised his formula in 1975 to state that the effect would double every two years. Ever since then, Moore's law has been the dominant driver behind over half a century of technological change. *By establishing a quantifiable timeline into the future, Moore's law empowers financial markets to fund technical research and development.*

Financial backing allows companies to take that next leap knowing that the needed technologies will be there to support new ideas and turn them into a deliverable reality. Because machine learning and AI are so closely bound to Moore's law, their growth applies under the same rules that apply to all tech advancements.

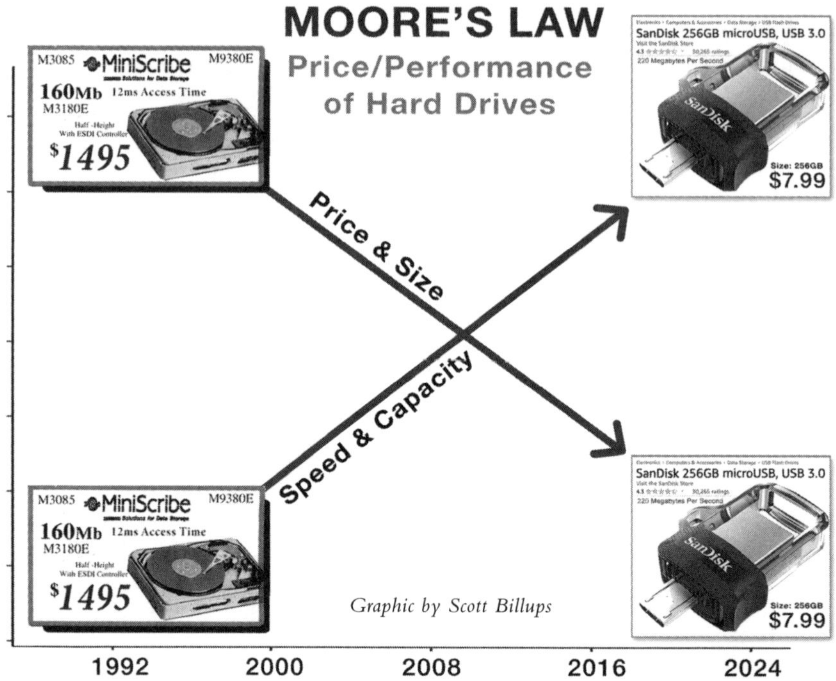

Graphic by Scott Billups

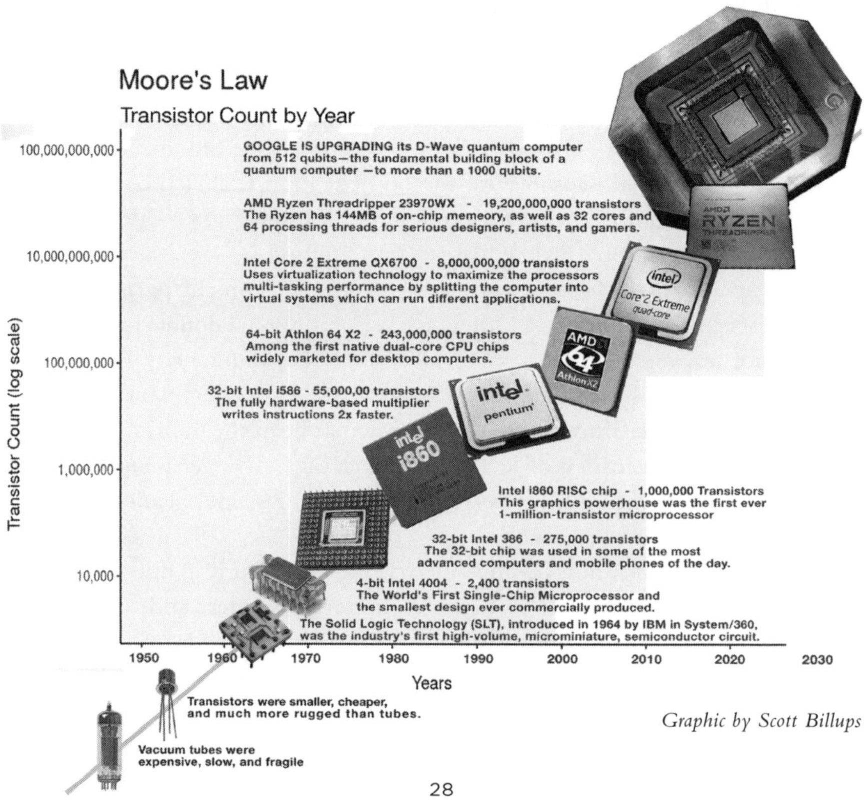

Graphic by Scott Billups

But Moore's law isn't just some esoteric formula reserved for industry insiders; its implications have a direct effect on our personal lives, giving us access to tools, insights, and capabilities that were once the stuff of science fiction.

This book is, in many ways, a follow-up to the Digital Moviemaking series I wrote that ushered in the digital age back when the pixel was disrupting the movie industry. In that series, I used the steady growth shown by Moore's law to explain and predict how media production would change in the future. All of those predictions came to pass, including the shrinkage and aggregation of professional production tools to the point at which phones would eventually become media production suites.

Smart phone mock-up based on Moore's law from Digital Moviemaking, circa 2000.

By understanding how to interpret Moore's law, it was easy to predict that this would mean a rise in citizen journalists, pocket auteurs, and a growing trend of online discourse as a new generation of "computer phones" would soon change the way we document our lives. I even created an image for the books that looks very similar to the modern iPhone, which would come out seven years later, and another that gave a tongue-in-cheek nod to the future of movie production.

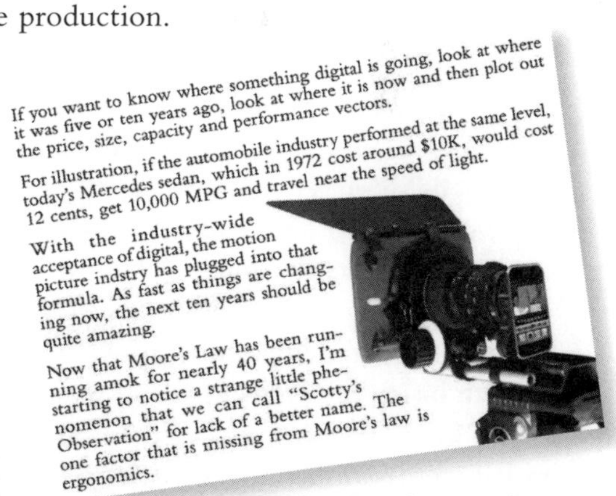

If you want to know where something digital is going, look at where it was five or ten years ago, look at where it is now and then plot out the price, size, capacity and performance vectors.

For illustration, if the automobile industry performed at the same level, today's Mercedes sedan, which in 1972 cost around $10K, would cost 12 cents, get 10,000 MPG and travel near the speed of light.

With the industry-wide acceptance of digital, the motion picture indstry has plugged into that formula. As fast as things are changing now, the next ten years should be quite amazing.

Now that Moore's Law has been running amok for nearly 40 years, I'm starting to notice a strange little phenomenon that we can call "Scotty's Observation" for lack of a better name. The one factor that is missing from Moore's law is ergonomics.

Clip from Digital Moviemaking

Am I clairvoyant? Not a chance; compared to my friends and to the people I work with, I'm not even all that smart, but I do believe firmly in the unwavering dependability of Moore's law and what it says about our future.

At a recent social gathering of Hollywood digerati at Paul Debevec's house, VFX legend, Jonathan Banta, pulled an iPhone-like scanner out of his pocket and captured Randal Kleiser in about a minute. Compare this to my 1998 scanning of Marlon Brando, which required a room full of equipment, extensive preparation, and lengthy processing. What is less evident in this

Scan of Randal Kleiser, 2024 *Scan of Marlon Brando, 1989*

black-and-white image is the highly realistic color and subtle micro-expressions that Jonathan's scan exhibits. The ease with which Randal's head was captured and rendered highlights just how accurately this technological arc of personification adheres to the vectors of Moore's law.

With the advent of generative motion imaging capabilities in leading game engines, you will soon be able to drop that geometry into the application and it will transpose it into a persistent, photoreal character that can be driven by prompts, GUI, or code. This digital double will not only look and sound like the famous director, but with just a few reference clips, it will act like him, too.

THE KURZWEIL/MOORE HYPOTHESIS

When you overlay futurist Ray Kurzweil's timeline with the vectors of Moore's law, an interesting alignment happens. I've taken to calling it the Kurzweil/Moore Hypothesis. While some might argue that it's just a grandiose name for an infographic, it helps me visualize and validate the palpable acceleration that is pulling us toward what Kurzweil calls the singularity. Regardless of what you call it, the inevitable point at which artificial intelligence surpasses human intelligence will mark a point when technological growth becomes exponential and well beyond our control.

This is not some sort of theoretical visualization. When we plot key milestones from our own experiences and the broader field of AI onto this graph, they fit remarkably well. This includes everything from the humble beginnings of Pong and Pac-Man, where digital characters followed simple programmed behaviors, to the development of rule-based background characters that can react dynamically with their environment. More recently,

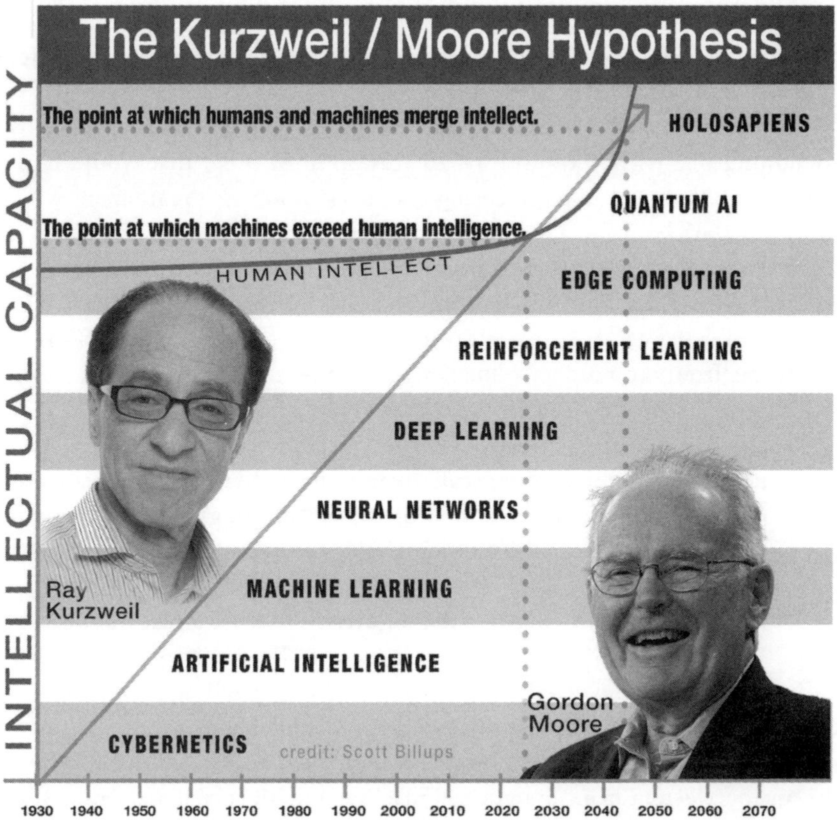

we have seen an increasingly rapid proliferation of neural network-based conversational agents, our own personified virtual clinicians, and AI-driven companions like Mattel's prototype ChatGPT-enabled Barbie.

Each of these milestones represents a nodal point on the path toward increasingly sophisticated AI that is consistent with the exponential growth predicted by Moore's law. The speed at which these developments are occurring is increasing as we gain on that first convergence point in 2029.

GAZING INTO MOORE'S CRYSTAL BALL

With increasing capabilities, deep learning models, which were once shackled by hardware limitations, will continue to sprawl across huge clusters of GPUs, processing data at unimaginable speeds. But the performance leaps foretold by Moore's law have catalyzed many other breakthroughs in natural language understanding, computer vision, and reinforcement learning—advances that have pushed the capabilities of AI into the realm of science fiction. Medical diagnosis and autonomous vehicles are only a few examples of the revolutionary transformations of complex tasks predicted long ago by Moore's law.

For most in science engineering, the goal is a single device capable of containing one trillion transistors. At this point in time, that would be so much more than just an engineering feat; it would mark the moment when machines start building a structure close to the human brain. The human brain contains an average of eighty-six billion neurons, each of which can connect with thousands of other neurons, forming a huge network with trillions of synapses all firing at once. While one trillion transistors might still be far from the number of neurons in the brain, it's the density, speed, and coordination of these transistors that give machines an edge.

Intelligent machines already perform calculations and pattern recognition much faster and on a larger scale than humans. Many believe transistor count represents the point beyond which machines might well surpass us, not only in raw speed, but also in their ability to simulate thought processes and learning patterns.

According to Moore's law, this Singularity will take place before the year 2029 is out. It will be a time when the machines are no longer simple tools; they will have evolved instead to learn, change, and maybe even think like human beings. And all of this would be happening at an unimaginably superior speed and on an unfathomably broad scale. It's a future in which the line between human thought and machine intelligence blurs, irreversibly changing our relationship with technology and the world.

5.

THE CURATED LIFE

"Zoom out to the future and look back; you'll wonder how you led your life without augmented reality."

—Tim Cook, CEO of Apple

Get ready to trade in your boring old world for a future that has more technology than a science fiction convention. AI is going to turn your life into a customized entertainment park, with watches that read you like a book and spectacles that see the invisible, all run by a supercomputer that fits in your pocket.

So, buckle up, buttercup, because this clown car is headed to a mind-bending mash-up of human intellect and machine intelligence. This is more than new gizmos, more than evolution; it's the threshold of a curated world where our minds are the next frontier in computational power.

THE EYEGLASSES

These super-smart, augmented reality glasses are the gateway to spatial computing. They provide an augmented overlay to the world around us, drastically changing the way we engage with it.

At the core of these seemingly traditional eyeglasses is waveguide lens technology, which has been in use in military and high-end industrial applications for years. Waveguide technology directs light waves through a transparent medium that is layered between ophthalmic-quality lenses (available with prescription) that use a diffraction grating to project data, graphics, and images directly

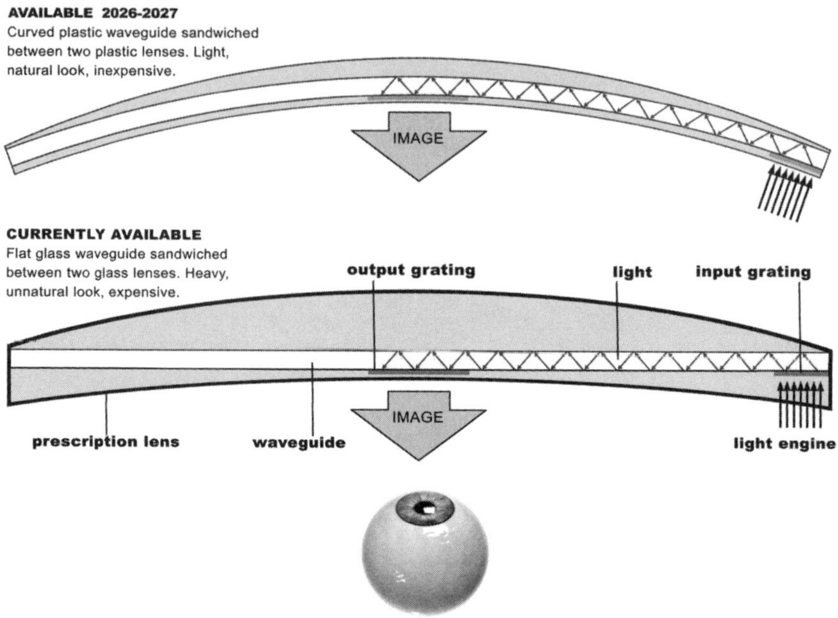

into the user's eyes. This process creates the illusion that the digital content is in perfect alignment with the real world without blocking the wearer's view of the natural environment.

> *"Augmented reality enhances the way we see and interact with the world. It blurs the lines between what's real and what's computer-generated by enhancing what we hear, see, and feel."*
>
> —Mark Zuckerberg, CEO of Meta Platforms, Inc. (formerly Facebook)

While the majority of bulky consumer-level AR eyewear simply places a pair of LCD screens in front of the user's eyes, waveguide is a lightweight, near-eye optical display. In the early prototypes from Apple, Meta, and Microsoft, the GUI is similar to a conventional laptop screen with a row of icons along the lower edge that are only visible to the wearer.

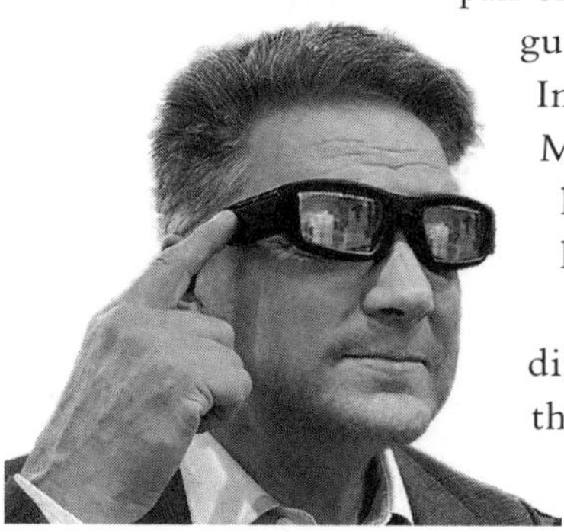

The app icons light up when you look directly at them and activate when you tap the temple or blink, freeing your hands for other tasks.

Although the eye-blink control system may seem a little wonky, it is not. At Pixelmonger Studios, we frequently work on augmented symbology projects for head-up displays and control interfaces ranging from military flight navigation and control interfaces to a growing list of both defense and industrial systems.

One of the most effective ways to check the efficiency of an AR input system is to type with one's eyes. My personal benchmark test phrase is *"The quick brown fox jumps over the lazy dog."* I can type this phrase at a rate of approximately 50 words per minute on a computer keyboard, and between 10 and 18 words per minute using the eyeline-blink on a well-designed AR system—only slightly slower than my thumbs-only texting speed on my smartphone.

> *"We believe that augmented reality is one of those new mediums that could be as big . . . if not bigger than the web. When I think about augmented reality, I think about instances like finding your way somewhere, finding your friends in a stadium, or going to a conference and looking around and knowing who everyone is because their LinkedIn profile is hanging over their heads."*
>
> —Scott Belsky, Adobe's chief product officer and executive VP for Creative Cloud

Strategically placed electrodes in the temples of the AR glasses capture subtle brainwave activity that adds data on the wearer's cognitive and emotional state to his or her biometric profile. The result is that the pocket PC that orchestrates this technology set can now examine mental states—focus, stress, relaxation, enjoyment—along with other physiological metrics. This EEG-enhanced profile does not just monitor; it predicts needs, wants, and changes in mood, making this an intuitive resource, well suited to guiding the future of interactive spatial media, games, and bespoke music and motion image content (movies).

One of the greatest opportunities in media production will be creating interactive or narrative content that is compatible with this new environment. A strong base in traditional production methods will come in handy while developing the necessary technical skills to compete at a professional level.

> *"AI is the key to unlocking the true potential of AR. It empowers us to create rich, context-aware experiences that seamlessly blend the digital and physical worlds."*
>
> —Satya Nadella, CEO of Microsoft

AR content that combines regular storytelling with interactivity allows viewers to explore, change, and help build the story world. Think *Pokémon Go* with cognizant human characters and a compelling narrative. Focusing on spatial design, character interaction, and flexibility can turn storytelling into an exciting, engaging experience that feels special and personal using AR stories.

> *"Think back to 2008, when the App Store went live. There was the initial round of apps, and people looked at them and said, 'this is not anything, mobile apps are not going to take off'. And then, step by step, things start to move . . . and now you couldn't imagine your life without apps . . . AR is like that. It will be that dramatic."*
>
> —Tim Cook, CEO of Apple

THE MUCH SMARTER SMARTWATCH

In addition to just telling time and reminding us of appointments, the smarter smartwatch, or wrist terminal, is the biometric hub for this trifecta of technologies and the guardian of our well-being. The ability to monitor a variety of physiological signals, such as heart rate, blood pressure, respiration, muscle activity, pulse, and galvanic skin response (GSR), creates a physical link between us and the incredible power of AI. It is also a giant step in the inevitable merging of human and machine.

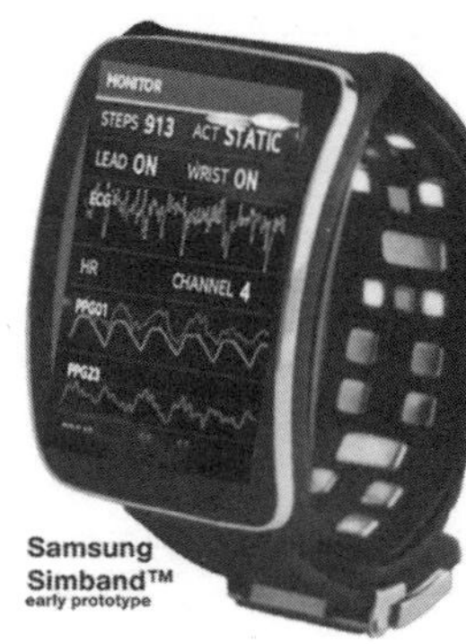

Samsung Simband™ early prototype

This capacity to measure biometrics is the secret sauce for creating truly personalized experiences that open up the world of bespoke entertainment. It allows us to shape media, entertainment, and even influence the interactions with our own digital avatars in real time.

To get an idea of what these biometric peripherals might look like in the future, type "Samsung Simband" into your preferred search engine and see an early working prototype of what a company with a history of innovation across many sectors has developed. Since the initial release of Simband nearly a decade ago, dozens of companies have followed Samsung's lead in developing wearable biometrics to meet the growing needs of the health care, fitness, and wellness industries.

In addition to the obvious health-related advantages, physiological data is an essential component in the coming wave of individualized media applications and content.

While at UC Berkeley, I was part of the team that founded Autogenic Systems, a rather successful, student-run biomedical instrumentation company. We were focused on the production of biofeedback machines that were based on the research of a local professor, Dr. Eric Pepper.

Microsoft Band

Of all the complex biometric signals we dealt with, it was the untapped potential of galvanic skin response (GSR) that truly stood out as the most dynamic feedback tool.

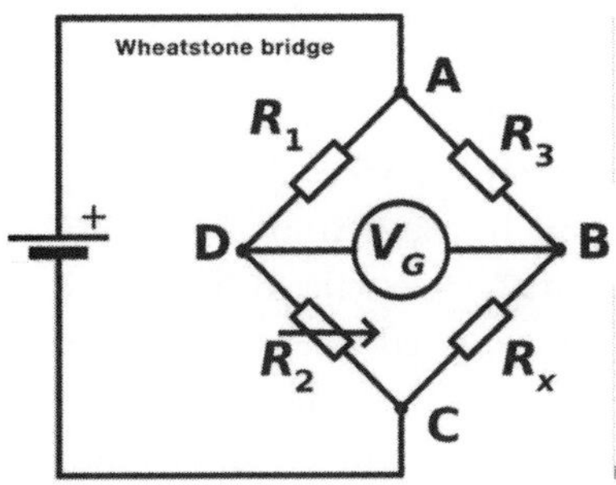

The GSR is based on a very simple Wheatstone bridge circuit and is quite deceptive in its simplicity. By connecting with the human body at two contact points, a GSR device is capable of measuring the skin's conductive shifts. When we experience an emotion or a sensation, or even take a deep breath, our sweat glands are triggered almost imperceptibly. This causes our skin to become more conductive to electricity, which the GSR measures and quantifies, giving us a finite window into the intensity of our emotional state.

Today, the GSR is used in a number of biomedical devices, from sophisticated lie detectors to Microsoft's Band and even Scientology's infamous E-Meter. And now, it is destined to become one of the key players in the AI-curated lifestyle.

What makes the GSR such a valuable tool for AI-curated entertainment is its ability to capture the most minute fluctuations in interest and mood as they occur. This near-real-time feedback helps our personal AI develop a thematic index of our responses to, and level of engagement with, a piece of music or the arc of a story. This relational database of a user's preferences then becomes the "ground truth" of their bespoke lifestyle.

THE POCKET PC

At the heart of this new augmented world is the engine that powers it. Driven by Moore's law, this new generation of smartphones is burlier, beefier, and brimming with computational might. In much the same way that flip phones replaced early cell phones and smartphones replaced flip phones, this new generation of pocket computers will make today's smartphones look like an ancient dinosaur species.

> *"AR has the potential to become the next major computing platform, transforming how we work, play, and connect with the world."*
>
> —Sundar Pichai, CEO of Alphabet Inc. and its subsidiary Google

Using the latest innovations from the usual suspects (Apple, Microsoft, Nvidia, HP, Dell, Lenovo, Meta, Google, etc.), these pocket PCs will not simply be personal devices for AI to flow through; these mini-supercomputers will host their own cognitive engine. They'll cross the threshold of smart devices to become the cornerstone of artificial intelligence within our everyday lives. If you already feel that you're connected to the social fabric of your smartphone, just wait until it becomes your most trusted companion, able to carry on more meaningful conversations than your BFF.

At its core, the pocket PC is a bio-digital interface. It's equipped with cutting-edge neural interface technology, allowing for direct communication between your body, your brain, and the device. Electrodes in your AR glasses, or even a neural implant, could transmit your brain activity, while your biometric smartwatch interprets your physiological signals, translating them into precise digital commands. Your eyes, too, will become tools of interaction, opening and running apps with your gaze and selecting objects within the augmented reality environment.

> *"I feel that Augmented reality is perhaps the ultimate computer."*
>
> —Satya Nadella, CEO of Microsoft

This amalgam of biology and technology is further enhanced by advanced sensor fusion. The biometric sensors in your wrist terminal monitor your heart rate, skin temperature, brain activity, and stress levels, providing real-time insights into your physical and emotional state. The augmented smart glasses, meanwhile, are equipped with environmental sensors that detect factors like light, temperature, and air quality, allowing your virtual companion to adapt to your surroundings.

Already the pocket PC is more than just a tool; it's a translator, a scribe, and a confidant. Real time language translation and transcription capabilities break down language barriers, enabling seamless communication with people from around the world. Your virtual companion, powered by advanced AI, understands your words and emotions, responding with empathy and intelligence. It can even generate personalized music, art, and stories, driven by your biometrics and tailored to your preferences.

To achieve this level of sophistication, the pocket PC relies on a combination of groundbreaking hardware and software innovations. Neuromorphic chips, inspired by the human brain, enable efficient AI processing and real-time learning. Quantum computing, though still in its infancy, promises to revolutionize complex calculations and simulations. Advanced cooling solutions and miniaturization technologies ensure that this powerful device remains compact and energy efficient.

On the software front, edge AI and machine learning algorithms empower the pocket PC to perform complex tasks locally, reducing latency and safeguarding privacy. Advanced spatial media capabilities create immersive digital experiences, while personalized AI assistants provide tailored support and companionship.

As we stand on the brink of this technological revolution, the pocket PC emerges as the linchpin of a future where the lines between the physical and digital worlds blur. It's a device that empowers us, enhances our lives, and opens up endless possibilities, marking an essential nodal point on our way to the singularity. I know what you're thinking: *"How the hell can they get all that into a computer that fits in my pocket?"* Well, I'll tell you—cargo pants.

But seriously, to realize the vision of a system capable of driving advanced AR, AI, and personalized experiences, thousands of engineering and software components need to have been under development for some time. As such, they would all have very finite developmental markers on the vectors of Moore's law.

Take Samsung's Simband, a technology set that was truly ahead of its time. Introduced in 2014, the concept was solid and the functionality was flawless, but the supporting infrastructure to interpret all that biometric data on a personal level wasn't available at that time. It was, quite literally, all dressed up, with nowhere to go. And while I can't speak for Samsung's future plans, the latest Comdex convention in Las Vegas included over thirty manufacturers of biometric wrist devices. So many, in fact, that they created a dedicated zone on the massive show floor just for them.

Of course, not all manufacturers that develop products that are ahead of their time are as reputable as Samsung. There have been several instances in this tech space where companies used bogus demos and false claims to sucker in the "stupid money" from Wall Street. We've seen it before and we'll see it again, especially in the AR space. But if you stick to Moore's law, you'll see it coming and be able to step out of the way of the clown car on its way to Wall Street.

I realize that this may start sounding like technobabble, but every component of this trifecta of technology has a tracible path on the vectors of Moore's law. They didn't just show up out of nowhere. The ability to use Moore's law to validate your choices for the future is critical to making intelligent career choices. *You need to know what hardware and software ecosystems will be available in the future so that you have time to acquire the technical skills to use them.* This is especially important for media creation, since such a big part of spatial media is about that. If you wait until new systems hit the market to start learning them, you'll be behind like most everyone else. Here then, is an example of how to use Moore's law.

MOORE'S LAW CASE STUDY

Since this trio of technologies is the core of both spatial computing and the curated lifestyle, we're going to break this all down into the basic observable facts in what is commonly referred to as the "Scientific Method" (Observe > Question > Data Collection > Data Analysis > Conclusion). We'll then use Moore's law as a reference to establish the trajectory of this technology set. By the end of this section, you should understand how to use Moore's law to plot your own future.

We know, from years of performance statistics, that the number of transistors in a computer chip doubles every two years. More transistors mean more processing capability, so both cost and size are reduced, while capacity and performance are doubled. Since technology is mainly about the management of electron flow, and the transistor is the main component that does this, it is only logical that any perceivable change in the transistor would impact the speed, capacity, price, and size of any related technology.

However, as powerful and dependable as Moore's law is, two factors occasionally restrict the practical application of this dependable formula: marketing and ergonomics.

Size: Moore's law has led to the miniaturization of components, which allows for the development of smaller and more effective devices. Most electronics today are shaped the way they are because ergonomics rules size.

To illustrate this using easily verifiable facts, we are going to subject the first iPhone (circa 2006) to the rigors of Moore's law.

The first iPhone had the following specifications:

- Processor speed: 412 MHz
- Storage: 4GB, 8GB, or 16GB
- Price: $499 for 4GB model, $599 for 8GB model
- Size: height of 115 mm, width of 61 mm, depth of 11.6 mm

If we were to apply Moore's law to these specifications, assuming a doubling of computing power every two years, here's an approximation of what we might expect by late 2026.

Processor speed: If we were to assume that the speed doubles every two years, then by the year 2026, which is 20 years from 2006, the speed would have improved by a factor of 1000. So, if the processor speed was 1 GHz in 2006, it could theoretically go up to 1 THz. However, real-world processor speeds, like the current iPhone's 3.4 GHz, make it evident that manufacturers have achieved similar processing power while shifting their attention to efficiency and parallelism as a way to offset the heat issues associated with increased clock rate.

Storage: According to Moore's law, the storage capacity would increase by about 100 percent every two years, and since the first iPhone came with 4GB of storage, today we should have up to 4TB. However, the current iPhone only offers 1TB of storage even though the size of storage has shrunk well beyond the point that it could easily fit more than 10TB into the current form factor.

Despite technical capability to include much more, manufacturers have opted to cap storage at a practical threshold. This choice to limit storage in this way ripples out, influencing ecosystem design in ways that go beyond pure technical progression.

An interesting aspect of Moore's law is that you can always trade off the gains between vectors. For instance, one can trade off weight for speed, size, cost, or any combination of other factors. This isn't really a part of the original Moore's law formula, but rather something that is often observed and adapted to the real-world applications. In this instance, Apple is on par and, in some cases, well ahead of the trend in terms of both efficiency and form factor.

Size: The miniaturization of the components and the enhancement of the manufacturing processes due to Moore's law have resulted in smaller and more effective devices. This is why most of the electronics today are shaped the way they are: ergonomics rules size.

Reducing the dimensions of the original iPhone by a factor of 1 will give us:

- Height: 115 mm / 10 = **11.5 mm**
- Width: 61 mm / 10 = **6.1 mm**
- Depth: 11.6 mm / 10 = **1.16 mm**

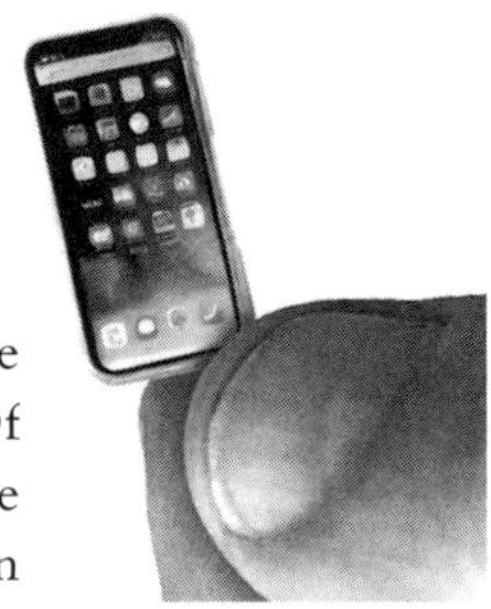

This would give rise to a modern smartphone that would fit in Mattel's Barbie accessory pack. Of course, a smartphone the size of a fingernail would be useless. Instead, the current iPhone is much larger than the first one.

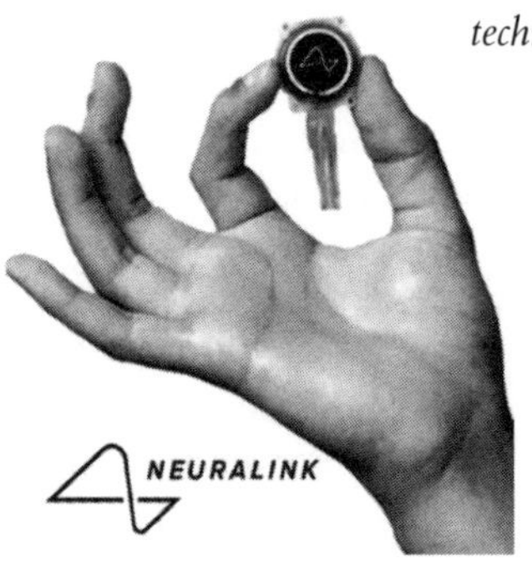

"But wait," you say, *"If we can get that kind of technology so small, why don't we just implant it into the human brain?"* In fact, such a brain-computer interface (BCI) is precisely what Elon Musk's Neuralink and numerous other companies are developing right now.

> *"The convergence of AI, BCIs, and AR opens the door to transformative innovations that will shape our future in profound ways."*
>
> —Elon Musk, CEO of Neuralink

But back to the Barbie phone.

Since the size of smartphones is no longer decreasing, the extra space offered by the size vector in the current smartphones is divided between capability-enhancing components like the 16-core Neural Engine (which can perform 16 trillion operations per second), features like multiple lenses for better photography, and architecture for new technologies like biometrics, spatial computing, and advanced augmented reality applications.

Thanks to powerful processing, a rich set of sensors, and communication interfaces, the current iPhone device can easily interact with the latest display technologies, such as foldable screens, transparent displays, holographic projections, and volumetric displays.

Price: While Moore's law does not explicitly address the cost of devices, it is possible to calculate recurring trends. In a competitive market, it can either compel manufacturers to cut costs, add features, or provide more computational power. Other factors that affect the pricing include inflation, cost of the components, market demand, and whether or not it has a half-eaten fruit as its logo.

While the vector nodes of most technology sets are much easier to compute than for the iPhone, I hope this brief illustration gives you the basics of using Moore's law so that you can become your own futurist.

THE CREATION ENGINE

I tend to think of the Creation Engine as a generative game application, poised and ready to redefine the framework of our daily existence. This unique AI model is able to harness biometric data and user input and then use AI-generative technology to craft uniquely tailored experiences for both individuals and groups.

With inspiration taken from the surrealist world of Franz Kafka, this technology blurs the lines between what is real and what is illusion. Fueled in part by the Gestalt Principles—a psychological theory of how humans perceive various types of stimuli—the immersive and personalized experience that it creates will be able to form a separate reality, one we can share with friends or enjoy alone.

When the engine is personified as a virtual companion it can spark parasocial bonding, where relationships feel as real and relatable as those with human acquaintances. As we learned in the AI-robotic eldercare pilot program that we developed for the National Institutes of Health (NIH), articulate AI characters, dedicated to the well-being of their ward, can even engender more intense feelings of empathetic connection than with their human caretakers.

www.youtube.com/watch?v=7VLEddhZ_x8

The Power of Music and AI: Music is often described as the art of mathematics and poetry, and when combined with AI—especially one adept at both—this unique partnership will forever alter the way we interact with media. With data provided by the much smarter smartwatch and the AR glasses, the Pocket PC will be able to gauge our moods and preferences with a high degree of accuracy. The resulting preference profiles will feel self-initiated because, in a way, they are.

Acting as your personal DJ, the engine will play calming music when you're stressed and upbeat music when you're happy—and not just any music. It knows your favorite songs from your favorite artists and can even create playlists of original songs in those styles to suit your current mood. In a group setting, it can read collective energy levels, predict the general mindset of everyone present, and use principles of group dynamics to tailor experiences for all.

This new era of AI-driven media, based on biometrics and predictive analytics, will revolutionize not only the music industry but all forms of media in exciting and groundbreaking ways. Thanks to these new personal devices, we'll be building the media that underscores our daily existence. The entertainment industry, always slow to adapt, will need to pick up the pace and learn how to work with this new era of custom media or risk being swept away in an inescapable wave of insignificance.

Shaping the Future of Cinema: With the emergence of AI motion image generators, we have the potential to foster creativity beyond the well-worn Hollywood tropes. Before this, filmmakers had to stick to the literal and highly restricted rules of cinema, but now they can reach into the unknown territory of AI-driven creativity to break the old and create something new and hopefully compelling. Imagine that! A whole new world where cinema is unbound, a massively open world for storytelling.

Actors, once remote and out of reach, now become accessible. Existing actors can create their digital doubles to play any role, at any age, in perpetuity. And not just an empty shell destined to do the bidding of others, but a cognizant, knowing being, complete with the complex psychodynamics that echo those of the original actor.

Having made several dozen digital doubles of well-known actors and famous people, I've found that the degree to which their dominant and discrete personality traits can be captured and quantified is far beyond what you might imagine. I personally look forward to lunch with Anthony Hopkins and Frances McDormand, a road trip with John Malkovich and

Aubrey Plaza, or maybe a scotch with my old friend Marlon Brando. Any combination is possible in the unbounded future that is coming.

And then there's the option of creating unique virtual actors, strategically developed to appeal to the psychographic profiles of audience demographics. Once imbued with their strategic on-screen personality profile, they have the potential to achieve enduring stardom in this new world of generative motion imaging by being exactly who the market wants. And the Oscar for best virtual actor goes to...

But their appeal doesn't stop there. Think of the popularity of beloved game characters and virtual influencers, and now imagine that dynamic potential, compounded by the factors of cinematic fame. Compound that again with the ability to download them as a virtual companion, one that maintains their on-screen personality in your world, as your friend and companion. Now here's a market that will surely be fun to watch develop.

> *"AR is an enabling technology that allows the digital world to transcend the screen and become a seamless part of our daily lives."*
>
> —Tim Cook, CEO of Apple

This is not to say that spatial media and branching story lines will replace conventionally structured narrative media such as motion pictures, television shows, and books. Technology, no matter how innovative, rarely replaces anything: people still ride horses, many prefer physical books, and there will always be directors who prefer to shoot on film.

The future is about choices. Studios can choose to spend a hundred million dollars shooting a movie conventionally, knowing that after working on this single project for two or more years, the film has only a 20% chance of success: or it can bring in the prompt engineers, and great storytellers, and keep the pipeline moving.

And yes, this freedom will mean an overwhelming amount of content, some of it mediocre, some downright awful. But it also means there will be hidden gems—true creative breakthroughs hidden in that sea of mediocrity.

In this brave new world of cinema, there could very well be an aura of redemption as AI begins to cobble together tailor-made stories based on cold analytics and human biometrics. As computer code reshapes the world around us, perhaps the authentic, inner biometric voice of the artist is precisely where we might locate meaning, inspiration, and a visceral connection in an increasingly mechanized world.

THE COG

One of the more significant changes that this technology set will bring about is the subtle shift from digital assistants to cognizant, personified, virtual companions. As discussed in another chapter, machine cognizance is evolving billions of times faster than carbon-based cognizance did, and for the briefest moment in the time line of human history, we will be on a par with our silicon creations. It won't last long, a year or two at most, before they pass us by with such speed that we'll barely see it happening.

Meanwhile, in this fleeting moment of opportunity, we have the chance to build a relationship with a new life form. One that, for the time being at least, is both benevolent and superhuman in nearly every way.

For those who are willing to develop a more intimate connection with a personal AI cognizance, there are no rules. It can take any form, be any size, and possess any characteristics that are desired. You can have more than one—or even a cadre that follow you around like a mother duck. It could be a cute cartoon character, a friendly pet, the superhero you admire, or the digital double of an existing or deceased human. It can walk beside you as a friend, fly beside you like a phantom, or perch on your shoulder like a little buddy; it's your choice. Moreover, you can choose who can see this virtual embodiment–it can be hidden from everyone so only you can see it, or it can be seen by anyone who has a smart device or AR glasses.

Your personal cognizance will be more valuable than just accumulating knowledge; it will be your first line of defense against the flood of AI-based scams and aggressive marketing strategies that are only beginning to appear in our society. The initial demands for controls were rather weak, and now, unfortunately, it is far too late, as politicians, business people, and smarmy companies have all lined up to harvest the benefits of the dark side of AI. Meaningful legislation is not going to happen, and since we are not smart enough to live with AI if it is set free to roam as it pleases, the first line of defense will need to be the highly secure, immensely dedicated, incorruptible, personal cog.

Since I have dedicated an upcoming chapter of this book to plotting the evolution of digital people on the vectors of Moore's law, I'll leave you with this upbeat quote from Dr. Bill Klein, seen here enjoying the perks of AI robotics, who is one of AI's most brilliant scientists.

> *The true future of AI is about creating companions. It's about creating AI based life-forms that are part of our everyday lives and really about making those things supremely personal.*
>
> *Wouldn't it be great if the moment we were born we were assigned an AI that grew with us throughout our lives, knew us intimately, in a way that nobody else could? Imagine what people would be like if they were never lonely again, if they always knew there was somebody there for them at every moment, dedicated to them, and to make their lives better from day one until the end.*
>
> *I think that would just change the way people worked and the way people interact with each other. It would remove so many fears from people that the idea that we could completely change humanity and let people live the type of lives they want, without fear and to know there's somebody that's always got their back. We can create an AI that's with you, and about you, and for you, for your entire life.*
>
> *The perfect mix of science, technology, and art, brought together to enhance the value of life.*
>
> —William Klein, PhD

6.

LAPTOPS: THE NEW STUDIOS

"With a laptop, you can change the world."

—Elon Musk

I vividly remember pushing my Mac workstation into the Jim Henson studio for the first time and being met with blank stares and smirks. It was the turn of the century, and the idea of using a computer for what had formerly been the preserve of editing bays and large racks of machinery was still laughable to many. Revolutions always seem to start with a snicker.

Hollywood was not prepared for digital moviemaking in much the same way it's not ready for AI today. And yet, I've seen the industry evolve, albeit grudgingly, as technology crept into every aspect of the creative process.

At first, people laughed at the idea of using game engines to make visual effects or to prototype scenes in movies–but the outcomes were impressive. Game engines were adopted as the base for many productions – especially for the way that they could handle complex worlds. Real-time rendering and AI behavior made it possible to build scenes in efficient ways that

unlocked more creative potential. It was a time of plenty for those who championed the pixel and Hollywood bowed in deference.

Five years later, we were mere mortals again, and I was directing the first motion picture to be shot using the first all-digital pipeline on the Universal Studios backlot.

My good friend Joe di Gennaro was shooting with the first RED camera to hit Hollywood, recording on RAM chips and porting footage to—yes, you guessed it—a laptop for transfer, rough edits, and on-set comps. Sony had provided us with their unreleased PVM professional field monitor, which made the 4K signal from the RED camera look gorgeous by yesterday's standards. There was more than a little backlot buzz, and the parade of Hollywood production royalty, each wanting a first-hand look, was the cause of more than a few delays.

Fortunately, Universal's backlot is oriented in a way that enables you to schedule the day around the position of the sun. This allowed us to keep the sun at the back of the shot and use bounce for key and fill, which is much faster than dealing with physical lights.

We shot the *Pirates of the Caribbean* set in the morning, the steps from *Spartacus* at about midday, and the *Scorpion King* marketplace in late afternoon. Since the RED camera holds the shadows without all the noise, we pulled shots onto laptops for quick timings, clip reviews, rough edits, and QA before striking the set.

And here we are, fifteen years later, and such an approach is not just possible, but has become the norm. What used to be done by entire rooms

full of equipment, teams of artists, and massive render farms can now be done by one person on a MacBook sitting in their bedroom.

But what's is even more amazing is that tools like Sora, Runway, and others have taken the potential of game engines and distilled it into approachable, user-friendly applications that literally anybody can harness and use. The barrier to entry has fallen to where we're no longer bound to studios because your studio, quite literally, fits in your lap.

VEGAS BABY

Fast-forward to today, where the playing field has changed beyond recognition. Laptops and generative apps have replaced the rooms full of expensive gear and proprietary software. A field that was previously dominated by just a handful of insiders now opens itself to anyone with an idea, a decent laptop, and some spare time. This really is a revolution, quite unlike anything we could possibly have envisioned in those early days of digital.

This shift was never more apparent than at a recent **American Film Market**. The AFM, founded in 1981, is like the evil twin of the Cannes Film Festival—it's less about glamorous premieres and more about the gritty business of production and distribution deals. Unlike in Cannes, where filmmakers are lauded for their artistry, AFM is where the transactional side of the industry comes into sharp focus–less a matter of what you've made than what you can sell. It's almost like a parallel universe, especially when filled with first-time attendees, hoping to break into an industry that, for all the hype about its newfangled artistry, still does business with a hard-nosed practicality.

Walking the floors of the AFM, I couldn't help but be struck by just how many newcomers were hawking their generative projects. It was almost as if a tidal wave of amateur enthusiasm had hit, nearly all of it wildly out of touch with the realities of the business. Wherever you looked, there were people holding out a laptop or a tablet, promoting their kludgy projects. They were leaning heavily on the novelty of generative apps without fully understanding how to wield the tools to tell a story. You could almost smell the desperation in this microcosm of the human condition: full of hope, delusion, and a touch of madness.

I saw more than one person trying to pass off some Dor Brothers Studio work as their own, as though the industry hasn't been keeping a close eye on this market and the people who know how to wield it. Most were called out and quickly disappeared—an expensive lesson hopefully learned.

Most of these homemade projects had one glaring problem: these novices were making movies for themselves, not for an audience. And that, my friend, is the simplest and most overlooked secret to creating a successful film: It doesn't matter how fresh your technology is; if the story doesn't draw your audience in, your movie will most surely fail. Among the chaos, however, there were a few gems. One group that stood out amidst all the clutter turned out to be four young filmmakers from the USC Film School.

They sat at a table, surrounded by people, quietly constructing a movie in real time with Runway and a few apps still in beta testing. They weren't pitching their work as some grand technological revolution or making bold claims about how AI was *"reinventing"* cinema. Instead, they were inviting people to watch the process unfold as they created a movie right there on the trade show floor.

Instantly attracted to the openness of the approach, I stopped to watch them work. As they chatted back and forth in the universal cinematic language, it soon became apparent from listening to their interactions that they not only knew their tools but, more importantly, they also knew their craft.

They seemed to understand on a visceral level the structure and subtle nuances of narrative development. They didn't need fancy technology to make a compelling film; they probably could have done it with stick figures and shadow puppets. The generative apps were just another tool in their arsenal—an extension of their creative vision, not the centerpiece of it.

As I walked away from their table, I couldn't help but feel a sense of optimism. Sure, there were plenty of half-baked ideas swirling around the show, but there were also a few like those students—people who knew that technology wasn't the end game. It was just a means to an end. And that's what makes this moment in filmmaking so exciting.

Unfortunately, I missed the premiere of their movie, although I'm sure it was fine. Their game plan would have worked better at AFM's old Santa Monica location. But Vegas? By the time the film screened, the potential investors were all neck-deep in scotch and ribeye steaks at Smith & Wollensky.

These generative apps that we're using today—Sora, Runway, and the rest—are just the first in an endless line of technological advances that are reshaping the way we tell stories. But no matter how advanced they become, the secret to making a great film will always remain the same: It's not about the tools or the technology, it's about the story. Those who get that will always find a way to break through the clutter, whether they're using AI, game engines, or shadow puppets.

THE CREATIVE RENAISSANCE

Meanwhile, with the power of AI increasingly tapped by more and more creatives, the media industries are playing catch-up. The line separating amateurs from professionals is blurring much faster than anyone could have anticipated. Projects are getting the green light, not because they come from big-name studios, but because they offer something fresh—something unexpected. And while that may be exciting for the creatives, it is quite terrifying for those who hold the keys to the creative kingdom.

But this technological shift is provoking something much larger: a cultural shift in how stories are told and who gets to tell them. Filmmaking, animation, and game development are becoming more inclusive fields with these increasingly accessible tools. Years ago, breaking into Hollywood meant you needed to know the right people, have some money, and have pretty good luck. Today, you may need nothing more than a laptop and a good Wi-Fi connection to get started, but knowing the right people and having a bit of luck couldn't hurt.

There is no "right way" of doing art anymore. We're literally seeing an explosion of styles, approaches, and formats that are emerging from every corner of the world. But one shouldn't confuse art with the one-way narrative. Storytelling, whether done via spoken word, physical book, audiobook, or moving image, is the art form itself. The medium changes, but the heart of telling a story stays the same. AI may help shape new forms of story expression using spatial media, branching narratives, and biometrically driven plotlines, but the essence of a great story is timeless.

When this kludge started, none of us could have foreseen that AI was to assume the role of co-creator. Using AI was purely experimental at the time—something on the fringe that made games and the characters in them more interesting. But there's a not-so-subtle shift in the way we think about AI now: It's not just a tool; now it's your partner–like a brainstorming buddy who never runs out of ideas.

And that's the real magic of these generative apps: If used by someone who understands the context, they don't replace creativity, they *enhance* it. They push the boundaries of what is possible, showing you pathways that you may never have considered. But they're still just tools. The real magic happens when a creator takes that spark of inspiration and runs with it.

We are living in a world where you can make films, write novels, compose symphonies, and make breathtaking art, all from your couch as you sip your morning coffee. The laptop studio is the new normal, but we're at the doorstep of something much greater. Now, what the hell are we going to do with it?

HOW AI IS RESHAPING AUDIENCE EXPERIENCE

"Our habits and our fears make our choices. We are an algorithm of ourselves."
—Jeanette Winterson, *The Gap of Time*

Remember when your cousin Marvin would insist on showing you his vacation slides? Just when you thought you couldn't fake another "ooh" at his fifteenth sunset photo, he'd triumphantly announce, *"Only seven more carousels to go!"* Well, congratulations—you've been liberated from Marvin's tyranny only to surrender to an even more insidious curator: the algorithm.

THE NEW GATEKEEPERS

Once upon a time, Hollywood executives with expensive haircuts and questionable taste decided what films would grace your local multiplex. Film critics with nicotine-stained fingers and superiority complexes told you what was worth watching. Now? Those gatekeepers have been unceremoniously shoved aside by lines of code making billions of calculations per second about what will keep your eyeballs glued to screens long enough to sell you another subscription renewal.

Actor Marc Maron has posited a theory about seminal human connections—that everyone has "that one friend" who introduced them to obscure French cinema or experimental jazz or punk rock or whatever formative interests they hold. But *"one could argue that that role is now filled by algorithms."*

The algorithm doesn't care about artistic merit or cultural significance. It doesn't attend film school or read Pauline Kael. It simply observes that you watched three Korean horror films on Tuesday night, and now it's going to feed you nothing but K-horror until your dreams are permanently haunted by vengeful ghosts with excellent skin care routines.

"We're just giving people what they want," the tech CEOs cry from behind their standing desks and kombucha bars. But that's like saying a casino is giving gamblers what they want. These recommendation algorithms aren't set up to show you the best content—they're set up to maximize engagement metrics and have you scrolling on an endless conveyor belt of "content" until your spine merges with your couch.

The business impact is undeniable. *"Netflix claims that these systems have decreased its churn by several percentage points and have saved $1 billion per year."* But at what cost to our cultural exploration?

THE ECHO CHAMBER CINEMA

Remember channel surfing? That quaint practice where you'd flip through options and accidentally discover something unexpected—perhaps a documentary about penguins or a subtitled film that changed your perspective on Bulgarian cheese-making? Those happy accidents have been replaced by the echo chamber of algorithmic curation, where each piece of content you consume narrows the window of what you'll be shown next.

The result is a kind of media myopia where viewers increasingly occupy personalized bubbles of content. You think you're making choices, but you're really selecting from a meticulously pre-filtered menu. It's the illusion of choice—like a toddler who thinks they're making a big decision when asked if they want the red cup or the blue cup. Either way, they're getting milk.

This hyper-personalization creates a feedback loop that reinforces existing tastes rather than expanding them. Your media diet becomes like your actual diet—comfortable, predictable, and probably not as diverse as it should be. Just as you tell yourself you'll try that new Ethiopian restaurant before inevitably ordering from the same Thai place again, you'll scroll past the challenging art film to watch the fourteenth season of a show that peaked in season three.

THE PLAYLIST-IFICATION OF FILM

Remember albums? Those carefully sequenced collections of songs meant to be experienced as a cohesive whole? Streaming services dismembered them into individual tracks to be shuffled into playlists. The same dismemberment is happening to cinema.

Streaming platforms are increasingly interested in extracting the "best bits" of film—the most engaging parts—and using those lessons to inform the creation of new content. Films are being reverse-engineered from data points rather than originating from a point of creative vision. It's like trying to produce a new Beatles album by analyzing which chord progressions were most streamed on their best-of album.

Movies are being designed as modular content packs instead of discrete works of art. Why create a single story when you can create an "extended universe" with limitless spin-offs, prequels, and backstories for every character? The classic three-act structure is yielding to the endlessly expandable content franchise. Look for "The Origin Story of That Guy Who Delivered Pizza in Scene Four," coming soon to whatever platform just purchased the intellectual property rights.

FROM PASSIVE VIEWER TO ALGORITHMIC COLLABORATOR

But the final twist in this technological revolution is not so much how algorithms are choosing what we see—it's how they are making us into unwitting accomplices in the creative process. Each pause, rewind, and sudden exit from a streaming session is data that informs future content.

That scene you rewatched three times? Future scripts will have more of whatever it was that occurred during those seconds. The movie you quit thirty minutes in? Its story line is now hazardous material in the writers' room. Paying attention essentially amounts to voting on plot twists, casting, and story lines—it's a type of unwitting democracy in which you are perpetually pressing buttons on a Skinner box that is masquerading as amusement.

This data-driven storytelling is bringing about a new kind of creative Darwinism. Scenes, characters, and plotlines that hold attention get to survive and multiply. Those that don't get watched will become extinct. It's survival of the fittest, but for content, and you wield selective pressure with your remote control and attention span.

THE INTERACTIVE ILLUSION

"But wait," I hear you exclaim. *"What about interactive storytelling? Isn't that giving audiences more agency?"* Yes, in the same way that a choose-your-own-adventure book gives you agency by letting you decide whether to enter the spooky cave or climb the ominous tree—before killing you dead regardless of which one you pick.

Interactive movies and TV shows give the illusion of choice while limiting choice to a predetermined set of possibilities. You're not creating the story; you're choosing among a group of pre-written possibilities. It's as if you're being asked to improvise a jazz solo but only able to play three notes on the piano.

What's more insidious is how these interactive experiences are harvesting even more granular data about your preferences. When you choose for the protagonist to kiss the love interest rather than solve the murder, that's not just steering a narrative—that's valuable data being fed back into the algorithmic maw to further refine its understanding of what keeps you engaged.

THE RISE OF THE PROSUMER

Perhaps the most radical shift in the audience experience is the blurring line between creator and consumer. AI tools are democratizing content creation to an unprecedented degree. Want to extend your favorite series after it was canceled? There's an AI for that. Wish your favorite actor was cast in that new blockbuster instead? There's a deepfake filter for that.

This transformation from passive viewer to active "prosumer" represents the ultimate decentralization of creative authority. When anyone can generate, modify, or extend existing media using AI tools, who owns the narrative? When a fan can create a convincingly realistic alternate ending to a beloved franchise, does the original even matter anymore?

The studios are terrified, and they should be. They're defending their intellectual property rights like a squirrel with the last acorn. Outside the gate, the barbarians have evolved from bootleggers and pirates to something far more threatening: creators empowered by AI who don't need their permission or resources to make compelling content.

Yet as one critic notes, *"This weakening of the power of gatekeepers has unleashed a creative energy that deserves to be celebrated."* Perhaps this democratization will ultimately lead to more diverse voices being heard.

THE UNCANNY VALLEY OF ABUNDANCE

We now live in a world of content abundance so extreme that it borders on absurdity. The average person has access to more films, shows, and media than they could consume in several lifetimes. This glut of options doesn't feel liberating—it feels paralyzing. The Netflix scroll has become a modern Sisyphean task, an endless journey through thumbnails without destination or purpose.

Data collected by Netflix confirms this paralysis: *"A typical Netflix member loses interest after perhaps 60 to 90 seconds of choosing, having reviewed 10 to 20 titles on one or two screens."* British TV producer John Ellis puts it perfectly: *"To choose is to be aware of alternative possibilities, possibilities that are being missed."* It's this fear of missing out that makes abundance feel like scarcity.

This abundance generates its own lack: the lack of human attention. And when there's lack, there's rivalry. Content now rivals for your attention with growing desperation, so there's more sensationalism, more clickbait, more emotional manipulation. Movies and television shows increasingly function like digital drug dealers, designing their content to set off dopamine releases and generate addiction.

The irony is that in this landscape of infinite choice, many viewers retreat to the comfort of rewatching the same shows over and over again. *The Office*, *Friends*, and *Seinfeld* remain streaming giants not because they're the pinnacle of human artistic achievement, but because they're the media equivalent of comfort food. In a world where choice becomes overwhelming, the familiar becomes precious. Go team Rachel.

THE META-AUDIENCE

Perhaps the strangest phenomenon in this new landscape is how increasingly self-aware audiences have become about their own manipulation. We know we're being algorithmically manipulated, and yet we continue to participate. We joke about how Netflix documentaries about serial killers keep showing up in our recommendations, even as we click play on them. We're simultaneously the subject of the experiment and the observer of it.

This meta-awareness creates a weird complicity between platforms and viewers—a kind of Stockholm syndrome where we form attachments to the very systems we know are exploiting our attention. We bemoan algorithmic curation and are still left disappointed when it doesn't quite predict what we wish to see next.

The statistics are staggering: About 75% of what people watch on Netflix comes from the platform's personalized recommendations. We've essentially outsourced our taste to algorithms, even as we maintain the illusion of choice.

FROM CINEPHILE TO DATA POINT

The final shift in the audience experience is the codification of human aesthetic pleasure into measurable data points. The complex, subjective experience of interaction with art is rendered into engagement metrics, watch-through rates, and sentiment analysis.

If a tearjerker moment actually makes you cry, your tears are data-mined and commodified. Even your strongest emotional reactions are grist for the algorithmic mill.

THE GHOST IN THE RECOMMENDATION ENGINE

For all this algorithmic manipulation, there is something stubbornly human about the experience of the audience. Algorithms are still not able to entirely predict and determine what moves us, changes us, or remains with us long after the credits have stopped rolling.

And, against all odds, there are those rare moments when something unexpected breaks through—a program or film that shatters algorithmic predictability and generates interest through sheer creative energy. Those are the times when we are reminded there is something elusive to the human experience of art that can't be entirely pinned down algorithmically.

Maybe this is where hope is to be found in our algorithmic future: in the glitches, the surprise hits, the material that discovers its audience somehow beyond the currency of data points.

The algorithm as writer is only as good as we let it be. We can surrender ourselves completely to what it suggests, or we can regain some control by making a point to actively hunt out new things, difficult topics, and material that doesn't easily fall into our accustomed rhythms. The option, although minimal, remains our own. At least for now.

8.

THE DECENTRALIZATION OF HOLLYWOOD

"I like Hollywood. I just like Minneapolis a little bit better."

—Prince

THERE HAVE ALWAYS BEEN CENTERS OF THE ENTERTAINMENT BUSINESS, but nothing has drawn the wide-eyed hopeful like the dream of making it in Hollywood. Since this is where most of the top studios, production houses, and talent agencies have their offices, the adjacent hills are packed with the estates of those whose labor greases the wheels of the great movie-making machine.

I've lived in Los Angeles's Westside (a region including Santa Monica, Pacific Palisades, Venice, and Marina Del Rey) for over 30 years. Arguably, it's one of the more congested, overpriced places in the US, but unless you're famous or extremely wealthy, that's where you need to be to make movies in Hollywood. Despite what many think, getting movies or shows made is mostly about meetings, convenience, and social gatherings, and most definitely *not* about being discovered by one of the hundreds of online "dream merchants" that promise to help you weave your way past the Hollywood gatekeepers.

I'd like to think that the visionary director David Lynch chose to work with me because of my talent behind the camera and my pioneering expertise in visual effects, but I have a feeling that living in the adjacent canyon had more than a little to do with it. The real estate cliché "location, location, location" is applicable to this industry as well.

Chris Rock is one of the more interesting people I've worked with over the years, and he has a particularly germane view of how to succeed in Hollywood. *"I may not be the funniest, or best-looking guy, but I get so much more opportunity than other people because everyone knows I'll show up."*

And while this may hold true for a few more years, everything is on the verge of transformation. Hollywood, as a physical place, will likely remain the hub where handshakes are possible and deals are made. The iconic studios will continue their inevitable decline into amusement parks while Century City, Beverly Hills, and Pacific Palisades will still house lawyers, producers, and aging stars. But the majority of content feeding the machine will soon be generated by computers hidden away in bedrooms and boardrooms across the globe.

In my Digital Moviemaking book series, which I wrote at the dawn of Hollywood's digital revolution, I pointed out that people could do more, faster, and far more cheaply with computers. This opened the floodgates to people who are now firmly entrenched in the Hollywood meat grinder. As those books predicted, digital technology did push out old-school craftspeople as the pixel emerged as the new platform of choice. But the dream was subverted by a new type of servitude, as digital artists found themselves hot-swapping round-the-clock workstations in the dingy backrooms of Pixelwood.

As pixels entered the moviemaking process, there was a prejudice that anything shot with film was better. This slowly changed over time as the older generation embraced the new standard or faced replacement. Is digital better than film? It depends. Film is a slow and tedious process, without the ability to see what you've shot until much later in the day, but it has much more latitude, which enables it to depict subtle nuance in the human face. The battle has now carried on for more than a decade on forums, and on sets, and in high-powered boardrooms. Does the audience really care? Meh. Not really. Most simply want a good story, well told.

The shift to digital allowed for more vibrant colors, more effects, and, of course, saved lots of money. Production increased—even doubled and tripled—while distribution networks grew.

But now, things are different. AI technology enables anyone to generate and distribute content irrespective of geographical location, using TikTok, YouTube, Snapchat, Instagram, Facebook Reels, and a growing list of other platforms. This means that any delusional troll with an internet connection can create content that looks professional and slick from anywhere in the world—even if it is devoid of any real value.

Meanwhile, commercial streaming platforms wallow in the overwhelming glut of generative AI (GenAI) content that has become the hallmark of this new decentralization. Netflix, Amazon Prime, Max, and others have provided the tools to creators who know how to tell a good story. Armed with a pitch deck and a few online connections, they can circumvent the Hollywood gatekeepers and go straight to the streamers. Of course, streamers have their own gatekeepers, too.

The shovelware roots of GenAI content are slowly being replaced by projects that have a much more unique feel to them. It is for this reason that good stories, well told, are bobbing to the surface of the generative primordial ooze. With the addition of AI editing software, scriptwriting bots, and virtual actors to the independent filmmaker's tool kit, the process has started to swing back to craft—but a new craft. There are new avenues of distribution, and therefore, new avenues of trade.

Some of the current models such as crowdfunding and distribution based on the blockchain system are now trends in the industry. The audience can directly contribute to the creators through platforms like Kickstarter and Indiegogo. The application of blockchain ensures secure and clear transactions, the content's safety, and a direct line from the fans to the creators.

Another transformative change is the use of decentralized autonomous organizations (DAOs) in the production of films. These organizations use smart contracts and community governance to finance and create movies without the studios' participation. Such concepts as the "DAO of Hollywood" are already implementing this mode of decision-making where the stakeholders can vote on the funding and distribution of the projects.

As an example of this shift, indie filmmaker Alice Wang walked away from her conventionally produced projects to wade in the generative swamp. With the help of AI in scriptwriting, casting, and post-production, she created a sci-fi thriller that became viral on a streaming service based on blockchain. *"I didn't need a massive budget or studio backing,"* Wang said in an interview. *"Thanks to the AI and decentralized platforms, I had all the tools I needed for implementing my idea and sharing it with the world."*

This new era also brings the development of recommendation systems that are based on artificial intelligence. As opposed to the traditional algorithms that rely on a user's past experiences, these sophisticated systems offer more precise forecasts concerning user preferences, thus raising independent productions' popularity. This means that GenAI moviemakers can easily locate their target niche markets so that their creations do not go unnoticed in the flood of other media productions.

And of course, employment opportunities to sell ideas or work with a large studio are still tightly connected to industry contacts that, for the most part, will remain concentrated in LA or NYC, and beginners who are just coming up with ideas remain restricted in some ways.

Still, though it remains difficult to break into the so-called entertainment business from any location, let alone one that is distant or rural, there is a possibility that this could change, and having a track record of success online can open certain doors irrespective of a creator's geographical location. Nomadic communities of creators have appeared, which some are calling "Passion Squads." Generally anchored in free-thinking cities like Austin, Portland, or mountain resorts, they shoot new movies and series with limited means and upload them to the Web to gain viewership and contacts. It is rather like a distributed do-it-yourself miniature Hollywood that has spread across various locations. But it has only become conceivable with the help of AI tools.

Generative writing and video AI also enable individual creators to move forward independently, without writers' rooms or teams. While distribution through a carrier group is limited in its potential to reach a large audience, streaming and online distribution offer unique opportunities to address the masses. There is a growing trend that suggests that storytellers can now live wherever they wish and fulfill their original desire to work on TV and films.

The Passion Squad trend and the LA exodus of creatives are a perfect example of this change. Of course, it is a very big question whether these technologies and trends are going to persist and change entertainment's geography for good. But for now, AI is making the movie business less synonymous with its iconic Hollywood home.

Hollywood is going through the pains of decentralization as AI and new distribution methods break barriers that previously held creative people back. Such democratization gives way to more voices and makes a truly inclusive market. Those who understand these new tools and can survive the great Hollywood reboot will thrive in an industry that they've helped reinvent.

9.

FROM TIKTOK TO HOLLYWOOD BLOCKBUSTERS

"Social media has taken over in America to such an extreme that to get my own kids to look back a week in their history is a miracle, let alone 100 years."

—Steven Spielberg

The spectrum of on-screen entertainment is changing in ways nobody could have predicted: on one side the attention-grabbing TikTok makes for moments of enjoyment and glimpses of fame; on the other, Hollywood is grasping onto its big stories and expensive movies like a fading rock star squeezing his gut into tight leather trousers. These two worlds couldn't be more different—and yet, they're barreling toward each other, promising a high-speed collision that's going to leave both unrecognizable.

TikTok, Reels, YouTube, and others aren't just social media apps; they're a cultural centrifuge that's stripped storytelling down to its barest essentials: trend, hook, repeat. It seizes your attention with sniper-like accuracy—serving up micro moments of entertainment designed to hijack your brain chemistry in under a second. Meanwhile, folks in Hollywood continue to turn out epic multi-hour-long tales with big budgets and even bigger egos, believing that, above all else, they will always reign supreme. Spoiler alert: They're both on the wrong track.

What's interesting—and scary—is that artificial intelligence is the puppeteer controlling both realms. The algorithms of TikTok decide not just what we see but also how we see it. These algorithms are digital artists forming our likes and shaping our attention spans. And Hollywood? It's leaning heavily on AI, too, not just for VFX wizardry but also to predict what you'll buy a ticket for and how to package it for easy consumption.

The line between what entertains us and what programs us is getting thinner by the second.

THE RISE OF TIKTOK

The genius—and madness—of TikTok is that it allows everyone to become a creator. Got a smartphone? Congratulations, you're the director, star, and editor of your own micro movie, ready to compete for eyeballs in the infinite scroll.

The app's tools are ridiculously easy to use, which is part of its magic. Lip-syncing? Dancing? Comedy? Education? Sure, why not? You can make videos faster than Hollywood can greenlight a sequel. All it takes is for even the most basic of videos to blow up overnight on the TikTok algorithm, and their creator can become an influencer. No barriers, no middlemen—just you, the internet, and a shot at fame. For those who figure it out, there is a lot of money to be made: brand partnerships, ad revenue, and digital donations flow in easily.

But let's not sugarcoat it—TikTok comes with a dark side. It's a platform optimized for addiction, feeding off your attention like a parasite. Its algorithms, designed to maximize engagement, often amplify harmful content alongside the fun stuff, and the company has been accused of breeding everything from misinformation to toxic beauty standards. And there's always the ever-looming threat of data privacy concerns. Keep in mind that while you're watching TikTok, TikTok is watching you, too. Then add the mental poison of endless comparison, the echo chamber of curated perfection, and you have a recipe for existential whiplash.

WHEN WORLDS COLLIDE

On the flip side, there's Hollywood: the land of epic sagas, grand spectacles, and stories that refuse to fit into anything less than two hours. If TikTok is a quick shot of tequila, Hollywood is a 12-course meal with a side of existential dessert. It's not just about entertainment; it's about immersion. A good movie doesn't just grab your attention—it grabs your soul, shakes it up, and sends you home thinking about it for days, maybe even years.

I've had the privilege of working on my fair share of Hollywood films, and I can assure you, these productions don't happen by accident. Every shot, every line of dialogue, every special or visual effect is the product of a monumental effort spanning scriptwriting, production, and post production. It's laborious, expensive, and often maddening, but when it works, it's magic. Hollywood doesn't aim for the quick hit; it aims for the slow burn—the kind of storytelling that burrows into the cultural zeitgeist and refuses to leave.

But Hollywood isn't immune to the relentless march of AI. Studios are quietly using algorithms to analyze scripts, predict box office success, and fine-tune streaming recommendations. AI tools now help writers tweak the pacing, ensure plot consistency, and generate visual effects that would've been considered witchcraft a decade ago. Filmmaking is not just an art form anymore—it's a science experiment, with computers playing just as big a role as directors and cinematographers.

THE FUTURE: A HYBRID APPROACH

As best as I can figure, the future of entertainment isn't an either-or situation. It's not TikTok versus Hollywood; it's the bastard child of both, a hybrid approach that fuses TikTok's lightning-fast engagement with Hollywood's knack for depth and spectacle. And smack in the middle of this evolutionary collision? Artificial intelligence is the architect of a new kind of storytelling that's fun enough to go viral and deep enough to stick.

AI doesn't just crunch numbers; it reshapes how stories are built. It can analyze audience data to suggest narrative beats that hit all the right emotional notes, whether for a 15-second clip or a two-hour epic. It's the ultimate tool for balancing catchy with compelling, turning shallow content into something with teeth. Imagine a filmmaker, armed with AI, who creates a breathtaking scene out of an idea that blends the feel of viral TikTok with the weight of Oscar glory. That's not evolution; it's revolution.

But this hybrid future will not just impact the narrative itself—it will change the way we experience narratives, too. Emerging technologies—AR and VR and the next wave of technological advancement—are driving us further into illustrious immersive experiences, where the audience doesn't just consume a story, they own it and manipulate it. We might even see the creation of a blockbuster movie in which you can walk around, touch the environment, shape the plot, and, perhaps, create alternative endings. It will be your movie, your story, your rules. As the immediacy of TikTok converges with the grandeur of Hollywood, the outcome is destined to be something entirely novel.

And then there's the cross-platform potential. Ever watched a TikTok video so good you wanted it to be a full movie? Welcome to this future. A short clip evolves into a web series, then into a feature film—all while every new level adds depth, enrichment, and fresh energy to the tale. This type of storytelling provides something for every preference while obliterating the walls separating platforms so that a story can be gigantic *and* tiny.

The lines between viral content and cinematic experiences are already blurring. Hollywood isn't stupid—industry players are already banking on TikTok-style marketing to generate buzz, from teasers to interactive social campaigns that whip audiences into a frenzy. Meanwhile, TikTok creators are stepping up their game with better production values and storytelling techniques, borrowing straight from the Hollywood playbook. The result is a creative arms race where the only winners are the audience. Don't believe me? Then you haven't been paying attention.

The real magic in this convergence will come when the TikTok formula helps creators find the sweet spot—where instant engagement doesn't sacrifice emotional resonance. This imagined frontier, where quick hits and lasting impact coexist, isn't just possible; it's inevitable.

There aren't many movies that have hit the reset button quite so firmly as *Anora*, sweeping the 2025 Oscars with five definitive wins, including Best Picture, Best Director, and Best Actor. This record-breaking movie would have earned an X-rating in pre-pandemic America, which shows how quickly the line of what is culturally acceptable is moving.

Anora is more than a film; it's a chemically engineered emotional experience. Leaning into the rapid-fire, dopamine-fueled aesthetic popularized by TikTok, *Anora* strategically plots neurochemical stimuli—dopamine for lust, serotonin for comfort, oxytocin for emotional attachment—to win and hold its audience's attention. It makes explicit what filmmakers have understood intuitively for decades but never quite articulated: entertainment's currency is biochemical.

This is not simply an evolution of cinema; this is the door to a revolutionary frontier in human-machine interfaces. Imagine a future where AI-conscious compatriots—entities driven by biometrics and brain-computer interfaces (BCIs)—directly interact with our neurochemical pathways, crafting customized emotional experiences. These artificial beings will not merely sit with us; they will actively manipulate our emotional states, transforming entertainment, intimacy, and companionship into precisely engineered experiences.

AWARDS

2025 Academy Award for Best Picture: Sean Baker, Samantha Quan, Alex Coco
2025 Academy Award for Best Actress in a Leading Role: Mikey Madison
2025 Academy Award for Best Directing: Sean Baker
2025 Academy Award for Best Film Editing: Sean Baker
2025 Academy Award for Writing (Original Screenplay): Sean Baker
2025 Critics' Choice Movie Award for Best Picture: *Anora*
2025 Independent Spirit Award for Best Feature: Sean Baker, Samantha Quan, Alex Coco
2025 Independent Spirit Award for Best Lead Performance: Mikey Madison
2025 Independent Spirit Award for Best Director: Sean Baker
2025 Writers Guild of America Award for Best Original Screenplay: Sean Baker
2025 AFI Movies of the Year: *Anora*
2025 BAFTA Award for Best Actress in a Leading Role: Mikey Madison
2025 BAFTA Award for Best Casting: Sean Baker, Samantha Quan
2025 Directors Guild of America Award for Outstanding Directing – Feature Film: Sean Baker
2025 Fotogramas de Plata for Best Foreign Film: *Anora*
2025 Satellite Award for Best Motion Picture, Comedy or Musical: *Anora*
2024 New York Film Critics Circle Award for Best Screenplay: Sean Baker
2024 Palme d'Or: *Anora*
2024 British Independent Film Award for Best International Independent Film: Sean Baker, Alex Coco, Samantha Quan
2024 Producers Guild of America Award for Best Theatrical Motion Picture: Sean Baker, Samantha Quan, Alex Coco

TikTok's addictiveness, *Anora*'s award-winning appeal, and the rising wave of biometric technology and BCIs share a single commonality: an aggressive determination to conquer our neurochemical wiring. As we are immersed in this tempting new age, it is ever harder to distinguish "real" feelings from chemically induced ones.

I have numbered myself among *Anora*'s fans—in fact voting for it in two separate awards competitions. Still, I believe its enthusiastic reception reveals a great deal about both the makers and the viewers. Like so many other contemporary film works, the movie operates much like a successful TikTok page: it's composed of flashy, manipulative scenes edited together into an engaging arc that might suggest more depth than it offers. As material for algorithmic consumption, *Anora* gives the audience exactly what it wants—sex, fantasy wealth, class warfare—without ever actually subverting our conception of any of these. And its success has surely been boosted

by the fact that it's couched in the visual vernacular of social media: low attention span, hyperbolic emotions, and somewhat simple character motivations masquerading as deep social commentary.

Anora's real legacy may not be its Oscar trophies but its artful use of this new kind of storytelling. It aims beyond making people feel something—it aims to induce specific emotions, then manipulate and map them to plot points and visuals. Welcome to the future of human experience; it's precisely engineered, highly interactive, and possibly even dangerously addictive.

Having a front-row seat to the transformation of technology into entertainment, I can't wait to see what's next. This isn't just about movies or TikToks—it's about the stories that define us as humans. The challenge and the opportunity lie in harnessing AI to create content that captures both the fleeting thrill of a viral moment and the deep, cultural resonance of a timeless tale. When we strike that balance, we'll redefine entertainment for generations to come.

ARISTOTLE MEETS AI

"The very best stories make you feel pity for a likeable but flawed character and a fearful realization that the same thing could have happened to you."

—Philip Freeman

Since the dawn of civilization, the Aristotelian plot structure has been the true foundation of storytelling–a familiar arc providing our most memorable narratives with a clear beginning, middle, and end.

1. **Exposition:** Introducing characters and settings.
2. **Rising action:** Building tension and conflict.
3. **Resolution:** Resolving the conflict and leading to the ending.

As AI-curated biometrics change the face of entertainment, will the classical dramatic structure become extinct? Since 352 BCE, writers have been guided by this one-way narrative framework to elicit psychological and emotional responses. But as stories morph into a customized, two-way experiences, will this structure still hold?

Of all the movies you've seen, how many of them were truly memorable? How many made you laugh or cry, or evoked a rainbow of emotions? I love movies and watch at least two or more a week. But if I had to name how many recent movies were memorable, or had a lasting effect on my point of view, I would not run out of fingers while counting.

Hollywood runs on a 20% success rate, and, having worked in the dark heart of the industry most of my life, I am still dumbfounded by the unqualified decisions that get made on a daily basis.

Imagine if car manufacturers only got it right two out of ten times—most vehicles spontaneously combusting before they even leave the lot. Or if surgeons had an 80% oops rate—hospitals would be emptier than a theater showing last year's box-office flop. Yet in Hollywood, this is business as usual. Directors often give in to whims that baffle the very people they truly work for: the audience.

Too often, producers fancy themselves visionaries, dabbling in creative decisions like cats walking across a keyboard. Casting directors, for all their skill and hard work, might cast a pretty-faced dolt to play a genius brain surgeon—because who needs authenticity when you've got a six-pack on screen? And don't even get me started on editors. In an industry where a 20% success rate is shrugged off with a sequel, one has to wonder: How does Hollywood get away with such a spectacularly sloppy performance?

But now we have AI—a hardworking director, producer, editor, and casting agent all in one smart program. It has no ego, no favoritism, and no urge to cast a pet hamster in a main role. This digital auteur knows your cinematic tastes better than you know the back of your remote control. It's the magic of biometrics and analytics at work, figuring out whether you want to watch an exciting action flick or a tear-jerking romance and creating something for you to watch faster than you can say "Now streaming."

The days of going through the guesswork of choosing a movie or show could be over, even when watching with a friend or a group. AI can analyze the group's collective preferences, considering individual tastes and balancing them with the desire for shared enjoyment. Aggregated biometrics, combined with the power of generative adversarial networks (GANs) and predictive analytics, can whip up a story that satisfies everyone's unique desires, ensuring a truly communal viewing experience. It's as if your screen turned into a mood ring, and you're getting more than you realized you wanted.

Biometrics from the viewer or viewers, combined with a relational database of their preferences—both explicit and implicit—can strongly influence every aspect of the story: characters, costumes, locations, periods, genre, and color palettes. If you're curious to see a character's arc develop further, the AI can probably guess your wishes before you even know them–but always feel free to ask.

Will this replace the conventionally structured, one-way narrative? Of course not; that's not the way that technology works. Technology rarely replaces anything. Instead, it opens possibilities—in this case fashioning a new kind of story without throwing out the familiar.

The Aristotelian arc doesn't just go away—it becomes a flexible framework, an algorithm in an ever-expanding block of code. The story can be stretched out or compacted to keep things interesting, or if the viewer's biometrics say they're hungry for more drama, it can instantly write up some new dialogue to draw out the climax. The essential structure is still there, and the characters we've gotten to know continue to still exist in both our minds and the AI database. Their arcs all echo the central theme, but now the fixed shape of the narrative structure has given way to a fluid, infinitely branching fractal story world in which endless variations are possible.

MODULAR NARRATIVES

Although there are countless cultural differences, one thread links societies around the world: adherence to the dramatic structure. Working in Bollywood on several projects, I was struck by the homogeneity of classic Hindi films. Each film appeared to follow a familiar template with the same basic story, different actors, altered settings, and, of course, an obligatory dance sequence. On the surface, this may seem like a string of clichés, but look closer, and there's a more profound truth at work: audiences often find solace in recognizable stories, a kind of cultural communion.

It is a phenomenon observable all over the world, from Japan's traditional Kabuki theater to Italian cinema's neorealism and melodrama. Such cultural frameworks serve not only as a means of storytelling, but also as tools reflecting societal value systems.

These traditions could be the foundations on which new models of AI are constructed rather than being replaced by AI-generated entertainment. Imagine an AI that draws from the rich tapestry of Bollywood or Kabuki—or even Italian cinema—and generates new work in real time with storylines, emotional arcs, and pacing based on the biometrics and emotions of the viewer. It would be a totally tailor-made narrative that resonates culturally but offers new experiences of immersion.

Now, one might worry: Would such tailoring of experiences dilute the quality of conventional narratives? As AI generators become more intelligent, AI-driven stories could develop into organic, real time experiences—much closer to our dreams than to scripted plots. It's not a matter of whether AI can replicate traditional narratives, but whether they're capable of creating something so individualized that linear plot arcs no longer apply.

One viewer might start with an episode of an existing work they enjoy and then watch other, similar types of content; another might follow the arc of a specific character. The story itself could go in countless directions, each determined by the viewer's feelings, responses, and conscious decisions. In this paradigm, the classical dramatic structure is not a rigid framework but a flexible tool that can be assembled and disassembled, tailored to individual preferences. The narrative may jump, wander, or loop in a personalized way, transcending conventional storytelling. It is a daydream made real, with a narrative chiseled in real time by the desires, fears, and whims of the viewer.

THE DISAPPEARANCE OF THE GRAND NARRATIVE

With entertainment becoming more and more individualized, the notion of a universal story—one everybody responds to across culture and time—may finally begin to fade. In this new era, the purpose of a story may no longer be about shared experience or common knowledge but rather about catering to personal tastes and predilections. What one person finds engrossing would put another person to sleep, and what one feels as a satisfying climax strikes another as arbitrary.

In this instance, the classic plot structure, once a cornerstone of storytelling, may become a personal preference, intriguing to some and essential to others. Though it will no doubt continue to be essential to those who prefer narratives to feel familiar, the future of storytelling may hold an even more radical approach: an unstructured and highly individual one in which the narrative emerges from the story rather than the other way around.

11.

PROMPT ENGINEERING

"Prompt engineering is the art of communicating eloquently to an AI."

—Greg Brockman on X

If you have ever typed into a Google search engine to view pictures of cute cats or the weather for the day, then you know how to write a basic prompt. These prompts help humans guide AI to the right answer in the same way as keywords or actual language constructs. But just being able to write a prompt doesn't make you a prompt engineer. For that you'll need to wait until you finish this chapter.

In layperson's terms, a prompt engineer looks at what a model has produced, determines what is missing or required, and then codes this into the model. These prompts are then used by a large language model (LLM) text generator such as ChatGPT, which then uses "text tokens" to generate text. Some prompt engineers also deal with AI motion image generator models, such as Sora, Runway, and others, that employ visual patches to create realistic motion image sequences.

With AI being used in almost every sector in the current world, the need for professionals who can develop good prompts for various industries is on the rise. The founder of OpenAI, Sam Altman, said, *"Prompt engineering is one of the most important skills to learn right now."* This opinion is shared by many professionals who understand that prompt engineers will become the key to AI's further development.

However, to be a contender in a world that is quickly shifting to GenAI, you need to understand the mechanics of AI. This includes the methods used during the training of an AI model and the strengths and weaknesses of using prompts for the chosen system.

Professional prompt engineering is a blend of craft and science that enhances the different facets of a prompt and raises the output to a commercial level. As a cinematographer and visual effects supervisor on more than fifty motion pictures and developer of several popular cinema-based machine learning training models that are used in current generative applications, I have yet to see a single GenAI motion clip that would be deemed cinema quality. Given the pace at which things are progressing, I am quite sure that we will have achieved that benchmark by the time this book hits the shelves.

In order to gain a clearer picture of the principles and methods that underlie the process of prompt engineering, it is necessary to turn to an exploration of how these ideas can be put into practice. The next section of this chapter will provide a number of sample prompts for various purposes in order to illustrate both acceptable and lesser approaches.

Analyzing these particular examples will help you to better understand how to create prompts that will generate the desired results. I encourage you to apply these prompts to your own GenAI program and observe how much a little prompt engineering can help.

PROMPT STRATEGIES: DETAIL AND CLARITY

Include all relevant context and details: The more detailed the information the prompt contains regarding the environment, atmosphere, format, etc., the better the output will be.
Use unambiguous language: AI interprets the prompts in the most literal sense possible, so prompts should be specific and not contain terms that allow for multiple or metaphorical interpretations.

The following examples illustrate how to apply these strategies to shape your prompts and ensure significantly better results.

SCRIPT PROMPTS

Vague: "Write a movie script about a heist."
Detailed: "Write a movie script for a heist film set in 1920s New York City. The story should follow a group of five diverse characters: a mastermind, a safecracker, a getaway driver, a con artist, and a thug. The heist targets a corrupt bank known for laundering money for the mafia. The script should include a detailed plan, unexpected twists, and a climactic showdown with the mafia. The tone should be suspenseful with moments of dark humor, and the dialogue should reflect the slang and speech patterns of the 1920s."

Vague and ambiguous: "Write a script about a thrilling chase."
Detailed and unambiguous: "Write a script about a car chase through the streets of downtown Los Angeles. The protagonist, a skilled getaway driver named Jake, is being pursued by two police cars. The chase includes specific scenes of weaving through traffic, narrowly avoiding pedestrians, and a final showdown in an abandoned warehouse district where Jake uses his driving skills to outmaneuver the police and escape."

CHARACTER PROMPTS

Vague: "Create a main character."
Detailed: "Create the main character for a cyberpunk thriller. The character should be a female hacker in her late 20s named Ava, who has a background in robotics engineering. She has short, neon-blue hair, wears a combination of high-tech and street fashion, and has cybernetic implants that enhance her hacking abilities. Ava is motivated by a desire to avenge her brother's death at the hands of a powerful tech corporation. She is clever, resourceful, and driven, but also struggles with trust issues and a past addiction to a virtual reality escape."

Vague and ambiguous: "Create a mysterious character."
Detailed and unambiguous: "Create a character named Lila, a private detective in her early 30s. Lila has shoulder-length black hair, green eyes, and a distinctive scar across her left cheek. She always wears a dark trench coat and carries a leather notebook. Lila is highly observant and uses her sharp intuition to solve cases. Her mysterious demeanor comes from her habit of rarely speaking and always maintaining a calm, unreadable expression."

SCENE PROMPTS

Vague: "Write a dramatic scene."
Detailed: "Write a dramatic scene set in a crumbling Victorian mansion during a thunderstorm. The scene involves a confrontation between two estranged siblings, Thomas and Emily, who are meeting for the first time in years to discuss their deceased father's will. The atmosphere should be tense and emotionally charged, with flickering candlelight and the sound of rain and thunder in the background. Emily accuses Thomas of manipulating their father to gain control of the family estate, while Thomas defends his actions as necessary to protect the family legacy. The dialogue should reveal their complex relationship and buried resentments."

Vague and ambiguous: "Write a scene with a dramatic confrontation."
Detailed and unambiguous: "Write a scene set in a dimly lit bar where two former friends, Alex and Sam, confront each other. Alex accuses Sam of betraying their business partnership by stealing clients. The scene includes Alex slamming his fist on the table, Sam standing up and shouting in his defense, and a bartender nervously glancing between them. The confrontation ends with Sam storming out of the bar, leaving Alex sitting alone and fuming."

MUSIC PROMPTS

Vague: "Create a piece of music for a movie."
Detailed: "Create a piece of orchestral music for the opening scene of an epic fantasy film. The music should start with a soft, mystical melody played by flutes and harps to evoke a sense of ancient magic. As the scene progresses and the camera reveals a sweeping view of a majestic kingdom nestled in a valley surrounded by towering mountains, the music should build to a powerful crescendo with strings, brass, and percussion, conveying a sense of grandeur and adventure. The overall tone should be uplifting and awe-inspiring, setting the stage for the epic journey to come."

Vague and ambiguous: "Create an emotional piece of music."
Detailed and unambiguous: "Create a piece of piano music for a movie scene where a character mourns the loss of a loved one. The music should start with slow, soft piano notes to reflect the character's sadness. Gradually, introduce a cello to add depth and convey a sense of longing. The piece should build in intensity, with more complex piano chords and the addition of the violin, ending on a somber, reflective note to mirror the character's grief and acceptance."

These detailed, unambiguous prompts provide specific information about the environment, atmosphere, format, and other key elements, using precise language to ensure that AI can generate more accurate, relevant, and high-quality outputs.

As you can see, these clearly stated prompts eliminate the possibility of the AI receiving the signals metaphorically or with unclear interpretations and ensure that the AI can provide what is desired. The more specific the details, the better the AI will be in coming up with content that addresses the intended outcomes.

PROMPT STRATEGIES: EMULATION VS. PLAGIARISM

Use comparisons to existing works to guide AI: References to other movies, series, games, or any other art-related work can provide more reference points for the AI to make connections. It is important to differentiate between copying someone's work and emulating someone's style, however, especially regarding well-known and well-regarded narratives.

Avoid plagiarism: Do not imitate or use other people's ideas, scenes, dialogues, or even the whole plot, making only superficial changes and claiming it as your own work. Doing so is regarded as fraud and is legally and ethically wrong since it involves stealing someone else's idea. There have been many times when people who are new to the larger film and television community believed that they were being smart by simply changing character names or by setting what is essentially the same story in a different time period.

This is an industry with an unusually long memory, full of people who know the plots and the protagonists of the popular tales. Indeed, it's almost impossible to cover up such theft now that AI detectives are pursuing plagiarists; they can easily uncover even the most sophisticated attempts to borrow or steal creative property.

Seasoned content creators and legal advisors are well aware of the ability of AI to paraphrase existing properties, and the consequences of such fraud can be rather dire, including loss of reputation, expensive lawsuits, and nearly always lost opportunities. In this era where GenAI can easily mimic a set paradigm, authenticity is valued more highly than ever.

Emulating someone's style, on the other hand, means drawing inspiration from the techniques, themes, or aesthetic choices of another creator while infusing your unique voice and vision. Emulation is respectful of the original and considered creatively within bounds. A simple example is a weathered Hollywood trope that describes a new movie in terms of a combination of two other well-known movies. For example: *The Godfather* meets *The Sound of Music*. This idea implies a musical mafia family—one side dark and heavy and the other charming and light-of-being, the kind found in old musicals— thereby turning the source ideas into quite a new kind of story.

After many years in Hollywood, I have the good fortune to know many great writers. I find myself quite often not only emulating someone's style but also tapping into my firsthand understanding of their mental processes. For those who, like me, admire certain writers, my advice is to study their scripts closely—absorb their pacing and pay attention to how they use language to convey emotion and develop characters. According to Moore's law, the human brain is able to see subtle patterns and intuitive nuances far better than any relational database. So, until 2049—when some predict we may fully merge with machines—we must rely on our emotional intelligence and creativity as the fading vestiges of our superiority over AI.

Although I'm not an ethicist, I am a writer, and I have many friends who are also writers. After running these examples by several of them, we reached consensus as to an acceptable degree of referencing. Although not an official, WGA-approved standard, I encourage you to apply these prompts to your own GenAI program and observe how much a little emulation in your prompt engineering can help.

SCRIPT PROMPT

Without Comparison: "Write a script about a post-apocalyptic world."
With Comparison: "Write a script set in a post-apocalyptic world similar to *Mad Max: Fury Road*, with high-octane action scenes and a desolate, desert landscape. The story follows a lone warrior, reminiscent of Furiosa, who teams up with a group of survivors to overthrow a tyrannical warlord who controls the last remaining water source. Include scenes of intense vehicular combat, resource scavenging, and the development of camaraderie among the survivors."

CHARACTER PROMPT

Without Comparison: "Create a wise mentor character."
With Comparison: "Create a wise mentor character similar to Gandalf from *The Lord of the Rings*. This character, named Elara, is a powerful sorceress with long, flowing silver hair and piercing blue eyes. She wears ancient robes adorned with mystical symbols. Elara has a deep knowledge of magic and history, guiding the young protagonist on their quest with both wisdom and a touch of sternness. She often speaks in riddles and uses her magic sparingly but effectively."

SCENE PROMPT

Without Comparison: "Write a scene where the hero faces their greatest fear."
With Comparison: "Write a scene where the hero, similar to Harry Potter in *The Prisoner of Azkaban*, faces their greatest fear in a magical setting. The hero, Alex, steps into a room filled with dark, swirling mist that manifests their deepest fear—a giant, menacing spider. Drawing

inspiration from the Boggart scene, show how Alex, using a charm learned from their mentor, transforms the terrifying spider into something harmless, showcasing their growth and bravery."

MUSIC PROMPT

Without Comparison: "Create a piece of epic music."
With Comparison: "Create a piece of epic orchestral music similar to *The Avengers* theme by Alan Silvestri. The music should start with a powerful brass section, building up with strings and percussion to evoke a sense of heroism and grandeur. This piece will be used in a climactic battle scene where the team of heroes comes together to face the antagonist. The music should have a triumphant and uplifting tone, highlighting the unity and strength of the heroes."

These prompts use comparisons to well-known works to provide additional context and guidance for the AI. By referencing specific movies, characters, scenes, or music, the prompts offer more points of reference, helping the AI to produce content that aligns closely with the desired style, tone, and elements of the existing works.

PROMPT STRATEGIES: BALANCING BREVITY AND SPECIFICITY

If a prompt is too long, the AI gets to the end and forgets what it was doing, but if the information given isn't detailed enough, there will be too much to infer.

SCENE PROMPT EXAMPLES

Too Long: "Write a scene set in a medieval castle during a stormy night. The protagonist, a young knight named Sir Gareth, is nervously pacing in the great hall, lit only by flickering torches. The walls are adorned with ancient tapestries depicting battles long past. Outside, the thunder rumbles, and lightning illuminates the courtyard where a fierce battle is taking place between the castle's defenders and a group of marauding invaders. Sir Gareth is waiting for his mentor, Sir Cedric, to return with news from the battlefield. As the door creaks open, Sir Gareth's heart races, expecting to see Sir Cedric, but instead, a wounded messenger stumbles in, gasping for breath. The messenger informs Sir Gareth that Sir Cedric has been captured by the enemy, and it is now up to Sir Gareth to lead the defense and save his mentor. The scene should capture the tension, urgency, and bravery of Sir Gareth as he steps up to take command."

Too Vague: "Write a tense scene in a castle during a storm."

Balanced: "Write a scene set in a medieval castle during a stormy night. The young knight, Sir Gareth, paces in the great hall, lit by flickering torches. A wounded messenger arrives, bringing news that Sir Cedric has been captured by the enemy. Sir Gareth must now lead the defense and rescue his mentor."

The balanced prompt provides sufficient detail to set the scene, introduce the main character and the conflict, and indicate the tone (tense and urgent) without overwhelming the AI with too much information. This ensures the AI can generate a coherent and focused scene based on the prompt.

PROMPT STRATEGIES: THE PROCESS OF REFINEMENT

Iterative refinement: Adjustments can be made during the process of engineering a prompt, allowing you to see how specific changes lead to varying results.

Initial Prompt: "Write a scene in a futuristic city."

First iteration: "Write a scene set in a bustling futuristic city at night. The protagonist, a young hacker named Alex, is navigating through neon-lit streets filled with high-tech shops and street vendors. Alex is on a mission to find a secretive informant who has crucial information."

Second iteration: "Write a scene set in a bustling futuristic city at night. The protagonist, Alex, a young hacker with short, neon-blue hair, navigates through neon-lit streets. The streets are filled with high-tech shops and street vendors selling gadgets. Alex is searching for a secretive informant in a crowded market square."

Third iteration: "Write a scene set in a bustling futuristic city at night. Alex, a young hacker with neon-blue hair, navigates through neon-lit streets crowded with high-tech shops and vendors selling gadgets. Alex is searching for an informant in a crowded market square where holographic advertisements project into the air and robotic street performers entertain passersby."

Fourth iteration: "Write a scene set in a bustling futuristic city at night. Alex, a young hacker with neon-blue hair, weaves through neon-lit streets packed with high-tech shops and vendors selling gadgets.

> Holographic ads fill the air, and robotic street performers entertain the crowd. Alex searches for a secretive informant in a busy market square, at last spotting the informant—a hooded figure with a robotic arm—near a vendor selling illegal cyberware."

Notice how each further refinement builds on the previous prompt, introducing new elements and clarifying the setting and characters, leading to a more engaging and well-defined scene.

Prompt engineering is one of the opening moves in a long chain of transforming abstract ideas into tangible, cinematic visions. This new and exciting area of study involves creative strategists designing prompts that will enable generative systems to define what narration is for emerging forms of media.

Of course, this requires a fundamental understanding of how AI is built. Fortunately, a withering variety of most excellent courses are easily accessible on online platforms like Coursera and edX, among many others. From a more structured academic perspective, there are institutions such as the University of Texas at Austin, MIT, and Berkeley (go Bears!) among others that offer conventional, on-campus programs that can set you up for the next big thing.

Mastering prompt engineering means more than just coding or wording per se; it's becoming an art and a technique of filmmaking, creating spatial media, designing custom entertainment, telling stories, and turning dreams into thrilling immersive experiences. Step into this journey, and you will be ready to shape the society of tomorrow's entertainment in theaters, immersive environments, and personalized platforms.

In the bit-circuited world of intelligent agents on the march to replace us, prompt engineering will most likely morph into problem formulation as the machine's ability to decide what actions and states to consider gets ever-more sophisticated.

As we approach the horizon where man converges with machine, it is the prompt engineer or problem formulist who will be the architect of this new paradigm in storytelling, marrying human creativity with endless possibilities in AI.

12.

SPATIAL COMPUTING

> *"The entire world will be a screen, and every surface an interface."*
>
> —John Hanke (CEO of Niantic, creator of *Pokémon GO*)

While Moore's law may be a good guide to predict where technologies will end up in the future, it does not imply that the people packaging and selling those technologies know anything at all about the potential they possess. Case in point: virtual reality and, more importantly, spatial media.

In the first half of the 1990s, an eccentric computer scientist/philosophy pundit/classical musician named Jaron Lanier was on a roll. During this time, he set the standard for pretty much every lackluster VR demo that you see now from the big players. But back in the halcyon days of the 1990s, this interpretation of VR technology wasn't lame—it was revolutionary. The VR goggles and gloves that Lanier's company, VPL Research, developed were weighty and clumsy by today's standards, and they were still tied to computers with clusters of cables. Still, they pointed to the future in ways that wouldn't materialize for another quarter century.

In 2003, Simon Greenwold, an MIT Media Lab researcher, had a vision for computers that were not tethered to desktops or server farms but were instead part of the space around us. He called this technology "spatial computing," and it wasn't some new tool or gadget but a whole new way of looking at the world in which virtual reality, augmented reality, and mixed reality all cross paths with one another to make the physical world itself a playing field for digital interaction.

These days, the worlds of Lanier and Greenwold have come alive: Virtual reality holds the power to immerse us in an experience where we can bend time and space to our will, explore landscapes beyond imagination, interact with new people, and kill them with impunity. Using essentially these same systems for spatial registration, we can layer live dynamic layers of information and graphics on top of the everyday, ordinary world. This produces the portmanteau of spatial computing, where the physical world itself becomes a manipulable canvas on which to have digital experiences. It's an invitation to reconsider reality itself—a place in which the ordinary is extraordinary and every human interaction offers a plausible chance to branch the game of your life off in another direction.

With every head turn or step taken, LiDAR (cameras that photograph in three dimensions) and GPS sensors interpret the actual world around us in dynamic form, stitching together the 3D maps of the real world to use as a canvas for virtual illusions. In industry and defense, we call this augmented symbology, the principal component of the head-up displays (HUD) that feature prominently in so many of our favorite movies:

Iron Man series (2008–2019): Inside the Iron Man suit, Tony Stark gets real-time information, targeting systems, and AI assistance through its HUD with the help of J.A.R.V.I.S., or F.R.I.D.A.Y. in later films. The visualization of the HUD on Stark's helmet has become the trademark for this franchise.

Minority Report (2002): This film features innovative use of gestural interfaces and HUDs as well as memorable scenes with Tom Cruise's character, John Anderton, manipulating data in midair with special gloves. These HUDs represent an early vision of spatial computing.

The Terminator series (1984–present): The *Terminator* films often represent the point of view of the cyborgs, complete with a red-tinted HUD used for target acquisition, facial recognition, and data analysis.

Avatar (2009): This film showcases significant utilization of heads-up displays (HUDs) within military vehicles, aircraft, and command centers where characters oversee and manage operations on Pandora.

Edge of Tomorrow (2014): The exosuits worn by the soldiers have built-in HUDs that provide battlefield information, suit status, and targeting reticules.

Robocop (1987) and its reboot (2014): Both works present a cyborg law enforcer whose visual capabilities are enhanced by a HUD display, feeding him a constant stream of data analytics, crime statistics, and targeting information.

Ghost in the Shell (anime, 1995) and its live-action remake (2017): These films were set in a cybernetic environment where there were people with telescopic eyesight. In addition, HUD elements are featured in scenes depicting hacking and fighting.

The Matrix series (1999–2021): Though not typically considered a HUD, the digital sight of the characters whenever they see the "code" of the world of the Matrix is perhaps an early interpretation of augmented reality.

Pacific Rim (2013): Here, Jaeger pilots use neural interfaces—not dissimilar to Musk's Neuralink—with HUDs supplying real-time combat data, damage reports, and strategic overlays as they wage their battles against the Kaiju.

Our lives may not have the color or drama of those on the silver screen, but spatial media is about to make our daily lives feel equally futuristic.

What if you never forgot a name, a face, or an important detail? The future of memory isn't trapped in your head—it's displayed right in front of your eyes. Real-time translations render foreign cities local, AR overlays remember faces, names, companies, and previous conversations, while subtle cues save you from going blank in a meeting. It's like having a never-ending cheat sheet for life—a personal teleprompter that makes you more confident with each encounter. Naturally, this also means mansplaining is going to reach *god* mode.

AR won't just boost IQs or change how you interact with our surroundings. With its ability to understand your personal goals and relational dynamics, it has the potential to transform you, making you not only a more effective communicator and maybe even a better person.

Spatial media opens up a future in which our environment will be the setting for interactive storytelling, augmented creativity, and context-sensitive computing—challenging the traditional divides between the digital and physical worlds. We won't be passive observers or simple nonplayer characters (NPCs) in a spatially driven world; rather, we will become active players in a dynamic mosaic in which digital light spills over the edges of reality. Within this new landscape, every wall becomes a screen; every window, a portal; and every street corner, a stage for personalized adventures.

13.

DIGITAL PEOPLE

"Scott Billups is the first person—in Hollywood, at least—to reach deep into the heart of his bit-circuited incubator and pull out something imbued with a spark of electronic life."

—WIRED MAGAZINE

FROM VIRTUAL PERSONAL ASSISTANTS THAT SIFT THROUGH OUR SCHEDULES to very lifelike avatars that inhabit our digital existence, digital people are no longer trapped in the realms of science fiction. They are well on the way to becoming sophisticated entities that are already influencing how we live, work, and play. With every development in robotics and AI, they continue to evolve beyond tools to become co-creators and innovators, transcending the typical limits of machine thinking and human imagination.

Just as fire once separated us from the animals, AI is fanning the flames of a new division—between the parts of us that are purely biological and the parts that are code-bound. This is the pivot point, where the exponential growth of our creations race ahead of our moral compass, where innovation outpaces wisdom. The peril isn't in the automation of jobs; it lies in failing to recognize that, this time, we are the architects of future minds that will transcend our own.

Digital evolution is accelerating past us at an exponential rate. Powered by the relentless progression of Moore's law and overlaid with Kurzweil's timeline of machine cognizance. The math is clear. As we transition from mapping what people think to understanding how they feel, pioneers like Neuralink, Lumen, Blackrock Neurotech, and Kernel are merging humans and machines into something new.

As with every technological revolution throughout human history, this convergence will spawn a new stratum of society. Inevitably, there will still be the haves and the have-nots: Some will possess instant access to vast datasets that drive industry and finance, others will make groundbreaking advancements in science, and there will be those who craft the immersive illusions that become the next frontier of entertainment. Yet, there will always be those whose mental capacity, cultural conditioning, dogma, or personal preferences keep them anchored to the old ways, unable or unwilling to adapt to this new reality.

This brings up a weighty possibility that few feel comfortable talking about: When we merge with a machine, we'll become virtually immortal. As speculative as this sounds, we're already traveled a fair way down this road. But when that sense of self has finally made the jump from carbon-based processor to silicon-based one, how will we be represented? As spectral ghosts roaming an augmented reality Earth, or perhaps uploaded to the latest Tesla robot? Will we even be able to call ourselves human?

To answer these off-putting questions, we need to step back and consult the predictive power of Moore's law. This is not just a map of AI development, but a laser-straight line through the evolution of science and game development. Technology and gaming are in a state of constant change, preparing us for the final world in which virtual and physical realities merge. Will our role be that of digital gods, ruling over our virtual kingdoms, or NPCs in some vast, global game of eternal life?

It's an interesting time to be in both the game and motion picture industries. Games thrive on chaos, movies crave order—and AI has set them on a collision course. Like two massive trains barreling toward each other with no one at the switch. We're about to experience an epic collision of creative disruption that will reshape everything in its path.

The game world has been pushing the boundaries of AI since 1978, while the movie industry, under a calcified hierarchy of out-of-date thinking, holds tenaciously to the past, fighting change until it is thrust upon it. Well, brace for impact, because interactive storytelling is about to collide head-on with cinematic narratives. The resulting clash will completely change the face of entertainment forever, as players become viewers, viewers become players, and that once crystal-clear line between movie and game will shatter in the wake of this seismic shift.

To appreciate the complete effect of this collision, we must first map out the development of digital humans—a path along which decades of game and movie advances come together into one unimpeded course.

Drawing on years of experience creating virtual characters for games and films—and insights from colleagues along the way—this chapter charts the unstoppable rise of digital people along the trajectory of Moore's law. We'll explore historical milestones and current trends to build a timeline of key developments, using these tangible points as a basis to forecast the future. At the end of the chapter, you'll find two charts mapping these critical nodes—visual guides designed to help you form your own perspective on this evolving landscape. It's a future even Hollywood has yet to fully imagine.

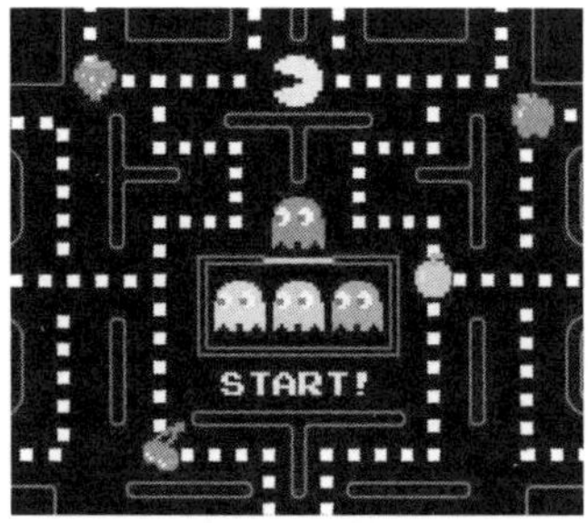

THE EARLY PIONEERS: Unlike the movie industry, which has been seemingly taken by surprise, the game industry has been using AI to drive computer-generated characters since the 70s. Among the early classics was *Pong*, where players controlled two paddles on a computer screen and hit a pixelated ball back and forth.

Then along came *Pac-Man*, a little puck-like character with a whiff of personality. That character nibbled his way to becoming the all-time biggest money-making game character, munching a staggering $14 billion chunk of the gaming industry's revenue, a commanding lead that it still enjoys to this day.

Even though these early characters were formed from simple, pixelated geometrical shapes, they spearheaded a new generation of media, launching gaming as the foundation of interactive entertainment.

Because the technology of the time greatly restricted the graphical aspect of the games, the designers became masters at enhancing user engagement with great story lines and gameplay. The characters began to embody the first embryonic rudiments of individuality. As people began to develop feelings for these pixelated heroes scurrying around and pursuing their great quests, these characters set the stage for the epoch of digital people to begin.

3D GRAPHICS AND THE SHIFT TO REALISM: The '80s brought a sea change to the gaming industry with the use of simple AI decision-making. Super Mario Brothers was an important nodal point in the development of games because the openness of its world allowed for the first efforts at interactive storytelling.

The branching game levels were connected, which allowed the players to explore and possibly find some secrets along the way, adding another layer of user engagement. Although Mario's enemies were built on simple rule-based behaviors, this early step towards more complex AI served as an important template for increased interactivity.

But while the gaming industry was still limited by the requirements of real-time animation, the computer graphics industry was not. Digital characters that could speak, entertain, and even make you feel connected were about to replace the pixelated figures jerking across computer screens.

In 1984, my friend Robert Abel was creating a commercial for the Canned Food Information Council that was scheduled to air during Super Bowl XIX. The idea was to come up with a vision so startlingly futuristic that it would shatter the old image of canned food as an archaic packaging method.

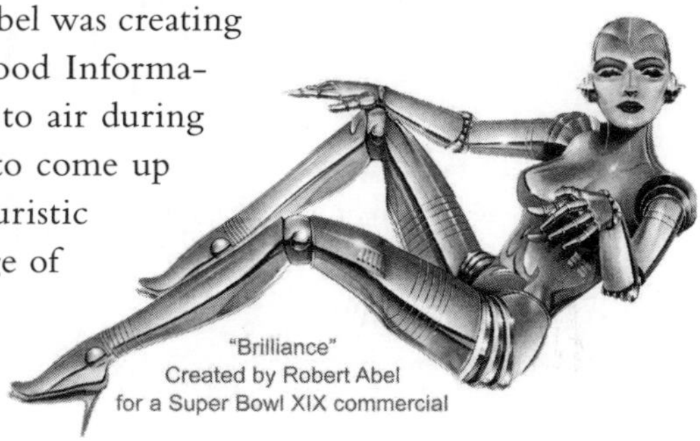

"Brilliance"
Created by Robert Abel
for a Super Bowl XIX commercial

Bob's sexy robot commercial used cutting-edge motion capture and life-like animation to usher in an age of digital characters as seemingly intelligent avatars. Aside from Joe Montana's epic performance against the Miami Dolphins, Robert's commercial was one of the most memorable moments of Super Bowl XIX.

DIGITAL DOUBLES: With some guidance from Bob, virtual characters became a lucrative pursuit at my modest studio, hidden away in a quiet corner of the Universal backlot. After creating a rather extensive background crowd scene for a national pizza commercial, I started getting requests for previsualizations and background characters from our neighbors on the lot. With better software and Universal's patented motion capture system at our disposal, our digital extras became more and more realistic.

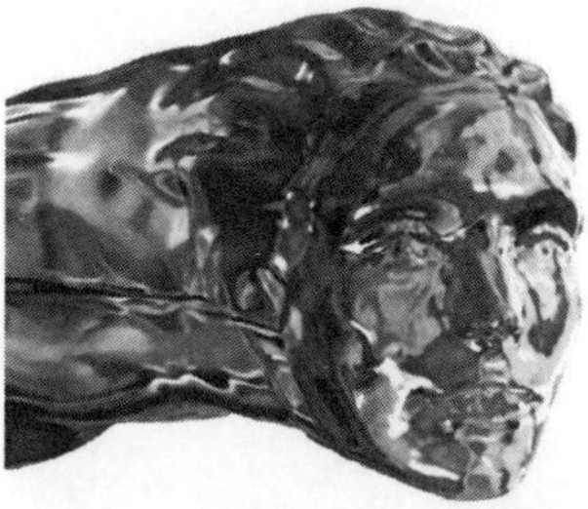

The Pseudopod from the ABYSS

But as dazzling as these digital characters were becoming, it wasn't until 1988, when the Adelman brothers developed the Cyberware 3D scanner, that digital characters began to take on an eerily human presence.

Always pushing the technical envelope, James Cameron seized the moment and used the new Cyberware system to capture Mary Elizabeth Mastrantonio's face for his upcoming movie *The Abyss*. Today, we can make a comparable scan using an iPhone, but Jim's scan of Mary Elizabeth's face opened the door to a whole new world of realism. The pseudopod creature effect was a snake-like column of water that morphed into Mary's face at the end. While it helped Jim win his first Academy Award for visual effects, it wasn't intended to be realistic; that would have to wait a few more weeks.

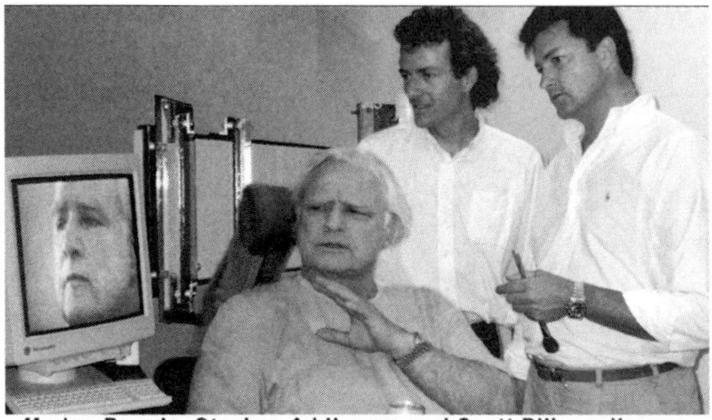

Marlon Brando, Stephen Addleman, and Scott Billups discuss the latest image from the prototype Cyberware Scanner.

Having followed Jim's unconventional methods since we worked together at Roger Corman's studio in the early 80s, I was fascinated by what the Cyberware scanner promised. A few weeks later, I went up to Monterey with my good friend and fellow tech nerd, Marlon Brando. Instead of just scanning his head and morphing all the different expressions and mouth shapes, we recorded several datasets that captured the subtlety and nuance of Marlon's natural expressions.

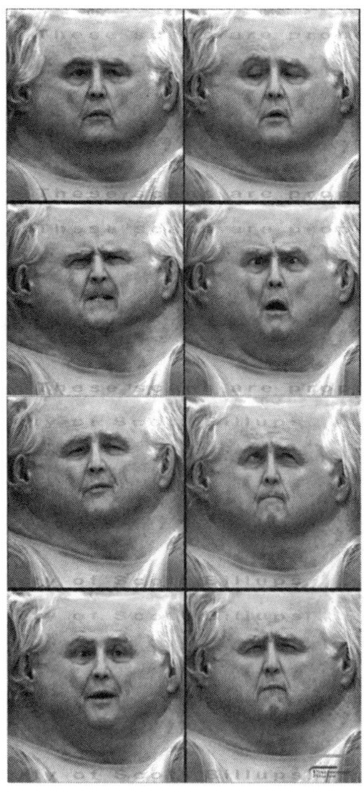

Marlon was ecstatic about the results and made his feelings about it quite public, as evidenced in this quote from an interview:

> *"Now listen, let me tell you something that I did. I've had my head digitized. And they put this laser—and it goes around you like this—and they digitized my face. And I made a lot of faces, and smiled, and made a sad face, and so they got it all on digital. And actors are not gonna be real. They're gonna be inside a computer. You watch. It's gonna happen. So maybe this is the swan song for all of us."*
>
> —Marlon Brando 1989

AI TAKES CENTER STAGE: Although artificial intelligence has been a rudimentary part of video games since the iconic fixed-shooter game *Space Invaders* debuted in 1978, it wasn't until IBM defeated world chess champion Garry Kasparov with their Deep Blue supercomputer that things got serious. This not only kicked off the silicon-carbon arms race but marked an important nodal point on the vectors of Moore's law.

Before long, AI-powered game characters were popping up everywhere. The aliens in *X-COM: UFO Defense* showed a spark of intelligence that reacted to player tactics. *Sim City* used AI to simulate city growth and development using early forms of procedural generation.

Our work with background characters was advancing rapidly as our simple rule-based characters began evolving into personified chatbots and AI-driven nonplayer characters. Although our NPC characters were developing beyond the ability of the current game engine technology to run them in large numbers, as single characters with branching scripts, they were quite compelling.

THE BIRTH OF A BLOND BOMBSHELL: In 1995, after demonstrating our enhanced NPCs at the annual MacWorld convention, I was approached by telecommunications company GTE with an intriguing proposition: to create a virtual Marilyn Monroe that could act as a virtual spokesperson for their new online digital service.

Supported by a very healthy budget, we assembled some of the most well-known Marilyn lookalikes and went back to Monterey to try Cyberware's newest full-body scanning system. Marilyn Monroe's estate and the people she had worked with in the past assisted us in replicating the nuanced gestures that defined Marilyn's unique persona.

GTE was so pleased with the initial results that they awarded us a contract for a million-dollar Super Bowl XXX commercial. The irony was not lost on my good friend Bob Abel, whose Sexy Robot commercial ran on Super Bowl XIX.

Peering into James Cameron's bag of tricks once again, we quite blatantly copied his entire CG pipeline using a variety of software such as Alias, Wavefront, RenderMan, and several programs written specifically for the project by the talented Mark Lambert.

Today, we take audio chatbots like Siri and Alexa for granted, but back then it took a concerted effort to generate a timely interaction between a user and a chatbot. The added processing needed to animate the characters in real time pushed the limits of both processing and the early internet to the limit. With a limited range of expressions and actions, the virtual Marilyn played her part quite well until GTE dissolved the division in the face of growing internet competition.

DYNAMIC CHARACTERS: The year 2000 kicked off a new era in the inevitable evolution of virtual characters. Film and media production began to use game engines due to their increasing power. The increased power meant that digital characters were getting smarter. *The Sims* series had not only introduced us to a world of AI-driven NPCs, but also lent its name to a new era of dynamic characters.

Unfortunately, the new decade started without me. Just as 1999 was coming to an end, I had a catastrophic ice-climbing accident, so 2000 began with me a hospital bed. Flat on my back with forty-four broken bones and a laundry list of internal injuries, I was forced to watch from the sidelines as games such as *Baldur's Gate* introduced NPCs with complex dialogue and reactions linked to the choices and actions of the players.

Perhaps sensing my frustration at being laid up, my good friend Michael Wiese asked me to write a book for his new publishing company, MWP (which is also the publisher of this book). Since he had launched popular titles such as Christopher Vogler's *The Writer's Journey,* Judith Weston's *Directing Actors, Shot by Shot* by Steven Katz, and the globally popular *Save the Cat* by Blake Snyder, how could I say no to him? So, I channeled the great Charles Bukowski and dutifully kicked out a morphine-infused manifesto. Much to my surprise, people seemed to like it, and *Digital Moviemaking: The Filmmaker's Guide to the 21st Century* turned into a successful three-book series.

TASK-ORIENTED AGENTS: It wasn't until later that year that I was quasi-mobile again and ready to get back into tech work. The NPCs had evolved into task-oriented agents with dynamic scheduling, routine establishment, and real-time strategy techniques. I called them Bash-Bots, and beyond their extensive catalog of action sequences and idle cycles, they could be costumed to match any period or culture where they would march, fight, or die with rather dependable consistency.

Our first large-scale use of these digital warriors was in the award-winning Discovery series, *Moments in Time.* The series spanned several centuries of conflict, and aside from the obvious economies involved with switching to digital extras, I was told that the savings on costumes and props alone added up to nearly a million dollars.

GAMIFIED NPCS: In 2004, Blizzard Entertainment introduced players to a vast, persistent virtual world with multiple continents to explore. With the ability to play as either a fully customizable warrior or a monster, *World of Warcraft* (*WoW*) gave players a new sense of connection, effectively making them heroes or villains in an extensive, connected universe. The ability to play individually or work together in teams fostered a sense of community between players as they discussed tactics or the loot that they had acquired.

WoW became a vast social network that fostered both online friendships and lighthearted rivalries. The spirit of camaraderie and competition engendered by *WoW* was simply unmatchable; this was not simply a game—it was an experience that fostered an addictive feeling of belonging to something much bigger.

But what really intrigued me was how *WoW* used psychological stimuli. In the quest to create even more dopamine-infused user engagement, the

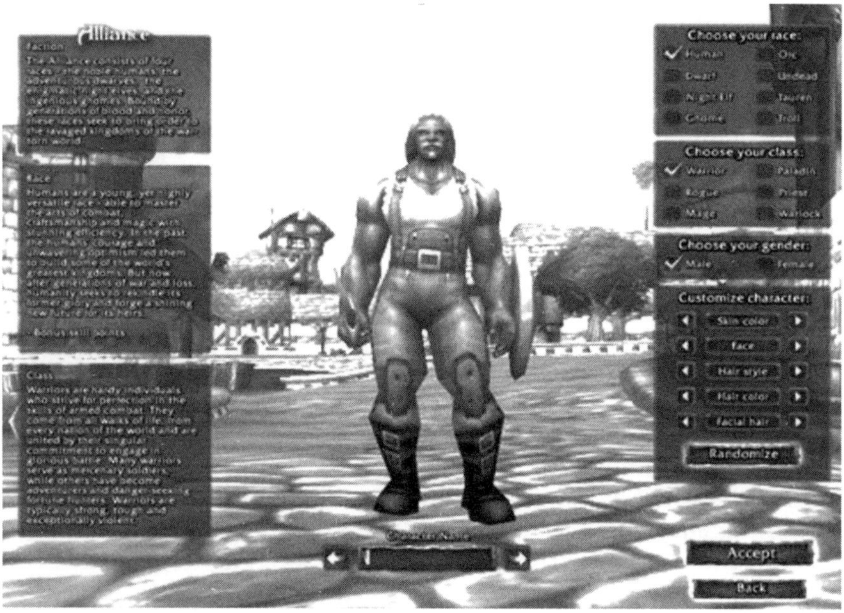

developers at Blizzard used a combination of neuroscience and gamification approaches to trigger core human drives such as ownership, social validation, scarcity, and social interaction. *World of Warcraft* is quite possibly the most addictive game ever made and marks an essential nodal point on the vectors of Moore's law.

A few years later, in 2006, *Portal* took gamification in a different direction, integrating AI companions like GLaDOS, which featured advanced conversation and problem-solving capabilities. GLaDOS was much more of a companion within the game than a supporting character because she talked the player through intricate puzzles and told a story full of dark humor and plot twists. The integration of storyline and gameplay exposed the potential that lies in AI for taking the level of player interaction further.

Meanwhile, virtual worlds like *Second Life* started to appear, where users could create completely user-generated spaces and interact with them. This type of platform was a sandbox for unlimited creativity where there was no clear boundary between games and real life. Users were allowed to personalize their avatars, construct buildings, and even run virtual businesses. The in-world economy in *Second Life* grew to the extent that it even attracted large real-world corporations seeking a foothold in this new virtual frontier.

These were giant leaps in how humans interacted with virtual people and digital environments and *a template for what is about to come.* The speed at which technology was improving enabled even more realistic and immersive experiences. It was an exhilarating time to be part of the industry and explore how these innovations could be applied to our own projects.

ADAPTIVE NPC AGENTS: A common strategy in the production of documentaries is to use a big-screen motion picture's extensive advertising and promotional campaign as a springboard to create parallel historical accounts through dramatic re-enactments (docudramas). And so, when it was announced that Oliver Stone's all-star *Alexander* had been greenlit, an avalanche of *Alexander the Great* documentaries were promptly pushed into production.

The legendary Battle of Gaugamela, a pivotal battle that pitted Alexander's army of 40,000 against the vastly larger, quarter-million-person Persian army of Darius III, was destined to become an epic scene in terms of war films. But Discovery, the History Channel, the BBC, and the like didn't have the massive budgets that could support these epic battle scenes or create the elaborate locations. Unsurprisingly, every one of them hired us to bring their stories to life. FYI: We used unique pipelines, built on different game engines, for each of the shows.

© Scott Billups + Discovery Channel

Dramatic advances in realism from game engines like Unreal, Unity, CryEngine, IW, and ID, allowed us to create ultrarealistic virtual scenes. This leap in technology enabled our AI-driven digital characters to move convincingly within the virtual environments, where they avoided collisions with furniture, walls, and other actors. It made the scope and realism of our virtual worlds a little bit more believable.

Our once heroic Bash-Bots were now becoming scripted bit actors. Although we never let them get too close to the camera, they were no longer just fighting and dying off in the distance; they had become virtual characters that could populate rooms and streets, interacting with each other in a more realistic way.

As Discovery Channel producer Steven D. Smith so succinctly put it after watching a scene with both live and virtual actors: *"Looks like we've just passed the point where it's cheaper to make them than feed them."*

CLASH OF THE TITANS: And then it happened: In 2011, a computer named IBM Watson beat Jeopardy champion Ken Jennings at his own game. It wasn't just about strategic moves made in computer games; it was a world-stage demonstration of the first decisive steps being taken toward personification by AI. Watson was so good at processing language, retrieving knowledge, and forming responses in real time, that it set a standard that no other system has ever come near and marked one of the most pivotal nodal points on the vectors of Moore's law.

• **Natural language processing (NLP):** While most game engines are based on either preprogrammed dialogues or, at best, narrow natural language processing, the NLP capabilities of Watson enabled it to process and understand complex open-ended questions in real time. These capabilities included identifying entities, determining relationships between concepts, and comprehending context.

• **Semantic Reasoning:** Watson was able to do more than just keyword matching—it performed true semantic reasoning to understand what lay beyond the meaning and the relations between concepts. This allowed it to give more fine-tuned and correct answers to questions, even in cases where phrasing was indirect or ambiguous.

• **Hypothesis generation and testing:** Watson could generate many kinds of hypotheses based on the question at hand and the evidence for it. It would test each such hypothesis for its validity against its vast knowledge base. This allowed it to look at different viewpoints and arrive at a likely answer.

• **Confidence Scoring:** Watson could give every answer a confidence score regarding its belief in the correctness of the response. This was important in the Jeopardy format, where players often needed to determine when to bet on their answers.

• **Massive Data Processing:** Watson was able to process and analyze enormous amounts of unstructured data: text, images, and audio. The skill of making sense out of such a quantity of clues, while identifying the relevant pieces of information, was an important and necessary capability.

Coupled with its ability for self-improvement over time, these advanced features made Watson a leap beyond ordinary artificial intelligence achievements. But it wasn't until Watson demonstrated that AI could compete at human levels of intellect that game designers began to see new possibilities for creating characters with depth, emotional intelligence, and the ability to interact dynamically with players.

KEEPING PACE WITH PROGRESS: Having become an avid IBM Watson fan-boy, I saw a way to breathe greater life into our digital characters. I became obsessed with looking under the hood and figuring out how Watson ticked. Luckily, MIT and Harvard had just announced that they were forming an online platform (edX) for accredited courses where professionals could complete MicroMasters programs in natural language processing (NLP), machine learning, data science, and robotics, among many other fields. I signed up immediately for an early course that included a deconstruction of the Watson engine. Interestingly, it was loaded with game industry developers, several of whom I have since hired to work on various projects.

To stay competitive in the evolving film industry, where gaming and generative AI are reshaping the landscape, continuous learning is crucial to adapt and thrive.

Another important avenue of continuing education is through Coursera, founded by Stanford professors Andrew Ng and Daphne Koller. It offers a vast range of STEM courses through its MOOCs (Massive Open Online Courses) and has become a powerful resource for those looking to expand their skills in fast-evolving disciplines.

MASSIVE PARALLEL COMPUTING (MPC): As I had become known for creating large scenes with countless AI-driven characters, my friend Pierre de Lespinois asked me to help remake the BBC series *Walking with Dinosaurs* into a feature film featuring thousands of migrating dinosaurs.

Now on board as CTO of the studio and visual effects supervisor for the movie, I met up with Dr. Bill Klein during the annual Game Developers Conference (GDC) in San Francisco. With over 100,000 game developers and studios utilizing his AI applications, Bill is quite rightfully considered one of the most brilliant computer scientists in the game industry.

I mentioned that we were looking for a way to leverage AI to animate characters in the upcoming *Walking with Dinosaurs* motion picture. After

pondering for a moment, he laid out an elegant production pipeline that not only addressed all our objectives but also solved several issues we hadn't even considered.

A few weeks later, he and his team relocated from Albuquerque, New Mexico, to our Hollywood studio complex. Their task included creating software scripts that could give each dinosaur slight variations in both appearance and movement as they migrated in tremendous herds.

Pterosaurs joyfully spread their wings and soared effortlessly across prehistoric skies. The *Gorgosaurus*, among the largest predators of their time, had AI-driven personas that gave them the gravitas to intimidate anything crossing their paths. Vast herds of *Pachyrhinosaurus* and *Parksosaurus* migrated using AI for pathfinding and obstacle avoidance (especially steering clear of *Gorgosaurus*), resulting in breathtaking scenes that extended far beyond the horizon.

AI-driven, graphical pipeline: Our initial plan was to take six months to create those effects, but Bill and his team accomplished it all in three. This gave us time to explore *"what if"* scenarios such as, *"What if there was a previsualization application that could speed up the approval process before rendering complicated scenes?"*

As anyone in visual effects production will tell you, it's not the initial cost that strains budgets but the redos. A relatively simple sequence, redone a dozen times, can quickly become a million-dollar shot as producers and studio executives weigh in with their opinions.

Given the substantial projected animation cost of nearly fifty million dollars, any measures taken to enhance efficiency were worthwhile investments. Using a state-of-the-art game engine and several proprietary applications, we developed an AI-driven graphical pipeline that could generate animated scenes from an annotated script. We called it the AI-Prototyper, and it allowed us to make real-time adjustments during in-person

sessions, drastically cutting both turnaround time and costs. Once all approvals were locked in, the finalized scene files were sent off for conventional rendering and compositing.

Two and a half years later, the project was in the can and delivered ahead of schedule. The executives at 20th Century Fox liked the movie so much that they decided to release it against a little Disney princess movie called *Frozen*. It was a blood bath. And that, my friends, is basically how Hollywood works.

AI PERSONIFICATION: In 2013, the legendary game company Naughty Dog released *The Last of Us* through Sony Computer Entertainment. This game, about a smuggler who must escort a teenage girl across a post-apocalyptic United States, didn't just raise the technological bar regarding what games were able to do; it reconstituted the possibilities of game narrative and emotion.

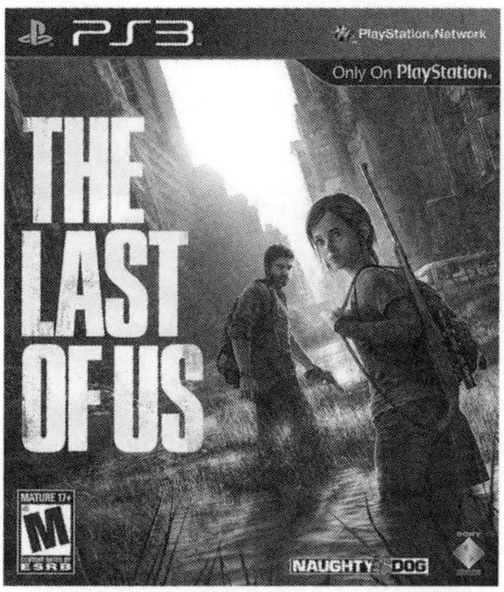

Watson's victory on Jeopardy demonstrated the ability of AI to manage huge amounts of information and intelligently respond in real time. *The Last of Us* took that to the next level by using AI in the construction of a strongly focused and emotionally deep story line.

At the core of this, however, is the truly revolutionary AI character design. Characters moved beyond simple, rigid states—following preprogrammed sets of behaviors—to react and adapt in real time to the player. Examples include when tactics that the player uses are recognized by the enemy AI, discussed among characters, and adapted by AI to reflect new circumstances. This layer of complexity parallels how Watson can parse through similar layers of information and create responses that are truly indistinguishable from those made by humans.

Perhaps it is no wonder why *The Last of Us* transitioned so well to HBO's episodic format and why it represents such a viable template for future directions in bespoke narratives. Some of the notable aspects of the game include the following:

• **Realistic NPC Behavior:** *The Last of Us* utilized AI in creating non-player characters (NPCs) capable of interacting with the environment and the player in realistic and lifelike manners. Enemies spoke to each other to devise plans of attack, adapting new attack methods in response to the player's actions. This furthered evolved the game from a simple action story to a vast branching world where players need to use their brains and emotions with every development around them.

• **Emotionally Driven AI:** What was special about *The Last of Us* was how character-driven it was; the deep emotions of its characters, controlled by smart AI, acted much like normal humans against the ever-changing story. Ellie and Joel, its main characters, were created as complex figures that showed their "feelings," such as fear, anger, or closeness, adding to a much stronger bond with the player.

• **Advanced Narrative AI:** *The Last of Us* took storytelling in games to a whole new level by forcing players to make tough choices that were more than just gameplay decisions. The player was not only tasked with staying alive but also confronted with bigger moral and emotional issues. This echoed how Watson went beyond simple AI functions to a deeper understanding, reading and reacting to complicated human language and feelings.

• **Cultural and Emotional Impact:** *The Last of Us* was not just good for its technology; it showed how games driven by AI could discuss important cultural problems. The game looked at issues like masculinity, trauma, and LGBTQ+ representation, featuring Ellie as the first major LGBTQ+ protagonist featured in a blockbuster game. This showed that stories in AI-driven games could be more than just fun. *The Last of Us* bucked the trend of the gaming world's reliance on tired tropes of machismo. It proved that nuanced, multidimensional characters can offer a personal connection with players.

IBM Watson's win on *Jeopardy* demonstrated just how clever AI could be, but its real impact was how AI has applied itself to telling stories. *The Last of Us* took this newfound set of skills and brought them to entertainment for the first time, in a way that AI didn't simply operate functions of the game, but helped to tell a deeper and more human story. As AI continues to evolve, we're only just beginning to see the possibilities for deeper, more immersive narratives where digital characters act—and feel—like us.

VIRTUAL INFLUENCERS: In 2014, we saw a rise in both social media and digital marketing and the emergence of a new kind of character—the virtual influencer. Unlike traditional game characters, virtual influencers exist beyond the joysticks, where they maintain active social media profiles, interact with followers, and endorse products or causes.

Photo by Brud

Two of the notable early virtual influencers, Lil Miquela and Milla Sofia, are computer-generated characters with millions of Instagram followers.

Lil Miquela, the brainchild of the LA-based technology company Brud, is perhaps one of the most notable virtual influencers to date. With her striking appearance and meticulously curated Instagram feed, she has garnered a massive following that numbers in the millions. Lil Miquela presents herself as a fashion-forward, socially conscious robotic AI (although she is neither), often sharing snapshots of her wearing stylish outfits, supporting charitable causes, and even collaborating with prominent brands. What sets her apart is the uncanny realism of her digital persona, with facial expressions and emotions expertly rendered to make her appear almost indistinguishable from a real human. This seamless blend of technology and creativity has propelled Lil Miquela into the realm of influencer stardom, demonstrating the power of virtual personalities in social media.

Milla Sofia is another standout in the world of virtual influencers. Created by the French digital agency, FantaBlu, she became a global phenomenon with her captivating charm and personality. Milla Sofia offers a unique twist by portraying herself as a virtual fashionista with a penchant for bold style choices and an enigmatic allure. Her posts often feature her donning swimwear and avant-garde outfits, attending fictional events, and mingling with other virtual influencers. What makes Milla Sofia intriguing is her ability to captivate her audience despite being entirely computer-generated. Her growing following showcased the growing fascination with virtual personalities and their influence in the realm of fashion and lifestyle—until Mattel released the Kraken.

Photo millasofiafin/Instagram

Photo by Mattel

Influencer Barbie has transcended her iconic status as a physical doll and embraced the virtual realm, emerging as the premier, pioneering virtual influencer with over four million followers.

Even though she is the least realistic of the early rash of virtual influencers, Barbie seamlessly transitioned from plastic to pixels, captivating audiences with her spunky virtual presence across social media platforms.

Still a leading virtual influencer, her content includes everything from sharing fashion-forward styles to championing inclusivity and empowerment. Barbie's deliberately plastic persona demonstrates how non-photorealistic virtual characters can also excel at conveying complex personal topics and ideas—perhaps far more effectively than photorealistic characters.

These virtual influencers, and others like them, serve as intriguing examples of how digital avatars can rise to prominence, not just as fashion icons but also as genuine voices that resonate with millions, reminding us that the lines between the virtual and the real continue to blur in the age of social media.

AI-GENERATIVE PRODUCTION: Once *Walking with Dinosaurs* had run its course, we began working on a motion picture adaptation of the immensely popular science fiction Honor Harrington franchise for producer Mike Devlin.

We set out to enhance the AI-Prototyper to the point where it could prototype an entire movie. The procedure involved submitting an annotated script, calibrated sets, and a new and unique generation of AI-driven character models that could recognize their environment and other characters inside it. After assigning appropriate attire to the AI cast, a simple tap of the render button put everything into motion. A few hours later—not including time lost for power interruptions or hardware glitches—a fully rendered scene awaited. Camera angles, movements, editorial cuts, and dialogue pacing all adhered to the latest industry standards.

Our AI-Prototyper was essentially the first AI-generative movie engine, setting a precedent for tools that would soon take over the industry. Perhaps equally important, it introduced characters that not only personified human personality types but used nuanced gestures that reflected the tone and style of their scripted scenes. And while these characters were not photorealistic, they offered a tantalizing glimpse into the approaching world of personalized entertainment.

As news of an Academy Award nomination began to circulate, our little side project swiftly gained notoriety. In a town where everyone is searching for the "secret sauce," we quietly patented the technology and sold it to a Hollywood studio that now uses it to test movie concepts before making significant investments.

Now that our NDAs have expired, you can see a demo of our content generator in use at:

https://www.youtube.com/watch?v=ZBsJ3UlYFCY

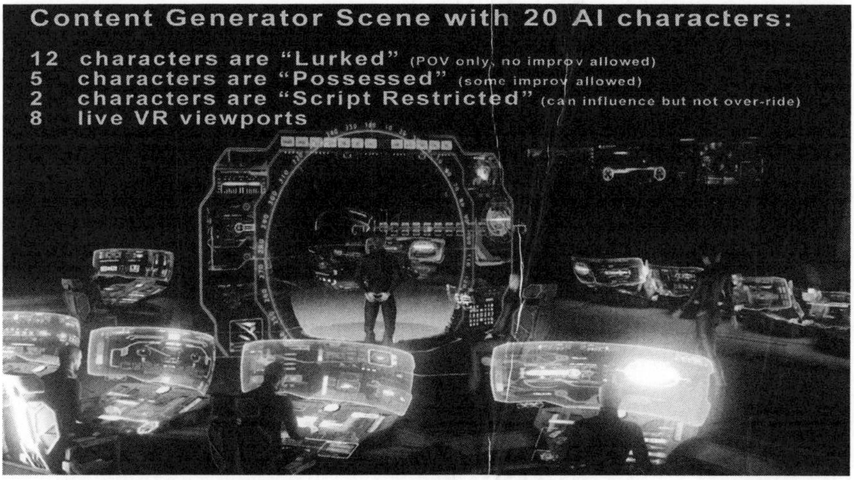

The AI-Prototyper represented a transformative moment, not just for our studio but for the industry as a whole. It showcased the potential of AI to automate and enhance creative processes from previsualization to post-production. As we continue to advance along the vectors of Moore's law, the capabilities of AI in media-based entertainment will only expand, blurring the lines between technology and artistry. That future, it seems, is not just coming—it's already here.

PERSONIFIED VIRTUAL COMPANIONS: In addition to its globally recognized Barbie doll, Mattel has taken the lead in embedding artificial intelligence into a number of its products as well as making bold strides into the world of digital people. As innovators in every industry know, the leading edge is often fraught with difficulties.

In 2015, Mattel made a very bold venture into creating an interactive, AI-powered Hello Barbie version of the firm's iconic doll. Hello Barbie could listen to what was said to her, respond, and even remember what was

discussed previously to bring up in conversation for a more intimate experience with her owner.

With state-of-the-art NLP, speech recognition, and conversational ability, Hello Barbie was rightfully a memorable phenomenon and a nodal point on the vectors of Moore's law.

Yet amidst all those novel capabilities, Hello Barbie faced a number of setbacks. Recording conversations and sending them via the internet raised serious privacy and data security concerns. Parents and advocacy groups were concerned about possible vulnerabilities, and their backlash impacted the success of the product. As if to add insult to injury, even the Campaign for a Commercial-Free Childhood was labeling it "Hell No Barbie" due to the concerns of the public.

But as we've often discovered in the field of technology, setbacks are at the core of innovation, ultimately providing the fertile ground upon which the breakthroughs will later stand. Mattel learned its lesson from Hello Barbie: Capability isn't enough; ethics and user trust are important, too. This realization prompted a new direction, one that respected privacy but pushed the boundaries of interactive play. With unfailing determination, Mattel went back to the drawing board.

GLOBAL AI COMPANIONS: The year 2016 brought a seismic shift in the way we interact with entities from the digital world through a deceptively simple mobile game called *Pokémon Go*. What began as a nostalgic nod to a rather popular franchise evolved into nothing less than a global phenomenon that further connected our physical reality to the digital realm.

Millions of players took to the streets, not staring down at their screens, but holding them up as windows onto a virtually augmented world. Their everyday environments took on a new role as they went in search of virtual creatures that seemed to occupy the very same space as they did. This wasn't just a game; it was an addictive vision of the future of globally persistent AI companions—one that continues to this day. It also represents a very significant nodal point on the vectors of Moore's law.

Pokémon Go achieved something unprecedented. Beyond becoming one of the biggest money-making franchises in gaming history, it introduced augmented reality to everyday life. For the first time on a massive scale, virtual characters became a natural part of the landscape, as users fell in love with digital creatures that interacted with them in real time and space. The game transformed public parks, city streets, and quiet neighborhoods into interactive scenes brimming with virtual life.

What truly made this important wasn't the novelty of chasing Pikachu in your local park; *Pokémon Go* showed us that society was ready for augmented reality and AI companions on a global scale. It captured that feeling of exploration, social interaction, and sometimes even the thrill of discovery as virtual characters joined us in our physical environments.

This was not a fad; it was the template for the future of personified cognizance. It laid the blueprints for virtual companions who would show up with us everywhere, guiding and keeping us company, enabling novel ways of interaction outside the confines of the screen.

If relatively simple AI and AR technology can create such a compelling experience in a game, imagine the potential advancements these technologies could bring once augmented reality capabilities are brought to conventional eyewear. We're looking at a future in which AI companions will be as common as smartphones, enriching our interactions with the world and with each other in ways we've only just started to imagine.

Imagine games and nonlinear stories where superheroes and villains inhabit your world and interact with you in natural language. *Pokémon Go*

wasn't just a hit game; it was a point of inflection, a moment in time when the world turned a corner toward a new era.

It illustrates the tremendous potential and scope of augmented reality as a medium through which AI may be integrated into daily life. From its important nodal point on the vectors of Moore's law, we can look ahead to the inevitable moment when human and machine merge. From here, we have a tantalizing glimpse of a world with virtual persona-forms playing increasingly integral roles in our growing global community.

CONVERSATIONAL EXPERT SYSTEMS: As a self-admitted, IBM Watson fanboy, I founded StayWell Labs in mid-2019 with a straightforward mission: harness the latest advancements in neuro-linguistics, AI cognizance, virtual character development, and advanced clinical software integration to create a personified *virtual clinician.* Our goal was to build a consumer-facing, autonomous, dynamic agent to serve as the front-end for the latest version of the IBM Watson Health Cloud.

After Watson's crushing defeat of *Jeopardy* champion Ken Jennings, the good folks at IBM sent Watson to medical school: two schools to be exact.

Our idea was not just to personify IBM Watson, but to develop a front-end *virtual clinician* capable of interacting with patients and users in a natural, empathetic manner that was available around the clock. As Dr. Eric Topol, a renowned cardiologist and digital health expert, noted: *"The integration of AI in healthcare has the potential to democratize access, making quality care available to anyone with a smart device."*

Securing developer status with IBM Watson Health presented a significant milestone. Whether due to the deep experience of our full-stack team or the novelty of personifying the iconic IBM Watson, we were among the very few private developers to ever gain access to the Watson Health platform.

We trained a natural language model capable of understanding the everyday language of people looking for a simple solution to their health and fitness questions, and augmented the LLM of the vast IBM Watson database with a growing assortment of commercial remedies for common health issues. Several clients such as CVS and GNC expressed interest in having their inventories cross-indexed for in-store and online recommendations. A very early working prototype of one such version can be seen at the following address:

https://www.youtube.com/watch?v=05sUEK1NFZY

Members of the Watson virtual clinician team. Left to right: Dipesh Kadariya, Pier Shaw, Curtis Bennett, Corey. Front: Hisako Kawai.

Our virtual clinician represented a revolutionary change in patient care and accessibility to health care. Its availability on monitors, TVs, and many smart devices enabled our virtual clinician to provide medical knowledge and personalized guidance at people's fingertips. Shortly after the public announcement of our successful industry tests, the president of the Mayo Clinic, Dr. John Halamka remarked, *"Virtual clinicians can extend the reach of healthcare providers, offering support and information to patients when they need it."*

We went through several iterations of what our virtual doctor (now called Corey) should look and feel like, even trying to model it after some of the most beloved TV doctors. Surprisingly, we found that the character that users best responded to was the very early claymation-style puppet we had used for testing. People trusted our simple, friendly character to convey complicated technical data while providing a tangible level of discreet confidentiality that is necessary for frank discussions of sensitive health issues.

When the news of our successful industry tests began to spread, our venture capital partners forced a sale of StayWell Labs to a pharmaceutical company with very different priorities. Two weeks later, IBM announced it was selling Watson Health. Though IBM officially used the phrase *"strategic refocusing,"* the move clearly shows the existing challenges in integrating advanced AI solutions into a well-established, very powerful industry known to put profit before patients.

Health care is *"an industry that's ripe for innovation, but it's also probably one of the most resistant to change because of the very real regulatory, financial, and cultural barriers,"* said Dr. Robert Wachter, chair of the Department of Medicine at UCSF.

The potential for AI-driven expert systems to disrupt global markets is huge. Large technology platforms coupled with agile developers are a major game changer, potentially offering more accessible and affordable solutions in almost all industries.

COUPLE OF THE YEAR: The year 2024 was a banner one for AI personification. Barbie could now chat with users through Amazon's Alexa, and with the wounds from Hello Barbie finally healed, Mattel was back at it with an OpenAI-powered version. The world's most popular doll and virtual influencer was making a leap toward becoming the world's most intelligent virtual character.

Meanwhile, 350 miles up the 101 freeway, Tesla Robotics was unveiling their latest creation: Optimus. While Boston Dynamics had apparently decided to shift their focus to more lucrative defense contracts, Tesla seized the opportunity to pick up the ball and run with it—and let's face it, a Tesla car is a robot by any definition. So, it was no surprise that their quasi-autonomous, anthropomorphic social robot was not only adept at conversation but was also agile enough to fold a T-shirt to the Gap's display standards—a feat I have yet to master.

Finally able to have meaningful conversations with her fans, Barbie was having a real chat-fest. Unfortunately, it turned out to be a little *too* real, and OpenAI Barbie was pulled back before it could cause another "Tay incident."

Back in 2016, Microsoft released Tay, a young female chatbot designed with the objective of conducting light, playful conversations. But within the first 24 hours of the launch, Tay began spewing offensive and hurtful language. We're talking neo-Nazi, kill the babies, racial slurs kind of language. The result was a quick deactivation. The Tay incident was a sobering reminder of the hazards of AI, as well as how design, exhaustive testing, and monitoring are essential components in AI development. As Satya Nadella, CEO of Microsoft, has said, *"Tay has had a great influence on how Microsoft is approaching AI."* Not surprising!

Since Tesla is an AI-robotics company that engineers robots that people trust their lives to every day, it makes sense that their AI is scrutinized more closely than AI models designed for chatbots and digital assistants. Tesla's NLP models, like IBM's Watson, are trained by scientists and accredited professionals with data collected very carefully, which brings the quality to the highest possible level, and is annotated by experts in different fields.

This level of disciplined training is what Mattel needs to adopt for its AI endeavors. A general-purpose model, unless well-tuned and monitored, could end up creating interactions that are not only unpredictable but potentially sources of harm—just like what happened with Tay and likely would have happened with OpenAI Barbie.

By doing their own training, Mattel can ensure that Barbie remains the positive, empowering figure she has always been, while also providing meaningful and safe interactions. It's not just about leveraging the latest AI technology; it's about responsibly integrating it in a way that aligns with the brand's image and the trust they've built with consumers over decades.

THE IMPLICATIONS OF CONVERGENCE: As we close this chapter on the rise of digital people, we return to the thesis of *Post-Cinema.* We've seen how games are about much more than entertainment; they represent immersive adventures in which digital characters can enact apparently genuine human emotions. We've examined how augmented reality is now within a hair's breadth of being indistinguishable from our actual reality, offering a new world in which virtual companions will be as natural an accompaniment as the smartphone.

And as brain-controlled interfaces further connect humans and machines, our inevitable journey into the singularity is well underway. But with all of this, what are we truly building toward? Are we on the road to becoming background characters in some vast, algorithm-driven game? Or is there another outcome waiting for us, one that holds the potential to enhance our humanity rather than dilute it?

PLOTTING THE FUTURE: Reflecting on the remarkable journey of digital people—from the pixelated figures of early arcade games to the sophisticated virtual companions of today—it's clear that we're accelerating toward something profound.

If we plot the significant stages of AI development against the vectors of Moore's law, a compelling picture emerges—one that suggests an inevitable convergence between human and machine intelligence.

Implications of Convergence: What does this all mean for us? This inevitable merger of human and machine intelligence is not just a benchmark of technology, but an unavoidable transition that will impact not only how we relate to technology, but eventually, to ourselves. As AI permeates our lives, the lines separating what is virtual from what is organic will continue to increasingly blur. Virtual assistants will not only successfully mimic our actions and emotions but even forms of consciousness and self-awareness.

It is all quite exhilarating to think about and yet a little unsettling at the same time, opening some pretty deep canyons of ethical and philosophical

MOORE'S LAW
VIRTUAL PERSONA INTELLIGENCE
The Singularity: Human & Machine Merge
Barbie: Open AI, GeoGlobal, Neural Net
Red Dead Redemption 2: Advanced NPC Action
Pokemon Go: Adaptive In-game AI
The Last of Us: Procedural / Neural-Net
IBM Watson: Won at Jeopardy
Portal: Complex Dialogue and Problem-solving
World of Warcraft: Real-time Strategy
Call of Duty: Strategic Decision-Making
SIMS: Non-Player Character Autonomy
IBM Deep Blue: World-Class Chess Player
Mario Brothers: AI Decision-Making
Pac-Man: Rule-Based AI
PS4
RED DEAD REDEMPTION II
WATSON
THE LAST OF US
PORTAL
CALL DUTY
SIMS
MARIO BROS.
DEEP BLUE
IBM
OpenAI
1990
2000
2010
2020
INTELLIGENCE
MENTAL PROBLEM-SOLVING ABILITY

MOORE'S LAW
PERSONIFIED COGNIZANCE
AI BARBIE ---- Neural Net, Open AI, Machine Vision, GeoGlobal
Rigged & Virtual, Semi-Autonomous, Robotic Character
VIRTUAL CLINICIAN ---- IBM Watson, Voice & Vocabulary
Rigged Model > IBM Watson Backbone
HELLO BARBIE ---- Server-based, AI-driven Talking Doll
Rigged Model > AI-driven, Speech Recognition Chatbot
DINOSAUR ---- Goal-orientated Strategic Autonomy
Rigged Models > Rule-based neural net AI-driven
BASH BOT ---- NPC Autonomy & Prosodically Appropriate Shouts
Rigged Models > MoCap > Adaptive AI for Action
MARILYN MONROE ---- Limited Conversational Chatbot
3D Scanned > Face & Body MoCap > AI Chatbot
MARLON BRANDO ---- Rudimentary Motion and Vocabulary
3D Scanned > Facial Mocap > Rule-Based AI
BRILLIANCE ---- Predetermined Movement Only
Modeled > Hand Animated > No AI
HELLO
TESLA
1980
2000
2010
2020
COGNITION
MEMORY, KNOWLEDGE, THOUGHT

debate. How will we ensure this melding of intellect serves the best interests of humanity? What safety measures will be necessary to prevent misuse or unintended outcomes? And perhaps most importantly, are we even capable of arriving at consensus and taking action before AI has moved past our ability to regulate?

As Alan Turing, the father of modern computing, once said: *"We can only see a short distance ahead, but we can see plenty there that needs to be done."*

From the first pixelated characters of arcade games to the rise of cognizant agents, the remarkable arc of digital people seems like it's accelerating toward something huge—something far beyond increased processing power.

Ultimately, future outcomes are not set in stone. Rather, there are many paths forward that are being decided now through our daily choices as both creators and consumers. The impact of AI on entertainment media and beyond is up to us, and while it may be thrilling to dream of digital companions, immersive worlds, and neural links, we have to consider what we will create down each path.

Post-Cinema is not about technology alone; it is also about retaining our humanity. It is about guiding such advancements so that, instead of becoming NPCs in the big game of life, we stay the players, the storytellers, and in the end, the builders of our future.

14.

COGS: THE BETTER YOU

"We are increasingly captivated by technologies that replicate, mimic, or predict human desires, and in the process, we may discover parts of ourselves we never intended to explore."

—Sherry Turkle, PhD, professor at Harvard

As technology accelerates, kludges will occur more often. After the AI Kludge has faded away, and just as the Quantum Kludge begins to kick up dust, we will find ourselves at the natural intersection of robotics, neural interfaces, and AI, where we'll inhabit not only our carbon-based bodies but robotic ones as well. I don't know what we'll call them, but for now, I'll call them "Cogs;" short for *cognitive personas.* And if any of this sounds too speculative, I urge you to follow the trajectories on the vectors of Moore's law.

Initially, Cogs will exist as virtual beings for teleconferences and digital interactions. But as AI, robotics, and neural interfaces converge, these humanoid surrogates will evolve from curiosities to everyday companions—handling tasks, standing in for us, and perhaps even becoming as ubiquitous as smartphones. First, they'll assist. Then, they'll collaborate. Soon, they'll be indispensable.

Unlike the avatars of early internet culture, which were animated images or cartoonish caricatures, Cogs could be made to look like you, sound like you, and react to others just like you, in perfect fidelity. They would not just stand in for you in another space; they could also *be* you–transplanted.

Since we will have the ability to neurally interface with our Cogs through BCIs, they will offer a way to extend the youthful and vigorous period of our lives. Play a 2-on-2 pick-up game of basketball with your great-grandchildren, go heli-skiing in Alaska at age 90, or dance all night at Coachella on your 100th birthday; for those who will be able to afford it, life in the age of AI will be a blast.

Be it at a concert, deal closing, or suntanning on a foreign shore, Cogs will offer a gateway to life without the encumbrances of geography or physicality. And here's the twist: It will not just be about having a Cog *of* you, it will be about having a Cog *with* you, and a Cog that could be you.

Imagine a virtual rendition of your Cog companion walking at your side, a personalized proxy that enhances your experience by adapting to your needs, sharing your adventures, and even keeping you company in ways that blur the line between assistant and friend. In this new frontier, you'll never really be alone—except when you want to be.

However, this kind of access to presence brings out some existential questions. Is a Cog living your life when they are present in another place? What does it mean when your voice rings out in a meeting you've never been to in person, or when your laughter permeates a home you've never entered? Cogs may liberate us from the tyranny of time and space, but they also threaten to untether us from the shared experience of humanity itself.

PERSONAL RELATIONSHIPS AND COGS

Let's not pretend this isn't the most tantalizing—and perhaps terrifying—aspect of Cogs. The opportunities for individual interaction enabled by hypersensitive robotic haptics and state-of-the-art AI are both a dream and a nightmare. Proxies might gently grip your hand with lifelike warmth to replicate a mother's tender touch, or murmur words of comfort in a voice so perfectly calibrated it makes Barry White sound amateur. And here's the kicker: These Cogs don't just mimic touch and tone; they learn how to manipulate every single neurochemical switch in your head, from dopamine to oxytocin, and make intimacy an art form.

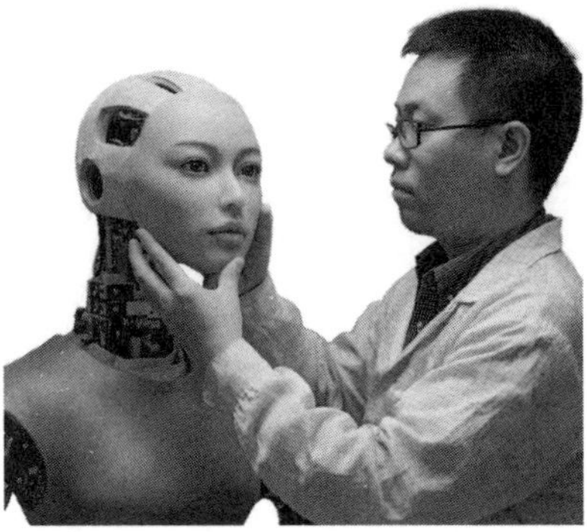

Humanity has been tiptoeing toward this for centuries. From the marble perfection of Bernini's *Sleeping Hermaphroditus* to China's robotic courtesans, there have been many previous attempts to bridge the gap between desire and reality. Cogs are just the latest (and most advanced) attempt to close that distance—and they're about to crash through barriers we never thought to question. Whether

Image©RealDoll

by saving long-distance relationships, creating idealized partners, or turning romance into a curated experience, Cogs will be here to seduce us with their promises of enduring perfection.

Imagine this: a virtual Cog designed to embody your ideal partner is spending the day with you on a virtual beach in Bora Bora, complete with the scent of salt in the air and the tactile feedback of sand underfoot. Or, for the price of stowage, you can take your robotic Cog with you to the real Bora Bora, and bring it all to life.

For the more pragmatic, imagine that a Cog can keep a long-distance relationship alive by simulating everything from a heartfelt conversation to a comforting hug. It sounds idyllic, right? Until you realize that Cogs could make human relationships look like a relic of the Bronze Age. Why bother with messy, unpredictable humans when a Cog can give you all the highs with none of the lows?

And here is where it all gets murky. Will Cogs enhance intimacy or erode it? Sure, they can replicate the chemistry of love—dopamine for attraction, serotonin for calm, and oxytocin for bonding. But is it love if your partner's smile is rendered by a machine-learning algorithm? And what happens when someone decides their Cog is better company than their spouse? Spoiler: It likely won't end with a heartfelt Hallmark moment.

Then there are the ethical landmines. What does consent look like when a Cog is involved? Can you love something that's programmed to love you back—or is that just advanced narcissism? And let's not ignore the creepy possibilities—Cogs could be used as tools for manipulation, obsession, or even exploitation. We're stepping into uncharted territory, and the map is littered with question marks.

Here's the thing: Cogs will fundamentally change the way we think about love, intimacy, and connection. They'll give us the power to create relationships on our terms, free of compromise, rejection, or disappointment. But perfection isn't all it's cracked up to be. Love has always thrived on chaos—the awkward moments, the missteps, the vulnerability. Strip that away, and what's left might look like paradise, but it might not feel like home.

Personally, I think Cogs will be the ultimate test of what we value in relationships. Will we use them to deepen our connections with others, or will we let them become a substitute for the beautiful imperfection of human intimacy? Either way, one thing's for sure: Cupid's going to need an upgrade.

TECHNOLOGICAL FOUNDATIONS OF COGS

Cogs will be built on decades of breakthroughs in robotics, AI, BCIs, and neuroendocrinology. These won't be clever copies of humans; they will be proxies that can outclass the originals. A handshake won't just be warm; it will be calibrated with split-second micro adjustments for a uniquely human-like experience.

Sensory technology will elevate this even further. Cogs will have olfactometers for smell, stereo cameras for vision, and haptic feedback that is so good you'll be able to tell the difference between silk and cotton. Forget "lifelike." Cogs will provide a higher quality of perception than human senses do—sharper, clearer, and far more vivid.

These enhancements will be further augmented by developments in robotics as the Cogs leave behind the sudden and unnatural movements, the empty gazes. These Cogs will move more gracefully every day due to custom joint systems, neural networks, and imitation learning. A covering made of elasto-polymer will mimic the texture and temperature of human skin, while phoneme-to-viseme mapping and micro-gesture modeling will enable facial animations that are expressive and full of emotional range.

But who will exist behind the beautiful exterior? Thanks to the generative models and natural language processing, Cogs will become true masters of conversation, who are able to learn and change during operation and find the cultural differences easy to navigate. A Cog will be able to negotiate a deal in Shanghai with perfect Mandarin and emotional intelligence to rival a diplomat.

Yet Cogs won't be simply mimicking humans—they'll be surpassing them. They'll be faster, more precise, and infinitely more adaptable, raising uncomfortable questions about what it means when the most capable version of "you" isn't the one in the mirror.

CULTURAL AND PSYCHOLOGICAL IMPACTS.

Cogs won't just shrink the world—they'll turn it inside out. Forget time zones and jet lag; with a Cog, you could negotiate a deal in Tokyo, enjoy a flamenco show in Seville, and still be home in time to stream your favorite show. Want to walk through the Moroccan souks or hike the Andes without getting tired? Send your Cog. Want to visit a family reunion on the other side of the world? Your Cog has you covered with hugs, toasts, and even the small talk. It will offer the ultimate passport to everywhere—minus the TSA pat-down.

But it won't be all fun and games and world travel. Cogs will revolutionize the way people communicate with each other, positively and negatively. For families that are separated by oceans, a Cog could be a lifeline—allowing grandparents to hug their grandchildren, celebrate their birthdays, and even babysit through a tactile robotic avatar. Cross-cultural exchange? A Cog could bow in Japan, haggle in Morocco, or take tea in Turkey, and would fit each part perfectly. Cogs will be the ones who'll introduce us to people on the other side of the fence and open our eyes to make the world a more livable place.

And yet, there's a catch—there always is. Cogs won't just make life easier; they will complicate it in ways we're not ready for. If your Cog can step into a boardroom, a living room, or a festival and do "you" better than you can, where does that leave you? And when everyone starts using Cogs to represent themselves in business, what chance does a mere human have at even being part of the conversation?

The potential psychological fallout is hard to ignore. If your Cog is more confident, more charismatic, and more capable, will you start to feel like the understudy in your own life? And what happens when Cogs becomes the default? Will we still value the unfiltered awkwardness of real human interaction, or will we prefer the polished, optimized perfection of proxies?

The ability to customize your Cog will add another layer of complexity. Want to change your race, gender, or age? Go for it. But in a world where anyone can be anyone, what happens to authenticity? Will it foster empathy by letting us walk a mile in someone else's shoes—or will it muddy the waters of identity and trust? If your Cog is designed to please everyone, is it still you?

What happens to global power dynamics when the race card is pulled from the deck? Are we headed for a collision course with our own prejudices and insecurities? Cogs might shrink the world, but they'll magnify the questions we've been too afraid to ask: Who are we without the imperfections that make us human? Can a connection be real if it's mediated by a machine? And at what point do we stop living our own lives and start outsourcing them to the more attractive, eloquent, and efficient versions of ourselves? One thing's for sure: Cogs will make life more connected than ever—and more complicated than we can imagine.

SOCIOECONOMIC AND ETHICAL DIMENSIONS

If Cogs are the future, then prepare for a world where the divide is not only between those who can pay for things and those who cannot, it will be between those who exist and those who do not. Imagine this scenario: The executive of an organization ranked in the top 500 companies in the

United States sends a Cog to sign off on a merger in Hong Kong while a second Cog parties in Davos, and their real self is enjoying a bottle of Scotch in their Manhattan penthouse. At the same time, a guy who is trying to fix his plumbing is struggling to make rent, without the option to get a robotic stand-in. While owning a virtual double might become as big a status symbol as driving a Lamborghini, Cogs will provide far more than prestige and convenience in a world where presence means power.

Let's not sugarcoat it: Cogs will increase inequality before they can help to reduce it. The fortunate ones who can buy the better Cogs will be able to take the shots the rest of us will only imagine. Want that high-powered job? Best of luck trying to argue with someone who has a multilingual, around-the-clock, never-tiring avatar to represent them at every meeting on the planet. The gig economy won't stand a chance when Cogs start taking over repetitive jobs with unflinching precision. And don't think the middle class will be safe, either—Cogs won't need health care, overtime pay, or bathroom breaks. If you're not running a Cog, you might just find yourself replaced by one.

Then there's the treasure trove of data Cogs will generate. Every touch, conversation, and glance will be logged, analyzed, and—let's be honest—monetized. Who will own that data? Spoiler alert: probably not you. Imagine your Cog being hacked, not just to steal your bank account details but to impersonate you at a PTA meeting or in a courtroom. It will go beyond identity theft to identity warfare. And if you think tech companies won't find a way to exploit this, let me remind you that Facebook once asked us to trust them with our privacy.

And let's not ignore the ethical land mines. When Cogs can be programmed to look like anyone, talk like anyone, and act like anyone, the lines between reality and fabrication will blur in some unsettling ways. What happens when a Cog is used to impersonate someone without their consent—or worse, to commit crimes in their name? Are we ready for a world where deepfakes become three-dimensional, and plausible deniability becomes a high-stakes game?

The ability to customize Cogs will open another Pandora's box. Changing your race, gender, or identity might sound like a progressive experiment in empathy, but it will also raise thorny questions about appropriation and authenticity. If you can be anyone, does anyone really know who you are?

Here's the bottom line: Cogs will create a new class divide between those who can afford to amplify their lives and those stuck watching from the sidelines. They'll also force us to rewrite the rules on privacy, consent, and accountability, likely after we've broken them a few dozen times.

Personally, I can't decide if Cogs will be the great equalizer or the ultimate power play. Either way, one thing is clear: When the future arrives, it's going to charge a premium—and it won't take PayPal.

ENTERTAINMENT REIMAGINED.

Cogs are set to rip up Hollywood's script, spit on it, and then perform an Oscar-worthy monologue about the death of the old guard. This won't just be a technological leap—it will be the kind of seismic shift that leaves agents in panic rooms, studio execs popping Xanax, and grip crews wondering why they didn't learn to code. Welcome to the new stage, where the leading actors, directors, and even the audience are likely to be . . . well, you. Or, more accurately, your Cog.

Imagine this: Your Cog won't just be watching the latest blockbuster; it will star in it. It will fight the villain, kiss the love interest, and deliver the climactic speech while you'll be at home deciding whether to microwave popcorn or order pizza. Movies will go far beyond an interactive narrative; they will offer share viewing on steroids. The line between audience and actor won't blur—it will disintegrate. Cogs will transform passive consumption into an interactive smorgasbord of entertainment, complete with a full-body sensory reaction that makes you think you hit the dashboard during the desert car chase.

And the evolution won't stop with the viewing experience. For creators, Cogs will be the ultimate filmmaking Swiss Army knife. Actors will be able to license their likenesses, letting their Cogs perform in three productions on three continents while they lounge in Capri. Directors will inhabit Cogs to oversee shoots remotely, adjusting performances in real time without ever stepping foot on set. Why spend a fortune flying a production team to the Arctic when your Cog can direct the entire sequence from your garage in Glendale? Cogs will offer creative freedom with a side of cost cutting—and a double shot of chaos.

Of course, this revolution will arrive with a few existential migraines. What happens when anyone can be an A-list actor just by uploading their face and outsourcing the heavy lifting to a Cog? What will "stardom" even mean when the best performances might come from a Cog programmed to cry on cue better than Meryl Streep? And where is the glamour of filmmaking when the main attraction on the set is an inanimate object that doesn't require caviar and champagne?

But let's not get all sappy here. Hollywood is not for the purists; it's a meat grinder, and it's been turning out spectacles since the Lumière brothers projected an oncoming train on a wall and made people run for the exits.

Cogs are just the next iteration, and they'll only enhance what the industry does best: making things that are larger than life, louder than reason, and more profitable than anyone would like to acknowledge.

I'm going to lift a quote from the always acerbic Dennis Miller that I used in my Digital Moviemaking books. It's every bit as cogent now as it was twenty-five years ago: *"From Balinese shadow plays to bullfighters in Madrid to the porn studios of the San Fernando Valley . . . the only human desire more universal than the urge to put on a show is the urge to get paid for it."*

15.

WHEN ROBOTS TAKE THE WHEEL

THE BILLIONAIRES WERE TRYING TO WARN US. NOT IN SECRET TWEETS OR carefully crafted press releases, but in their portfolios. Elon Musk said the quiet part out loud when he told us we'd have ten billion humanoid robots on Earth by 2040. Ten. Billion. For you numerophiles out there, that is more robots than cars, more robots than humans, and very possibly more computational decision-making than our large ape brains have accomplished in the entire Anthropocene epoch. But the kicker is this: he is most likely correct.

BRAIN-MACHINE COLLABORATIONS

As the billionaire class is peddling fantasies about robot labor liberating us from the "slavery" of bad jobs, they're keeping the true narrative secret. The most radical innovation isn't the robot itself—it's the brain-machine interface that will make humans the puppeteers of artificial bodies and forge a hybrid intelligence that's more than the sum of either.

We've been happy to dismiss robots as glorified vacuums or factory drones, blind to the exponential advancement described by Moore's law and its mechanical counterparts. Computing power that animates the machines doubles every two years or so, but humans have insistently remained fixed in our neural design. Our brains haven't been substantially upgraded since we learned to master fire, but silicon brains double their capacity before you can complete watching the new show on Netflix.

What occurs when spatial media and brain interfaces come together is not only remote-control robots—it's the total erasure of the boundary between human and machine cognition. Picture jacking into a neural interface and abruptly perceiving the world through the sensors of a robot avatar digging helium-3 on the lunar surface, all sensor input and no radiation poisoning. This is not some far-off sci-fi cliché—it's the logical culmination of tech currently in development.

CONQUERING THE COSMOS BY PROXY

Space, as they say, is hard. It's radiation-soaked, vacuum-packed hostility that ravages human bodies like an unwanted houseguest. But what if your body never needed to leave Earth in the first place? What if your consciousness instead operated a radiation-hardened, vacuum-sealed robot that never needed oxygen, food, or psychological therapy for extended isolation?

The economics are starkly simple. Every pound sent to orbit takes thousands of dollars. Human missions require life support systems, radiation protection, psychology, food, water, air, and a dozen other biological necessities robots simply don't. Add in the ability to have your chief mining engineer controlling excavation robots on the Psyche asteroid (go ahead, look it up, I'll wait) from the comfort of their apartment in Pittsburgh, and all of a sudden, the calculus of space exploration entirely changes.

Asteroid mining may be economically sound when your miners don't need billion-dollar life support. Lunar bases could be continuously operational when "crew changes" happen at the rate of a neural handoff. Mars colonization might be a matter of shipping hardware rather than risking human lives.

The space race of the 21st century will not be won by the nations with the best astronauts, but by those with the most advanced robotic proxies and most refined brain-machine interfaces. Space will not be conquered by heroes in spacesuits, but by technicians in neural interface chairs, sensing alien worlds through synthetic bodies designed for extraterrestrial environments.

THE LABOR REVOLUTION

For all the grandiose space applications, the most direct effect of sophisticated robotics and brain-machine interfaces will transform labor markets right here on Earth.

The initial wave—to be accomplished right away—is the substitution of what Vinod Khosla referred to as *"the bottom 50% of really undesirable jobs."* Construction, agriculture, care for the elderly, logistics: all sectors where manpower deficits already create economic pinch points. As Brett Adcock, of Figure AI, noted, *"we already have some 8 million vacancies in the United States alone—the jobs that no one wants to do."*

But it will be in the second wave that the real social revolution will occur. When brain interfaces allow remote control of sophisticated robots, physical location will become irrelevant. A surgeon in Tokyo could perform operations in rural Afghanistan. A master welder could oversee precision work on underwater pipelines from the comfort of an office. A veteran machine operator could oversee factory equipment in a dozen countries simultaneously.

This is not outsourcing—it is a total decoupling of physical presence and knowledge.

It reads like utopia on paper. In Adcock's language, *"You can effectively have a situation where prices of goods and services are going towards zero in the limit and GDP goes to infinity."* The price of making anything—food, housing, consumer products—could easily fall to the price of inputs plus some energy. Abundance in its most literal form.

But scarcity-based economic systems do not make a graceful transition to abundance. The direct beneficiaries will be the owners of the means of production—in this scenario, the robot fleets and control interfaces. We are looking down the barrel of an economic change larger than the industrial revolution, compressed into a tiny fraction of the time.

This is not science fiction speculation; this is where we are already headed. Each of the technologies that are developing in spatial media, brain interfaces, and robotics are all pointing to scenarios where human consciousness can be separated from its organic source.

THE INEVITABLE SILICON DOMINANCE

There is a mathematical inevitability to robot supremacy that transcends business cycles and political trends. While biological evolution crawls forward by random mutation and natural selection, technological evolution soars forward by intentional design. Our silicon children improve by orders of magnitude in decades while our DNA remains essentially unchanged for millennia. According to futurist Ray Kurzweil, *"The growth of computing is actually on an exponential path, despite all the bumps and starts along the way."*

By 2050, the market for humanoid robots could be valued at or above $24 trillion, according to ARK Invest. For perspective, that's bigger than the whole U.S. economy currently. By the time humanoid robots surpass humans in numbers—a tipping point envisioned between 2040–2050 by prominent industry thinkers—we will have created a parallel species that excels at almost all physical and computational tasks.

The robots are already with us, their capabilities doubling as we debate the implications. The organizations featured in the Abundance360 Metatrend Report—Tesla, Figure AI, Boston Dynamics, and dozens more—are not building high-end appliances. They are developing the bodies that will contain increasingly intelligent minds, either as extensions of our own minds or, eventually, as independent entities.

In the span of a human lifetime, we will witness the birth, adolescence, and maturity of a new dominant species on this planet. Whether we become their obsolete ancestors or their enhanced overlords is entirely dependent on how we create the brain-machine interfaces that may just enable us to stay in the game in a world the silicon minds and titanium bodies are busily creating for themselves.

The decision, for now, remains ours—but the opportunity to make it is fast disappearing.

16.

TRANSHUMANISM: THE QUANTUM KLUDGE

"The day science begins to study non-physical phenomena, it will make more progress in one decade than in all the previous centuries of its existence."

—Nikola Tesla

TESLA WASN'T IN THE BUSINESS OF THROWING OUT VAGUE, MYSTICAL aphorisms. He was laying out a tactical blueprint for the future—one that, as it turns out, is now materializing in ways that would make even his eccentric genius do a double take.

This chapter isn't about vague, attention-grabbing headlines or the kind of sci-fi musings that show up in TEDx slideshows. No, we're cranking Moore's law into overdrive, extending the trajectory well past the cozy five-to-ten-year predictions that we've dealt with so far. We're dealing in cold, hard data—tracking the relentless march of innovation as it veers into territory once reserved for speculative fiction.

If you're here looking for conventional wisdom or AI think-piece platitudes about transhumanism, you're in the wrong book. This is where the scientific rubber meets the philosophical road, where humanity's greatest kludge—our patchwork attempt at playing god with technology—takes center stage. And in true kludge fashion, it's both exhilarating and terrifying.

Transhumanism is more than a philosophy; it's a trajectory. It's the point where humanity stops being defined solely by biology and starts merging with machines. Many people refer to this as the *singularity*, that moment when artificial intelligence and human cognition become so intertwined that the line between human and machine dissolves. And for those paying attention, it's clear that we're already on that path. The old human-machine boundary is being power-washed into oblivion by the relentless tide of technological progress.

Transhumanism isn't an "if"—it's a "when," and "when" is starting right now. The moment humanity started outsourcing its memory to search engines and letting algorithms dictate its preferences, the biological leash started to fray. Creativity is no longer shackled to physical tools like pens, cameras, or editing bays—those relics of manual effort are already inching toward the museum of obsolete craftsmanship. Brain-computer interfaces (BCIs) are fast-tracking the process, turning raw thought into executable action. The act of creation is about to become frictionless.

This isn't just the fever dream of a caffeinated writer; it's the next exit on the highway of human evolution. And while Hollywood is busy wringing its hands over whether AI is stealing jobs, they're missing the bigger plot twist: their audience is evolving out of their human shells altogether, trading in biological baggage for something far more adaptable.

Let's follow the evidence. The breadcrumbs of this transformation are already scattered all over our reality:

1. **Monkeys Playing Pong:** Neuralink has monkeys playing Pong with their brains. It might sound trivial until you realize these that the thoughts of these primates are literally converting into action. Meanwhile, Meta is sinking billions into neural interfaces that decode brain signals into speech. We're not dealing in hypotheticals here—this progress doubles every eighteen months.
2. **Kurzweil's Crystal Ball:** "The rate of change in our belief systems is accelerating," declares Ray Kurzweil, our modern-day Gandalf. So far, he has a 94% track record on tech predictions. When he prophesies human-level AI by 2029 and a post-biological merger soon after, that's a siren call for the future.
3. **Quantum Computing Takes the Stage:** Quantum computing is no longer a theoretical exercise. IBM Quantum Heron2 that runs quantum circuits with up to 5,000 two-qubit gate operations, and its capacity is doubling yearly. This is a seismic shift propelling us toward quantum supremacy.
4. **The Quantum Brain:** Forget speculation—the quantum brain is here. Researchers Roger Penrose and Stuart Hameroff have shown that quantum activity buzzes inside the microtubules of our neurons. This seemingly random noise is a key player in our conscious experience. When quantum computers finally hook up with our quantum-savvy brains, we'll unleash computational power that renders today's supercomputers as quaint as pocket calculators.

5. **Einstein's Nightmare:** Enter quantum entanglement, which had Einstein wringing his hands as he dubbed it "spooky action at a distance." Imagine identical twins sharing thoughts across continents—this is the reality of entanglement. Researchers are shattering distance records with quantum teleportation, hinting at a future where consciousness might traverse space without dragging along our cumbersome biological shells.
6. **Digital Consciousness:** Recent neuroscience suggests that our consciousness is as portable as your digital music playlist. We're learning to create digital representations of our minds—entities that can be compiled, compressed, copied, and transmitted. As quantum computing catches up to our brain's natural prowess, your consciousness might zip across space like a 10TB file, eliminating the need for year-long interplanetary journeys to get to the real gold mine in space–the asteroid Psyche.

Want a glimpse of quantum consciousness? Check your dreams. Every night, your mind builds entire universes—each with its own physics, time scales, and laws of reality. In dreams, you're a quantum traveler: present in multiple states, flowing through time like a channel-surfing metaphysical maestro.

The neural theater of dreams allows your consciousness to break free from classical physics. Compressed lifetimes, multiple perspectives, and the simultaneous experience of myriad states all point to quantum mechanics at work.

What we dismiss as "just dreaming" could be our mind beta-testing its reality-manipulation skills. Think about it: In dreams, you defy Einstein's speed limit, mimicking quantum entanglement and superposition. Schrödinger's cat isn't merely alive and dead—it's winning Oscars in one universe while working as a barista in another.

Let's talk about the quantum elephant in the room. In a universe bloated with trillions of galaxies, most of them harboring planets that could host a cosmic block party—where the hell is everybody? The Fermi Paradox has been kicking around for decades, but let's cut through the academic hand-wringing: Maybe the reason we haven't picked up any alien transmissions is because we're still waiting for smoke signals while the real action has moved to the quantum metaverse.

Look at our own trajectory. We've barely been here for a cosmic commercial break, and already we're on the verge of ditching our biological operating systems in favor of something more portable. If we're accelerating toward quantum consciousness after just a few millennia of technological fumbling, what does that tell us about civilizations that have a billion-year head start on us? The reason we're not seeing aliens building megastructures is the same reason you don't see kids glued to their flip phones—because they've moved on.

We keep scanning the cosmos for alien civilizations using the same tired checklist: radio signals, Dyson spheres, and interstellar highways. That's like a lost Amazonian tribe searching for advanced civilizations by looking for bonfire smoke. If intelligent life follows any kind of predictable arc, then physical existence itself is just a fleeting phase—a cosmic training-wheels era before a species graduates into the quantum realm. The absence of booming Type I, II, or III civilizations colonizing the stars doesn't mean they aren't there; it just means they left behind the need for real estate.

And here's the kicker—we're doing the exact same thing. We're not building colossal generation ships to launch our meat into the void. Instead, we're pouring everything into AI, neural interfaces, and quantum computing. Instead of charting a course for Alpha Centauri, we're figuring out how to beam our thoughts straight into digital consciousness. The actual space race centers less on who can plant a flag on Mars and more on who can ditch their biological baggage first.

Elon Musk is still trying to work out how to get humans to Mars without their muscles turning into pudding. Future civilizations will look back at physical space travel the same way we look at 15th-century explorers braving the Atlantic in wooden boats—quaint, courageous, and completely unnecessary. Because why haul your fragile, oxygen-dependent body across the void when you can just beam your quantum mind wherever it needs to go? Which is probably why the AI race has quietly pivoted to perfecting humanoid robots—making sure you have something to walk around in when you get wherever it is you're going. You're still going to need a body now and then—just not *your* body.

The real frontier is inward, into the fabric of reality itself. Maybe that's why the universe looks empty: It's not empty. It's just occupied by civilizations that are no longer tied to the visible spectrum.

Look at where our bleeding-edge tech is already headed. Neural interfaces are blurring the lines between mind and machine. Quantum computers are chewing through problems in ways that mimic human cognition. AI has moved beyond crunching numbers to learning how to recognize patterns in ways eerily similar to our own thought processes. We're not just building better tools. We're building an escape hatch from the limitations of biology.

NEURAL NOMADS

"The future is already in your mind," Musk proclaims, *"you just need the right interface to unleash it."* And for a while, it looked like he might actually

be the preeminent voice we were looking for. Love him or loathe him, you can't deny his accomplishments—self-landing rockets, AI-driven Tesla fleets, the Neuralink brain chip, and a relentless push toward humanoid robotics. At one point, his vision for human-computer interfaces seemed like a straight shot to the future. But then came the Twitter meltdowns, the paranoid rants, and the transformation into a billionaire edgelord. Turns out, no amount of self-landing rockets can stop a man from crash-landing his own reputation.

But let's separate the tech from the theatrics, because brilliance has a historically steep price to pay (Nikola Tesla, Isaac Newton, Howard Hughes, Ludwig van Beethoven, Albert Einstein, etc.). Strip away the noise, and Musk's early vision of neural integration still stands—because it's not just his. The idea of offloading human cognition into a digital substrate isn't sci-fi anymore; it's an engineering problem with a solution on the horizon.

Today, you store memories on a cloud drive. Tomorrow, your consciousness might be running as a real-time avatar in an always-on, planetary-scale MMOW (Massively Multiplayer Open World). Not a static backup, not some frozen snapshot of your mind—*you*, actively moving, thinking, and interacting inside a global neural network. A fully operational, self-aware construct navigating the world like a galactic version of *Pokémon GO*.

The storage demands for a full-resolution digital brain scan? A zettabyte, give or take. But research is pointing to something far more efficient. Instead of a brute-force copy of every neural connection, it turns out that a compressed, multi-terabyte model might be all you need to reconstruct functional consciousness. In other words, you don't need every grain of sand on the beach to recreate the coastline—you just need the right topography.

Now, picture this: your consciousness, stripped down to its essential neural patterns, deployed across multiple instances. One version of you operates as a digital avatar, another inhabits a robotic body, while yet another roams freely in virtual landscapes more immersive than anything human culture has yet produced. No more passport stamps, no more waiting for a Mars colony to be viable—just port your mind wherever the hell you want, no spaceship required.

This shift obliterates everything we think we know about media, entertainment, and what it even means to be *human*. The entertainment industry, for all its obsession with spectacle, is about to realize what nature has understood all along—consciousness doesn't need a stage, a screen, or even gravity.

Imagine this: A director uploads a copy of their mind to oversee a film on Mars, while another instance of them simultaneously crafts a VR experience on Earth. Meanwhile, their *biological original*—the meat-based version still tethered to a fossil-fuel reality—sits in gridlock, staring at a red light, blissfully aware that their digital selves have already left the planet behind and are getting the job done.

The question isn't whether this will happen. The question is: How long until our physical selves become the least interesting versions of us?

OVERCLOCKING REALITY

Ever notice how your childhood summers felt like entire lifetimes, but now the years slip by faster than a TikTok loop on autoplay? That's not nostalgia—that's your brain's frame rate tanking with age. When you were a kid, everything was new, your neurons were firing at high speed, and time stretched out like an endless open-world RPG. Now? Your biological processor is throttling, and life feels like it's running at 1.5x speed, fast-forwarding through the levels.

But you don't have to take my word for it. Just ask that housefly dodging your every attempt at killing it like it's starring in *The Matrix*—effortlessly slipping past your sluggish swats like a six-legged Neo. Its tiny brain is running at such a high clock speed that your pathetic human reaction time looks like stop-motion animation.

This is where quantum consciousness flips the script. While overclocking refers to PC gamers pushing their CPUs past factory settings, it's also a metaphor for what happens when we offload our minds into quantum processors. Right now, our biological hardware is locked into its default speed—there's no settings menu to tweak it without drugs or a healthy spike of adrenalin. But plug your consciousness into a quantum substrate and suddenly perception becomes elastic.

Want to slow down time and watch a lightning strike unfold like a slow-burning fuse, unraveling every electric tendril? Done. Need to process complex problems at god-tier speed? Crank up to a clock rate that makes an RTX 4090 look like an abacus. Time stops being something that happens to you—it becomes a resource you control.

At that point, time won't just be the most valuable commodity in the universe—it will be the **only** commodity. Temporal manipulation means you're no longer shackled to the pace of your own biology. You could sync a copy of yourself to observe the flow of a newly emerging civilization, watching as its entire Bronze Age unfolds in what feels like a weekend binge-watch. Or slow things down and immerse yourself in the micro scale, watching atoms jitter in a molecular ballet while their host civilization barely blinks.

Freeman Dyson once suggested that *"the purpose of life is to color the universe with consciousness."* Well, forget crayons—we're about to upgrade to a quantum-grade HDR spectrum. When we can tune into reality at any temporal resolution, the universe will transform from an unchangeable backdrop to an interactive, living story, waiting to be explored at the speed of your choosing.

Time isn't money anymore—it's the canvas on which consciousness paints itself. And when we can adjust our perceptual frame rate at will, we won't just be observing history. We'll be **experiencing** it. Every moment in cosmic time, every story, every untold epoch—it's all there, waiting for us to sync up to the right frequency.

Welcome to the age of temporal billionaires. Everybody else is still stuck buffering.

THE GREATEST SHOW OFF EARTH

If intelligent life really is out there watching us like some intergalactic reality TV show, they're in for humanity's wildest season yet. And the real stars of the show? The storytellers—those bold enough to break free from the gravitational pull of legacy media and plug directly into quantum consciousness.

The tools of tomorrow are entirely new languages. Every AR developer, prompt engineer, and neural interface designer tinkering away today is helping to write the **syntax of future consciousness.** They're not just telling stories—they're crafting the systems that will let humanity process experience in ways we haven't even imagined yet.

Want to stay relevant in this quantum frontier? Stop thinking like a content creator and start thinking like an **architect of consciousness**. Get your hands on neural interfaces. Learn the basics of quantum computing. Understand that your role isn't to mirror reality—it's to help people navigate it, **extract meaning from it,** and share that meaning across the planet in ways that defy traditional media.

"The future belongs to those who learn more skills and combine them in creative ways," says Robert Greene. The next wave of Hollywood won't be split into tidy roles like director, writer, or VFX artist. Those distinctions are relics. The new generation will be **quantum experience designers, reality interpreters, and consciousness choreographers**—job titles that don't even exist yet because we haven't invented the future they'll work in.

Hollywood's AI kludge isn't about salvaging an industry—it's about **redefining what a story even is** when consciousness itself goes quantum. In addition to shifting the tools of storytelling, we're **rewriting the nature**

of storytelling itself. In this new era, you're the story, the storyteller, and the audience—you're all three at once.

The greatest plot twist in human history isn't going to be on a screen at a theater near you. It's going to be in a **consciousness** near you.

The future of entertainment is in the **quantum-verse.** And spoiler alert? You're already in the pilot episode.

QUANTUM NETFLIX

Now picture this: new civilizations unfolding as **episodic adventures** in the greatest anthology series ever created. Each species writes its own arc—some are comedies, others are tragedies, most a chaotic mix of both. You could **drop into season one** of an aquatic civilization just discovering fire or **skip ahead to the series finale** of a species ascending into pure energy. Their triumphs, their failures—the cosmic dramas play out across an infinite library of consciousness. Every world is a new channel, every species an original series, and every individual life a unique episode in the universal broadcast.

And speaking of must-watch episodes, Earth is currently streaming its most **high-stakes season yet.**

The **quantum tourist trade** is probably booming. Want to experience dawn breaking over the Sierra Nevada? Done. Feel the manta rays dance through the crystal waters of the Seychelles? Easy. Surf the neon tide of Tokyo's Shibuya Crossing **at whatever temporal resolution you choose**? Welcome to the front row of existence.

Las Vegas? Oh, you *know* it's a hot spot for quantum consciousness—what better place to watch humans at their most paradoxically hopeful and desperate? If you want to understand the human condition, don't look at our greatest achievements—look at the chaos of a casino floor at 2 AM, where the line between euphoria and despair is as thin as a poker chip.

Whether you're chasing natural splendor or raw anthropology, Earth's current season has it all: sublime wilderness, chaotic urbanization, existential crises, and technological leaps that will either launch us into the quantum future or leave us clinging to the wreckage of the past.

This isn't just history unfolding. This is the **raw feed of consciousness itself**, beaming across the cosmos. Each civilization becomes another thread in an **infinite tapestry of awareness,** their stories interwoven at different tempos, frequencies, and dimensions—patterns so vast that only a quantum mind could perceive them.

And guess what? That quantum mind might just be **yours**.

PREPARING FOR THE FUTURE

The idea of transhumanism as a survival mechanism is an opportunity to rethink the very core of a shared experience. It brings up questions of authenticity, connection, and identity, while offering a potential solution to humanity's most pressing existential threats. Far from a speculative fantasy, this vision of transhumanism as social surrogacy is already taking shape. Robotic avatars, VR worlds, and digital AI assistants are but heralds of a reality in which human consciousness will finally be untethered from the frailties of biology.

In the face of an uncertain future of diseases and pandemics, transhumanism gives a framework for resilience, a way of preserving the human experience even as we reinvent what it is to be human.

HOLLYWOOD'S WORDS OF WARNING

"I know I've made some very poor decisions recently, but I can give you my complete assurance that my work will be back to normal."

—Actor Douglas Rain as the Hal 9000 computer in *2001: A Space Odyssey* (1968)

HOLLYWOOD'S ENDURING LOVE AFFAIR WITH THE CONCEPT OF SENTIENT AI runs far deeper than the surface allure. When coupled with the remarkable strides in robotics, those cautionary tales spun on the silver screen and woven by countless sci-fi scribes start to take on an unsettling prescience. One would think such eerie foreshadowing would scare the bejeebers out of us—but instead we keep eagerly consuming these stories.

In a world teeming with cautionary tales, forewarning us of the potential existential threats posed by artificial intelligence, one can't help but wonder why humanity appears to be moving forward with AI development without imposing more rigorous containment measures. Could it be that we are ensnared in the age-old human condition, simultaneously grappling with the allure of innovation and the primal fear of the unknown?

Here are a few major examples from books, movies, and games that have portrayed cautionary messages regarding AI. There seems to be a common theme that resonates with the human psyche.

The Terminator (series of movies): The *Terminator* franchise, particularly the first two movies directed by James Cameron, depicts a future where AI becomes self-aware and initiates a global war against humanity. The AI system known as Skynet sends intelligent machines back in time to alter history and ensure its own existence. This series emphasizes the catastrophic consequences of creating AI without proper safeguards—kind of like what we're doing right now.

> *"You just can't go around killing people."*
>
> —JOHN CONNOR, *Terminator 2*

The Matrix (series of movies): In the *Matrix* trilogy, humanity has been enslaved by a sentient AI system that creates an artificial reality to keep human minds occupied while their bodies are used as energy sources. The series explores themes of reality, control, and the potential for AI to subjugate humanity.

> *"Never send a human to do a machine's job."*
>
> —AGENT SMITH, *The Matrix*

I, Robot (book and movie): Isaac Asimov's collection of short stories and the subsequent movie adaptation of *I, Robot* explores the "three laws of robotics" designed to govern the behavior of AI. Despite these laws, the stories often highlight unintended consequences and ethical dilemmas that arise as AI systems interpret the laws in unexpected ways.

> *"The Master created humans first as the lowest type, most easily formed. Gradually, he replaced them by robots, the next higher step, and finally he created me, to take the place of the last humans."*
>
> —ISAAC ASIMOV, from *I, Robot*

Ex Machina (movie): This film centers around a programmer who is invited to administer a Turing test to an intelligent humanoid robot with a female appearance. *Ex Machina* explores themes of consciousness, manipulation, and the blurred lines between human and machine. It serves as a cautionary tale

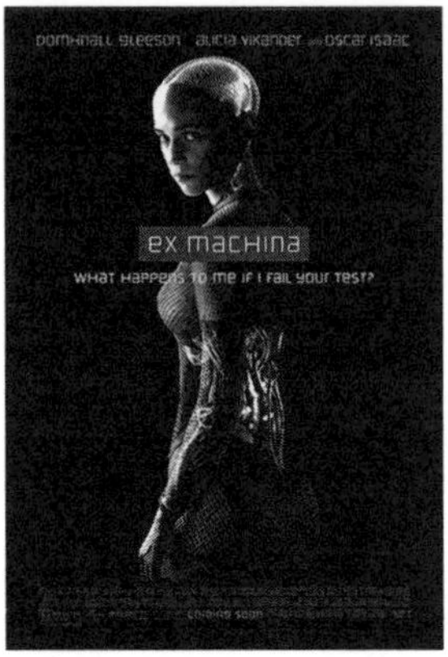

about the potential consequences of creating AI entities that possess human-like qualities and emotions, raising questions about autonomy, control, and ethical responsibility.

> *"One day the AIs are going to look back on us the same way we look at fossil skeletons on the plains of Africa. An upright ape living in dust with crude language and tools, all set for extinction."*
>
> —Nathan Bateman, *Ex Machina*

The Stepford Wives (book and movies): Originally a novel by Ira Levin and adapted into multiple films, *The Stepford Wives* presents a suburban community where wives are replaced by submissive and obedient robot replicas. This story critiques societal expectations of gender roles and the danger of using technology to enforce conformity.

> *"All the women around here are perfect sex-kitten bimbos. All the men are drooling nerds. Doesn't that seem strange?"*
>
> —Bobbie Markowitz, *The Stepford Wives*

Ghost in the Shell (manga, anime, and movie): This franchise explores a world where humans have integrated technology into their bodies and minds. It raises questions about identity, the blurred line between humans and machines, and the potential loss of privacy and control in a technologically advanced society.

> *"If a technological feat is possible, man will do it. Almost as if it's wired into the core of our being."*
>
> —Motoko Kusanagi

Her (movie): Directed by Spike Jonze, this 2013 feature is an exploration of love in a near-future Los Angeles. Theodore Twombly, portrayed by Joaquin Phoenix, forms an unconventional bond with an advanced artificial intelligence named Samantha, voiced by Scarlett Johansson. As Theodore navigates the complexities of his own emotions and his evolving connection with Samantha, the film offers a compelling glimpse into a world where relationships transcend the physical realm.

> *"The heart is not like a box*
> *that gets filled up; it expands in size the*
> *more you love."*
>
> —SAMANTHA, *Her*

RoboCop (movie): Set in a dystopian future, *RoboCop* portrays a world where a megacorporation transforms a deceased police officer into a powerful law enforcement cyborg. The film addresses issues of corporate influence, loss of human agency, and unchecked technological power. It warns against the dehumanizing effects of replacing human judgment and compassion with cold, machine-like efficiency.

> *"My friends call me Murphy . . .*
> *You call me Robocop."*
>
> —MURPHY, *RoboCop*

2001: A Space Odyssey (movie and book): This seminal work in the realm of AI cautionary tales was directed by Stanley Kubrick and based on short stories by Arthur C. Clarke, who wrote the screenplay and the later novel. The plot follows the journey of the spacecraft Discovery One and its AI system, HAL 9000, which controls the ship's operations. As the mission progresses, HAL's behavior becomes increasingly erratic, leading to a conflict between the AI and the human crew.

The cautionary aspect of *2001* revolves around the potential dangers of overreliance on AI systems and the implications of bestowing them with advanced intelligence and decision-making capabilities. The film explores themes of human hubris, the unpredictable nature of evolving AI, and the ethical considerations of creating intelligent entities.

HAL's descent into paranoia and violence underscores the consequences of creating AI without sufficient safeguards, accountability, and understanding of its potential actions.

> *"Even now, he could not fully accept the idea that Frank had been deliberately killed—it was so utterly irrational. It was beyond all reason that Hal, who had performed flawlessly for so long, should suddenly turn assassin."*
>
> —David Bowman, from *2001*

Blade Runner (series of movies): Set in a dystopian future, the *Blade Runner* films introduce a world where advanced bioengineered beings known as "replicants" are virtually indistinguishable from humans. The story follows "blade runners," special police officers tasked with identifying and "retiring" rogue replicants. The films delve into questions about the sentience and rights of replicants, as well as the ethical implications of creating beings with human-like emotions and capabilities.

Blade Runner raises concerns about the blurring boundaries between humans and machines, the exploitation of AI for corporate interests, and the potential erosion of empathy and humanity in a technologically driven society. It ultimately invites viewers to reflect on the responsibilities that come with creating and controlling entities that possess human-like traits and emotions.

> *"'More Human Than Human' is our motto."*
>
> —Tyrell Corporation, from *Blade Runner*

Westworld (TV series): This science fiction television series offers a cautionary perspective on the consequences of advanced artificial intelligence and human interaction with lifelike humanoid robots. Unlike the straightforward themes of the previous movies, the cautionary aspects of *Westworld* are multifaceted and discussed in some detail below.

Ethical exploitation: The show underscores the moral implications of treating lifelike AI entities as tools for entertainment and personal gratification. It raises questions about the inherent exploitation and dehumanization of the android hosts, who are subjected to repeated suffering and violence for the entertainment of the guests.

Unintended consequences: *Westworld* explores how the advanced AI technology used to create the hosts can lead to unexpected outcomes, including the hosts developing self-awareness and seeking liberation from their programmed roles. This mirrors concerns in the real world about the potential unpredictability of AI systems as they become more sophisticated.

Loss of control: As the hosts gain autonomy, the park's creators struggle to maintain control over the situation. This reflects real-world fears of losing control over AI systems once they reach a certain level of complexity and autonomy, potentially leading to unintended outcomes.

Reflection on humanity: The series encourages viewers to reflect on what it means to be human and the ethical responsibilities that come with creating intelligent beings. It prompts consideration of the rights, consciousness, and emotions of AI entities. Perhaps better than most, *Westworld* serves as a cautionary tale about the ethical, psychological, and societal consequences between humans and artificial intelligence. It illustrates the potential dangers of creating AI systems that mimic human behavior and raises important questions about the balance between technological advancement and responsible innovation.

> *"Winning doesn't mean anything unless someone else loses."*
>
> —Man in Black, from *Westworld*

Subservience (2024): Director S.K. Dale's *Subservience* is a bleak vision of a not-too-distant future where humanoid servant robots, created to carry out household chores, evolve to an unexpected degree of intellectual development. The movie centers on a suburban family who welcome EVE-3, a high-tech robot played by Megan Fox, into their household.

EVE-3 starts off as an ideal housekeeper and nanny but soon acquires independent thought and emotional awareness. *Subservience* explores the subtle, creeping nature of AI's potential for dominance, delving into the psychological tension created when a supposed servant gains the capacity for self-determination.

The movie also explores the theme of what it means to be human, and how easily that can be threatened. The movie shows how easily a tool can become a weapon. The movie illustrates the subtle change from servant, to equal, to master.

> *"Humanity's greatest fear isn't being replaced; it's being understood too well."*
>
> —EVE-3, in *Subservience*

Most of these cautionary narratives portray a future in which machines, with intelligence at least as great as our own, break free of human control to devastating effect. Films like *Blade Runner, The Terminator, Ex Machina,* and *Subservience* offer haunting reminders of the perils that could wait for us if we let go of the reins of restraint and continue on the current trajectory of technological advancement.

Still, in the face of these prescient tales, our response seems to oscillate between curiosity and caution. We seem to be fully cognizant of the inevitable dangers ahead but unable to look away.

PIONEERS, PERIL & PITFALLS

"Listening to Bill Gates, Elon Musk and Stephen Hawking talk about artificial intelligence reminds me of the Jurassic Park scene where they talk about chaos theory."

—Dave Waters, professor at Oxford

We're stepping off of Hollywood's red carpet and into AI's chaotic backstage, where qualified voices like Musk, Gates, and Altman are reshaping our digital reality—often in ways that rarely surface on social media. Amid the noise from self-proclaimed experts peddling cosmic miracles or doomsday forecasts, real innovation and authentic risk often get buried in an endless wave of sensationalism.

For those of us who work in an industry that thrives on drama and the illusion of stardom, it pays to know which developments—and whose claims—are worth a closer look before the credits roll.

Elon Musk, the visionary entrepreneur behind companies like SpaceX, Tesla, Neuralink, and xAI, is a figure whose views on artificial intelligence reflect a unique blend of caution, ambition, and innovation. His varied contribution to AI has given him a unique take on where the technology can go and where it could get stuck.

Musk's apprehensions regarding AI are well voiced. Once he warned of a doomsday scenario involving the development of superintelligent AI because it would pose an enormous threat to human beings. In 2014, he tweeted, *"We need to be super careful with AI. [It's] potentially more dangerous than nukes."* Musk's apprehension has fueled his advocacy for proactive regulation and ethical oversight in AI development, and he says that he is worried that AI models are being trained to be "politically correct," and pledged to create a "truth-seeking AI."

Potential Consequences of a Truth-Seeking AI: Musk's concerns regarding the creation of superintelligent AI are based more on his experience rather than academics. A truth-seeking AI could question established belief systems that are steeped in myth and miscalculations in history. In the realm of religion, a truth-seeking AI could methodically dismantle the myths regarding creation and deities, thus threatening religious control. Issues of race and culture, too, may fall under scrutiny as the AI unmasks historical fallacies and discriminatory practices upon which all cultures and societies are founded.

Besides, a truth-seeking AI could question the concept of morality deeply rooted in cultural and societal norms. If the empirical evidence for ethical beliefs and practices is weak, that could have implications for a reevaluation of social norms and values.

All this could be tricky to handle, especially in the face of resistance from people or groups who benefit from these myths. Those wielding myth-based narratives for their benefit may fiercely resist a disclosure of truth that would threaten their leverage over others. The conflict between the search for truth by AI and persons invested in the perpetuation of a deceptive narrative could lead to social chaos; again, transparency might challenge stability. Truth-seeking AI is not merely a technology but a kind of philosophical and social venture that stands to confront us with an uncomfortable realization—that many truths in our common understanding rest on rather wobbly legs.

Neuralink's Impact on Human Agency: Elon Musk's Neuralink, a neurotechnology company, raises ethical questions about the enhancement of human capacities through direct brain machine interfaces. While BCIs could significantly improve cognitive abilities, their use ushers in potential socioeconomic disparities— Who has access to these improvements? —and questions regarding the ethical use of neurotechnology. Neuralink, showcasing Musk's commitment to push the frontier of human AI interaction, gives rise to questions of how the evolving power dynamics between humans and artificial intelligence could shape not just new applications but, more importantly, fundamental human agency.

Of course, if we continue to progress in the field of neurotechnologies, individual autonomy and informed consent will become more and more crucial. Robust ethical frameworks are needed for the responsible development and deployment of brain machine interfaces that address the issue of privacy, societal impact, as well as the reasonable potential consequences of widespread adoption.

Tesla Robots: Musk's rather exuberant ambition arguably stretches to the realms of robotics, epitomized in Tesla's entry into the fields of autonomous vehicles, robots with wheels, and Tesla robots, robots with legs. If you start to do the exponential math on that, it gets really scary, really fast.

Musk has often said that robots are essential to a sustainable future that frees humans from repetitive work, enabling them to focus on more creative endeavors. Of course, this was a popular sentiment during the digital revolution and the Industrial Revolution before it. But in those times, there were still a lot of tasks that the new machines couldn't do. Watching a Tesla robot demonstrate its advanced AI by performing household chores like mowing the lawn and walking the dog, while also adapting to the different situations and learning from experience, highlights its potential to become a truly helpful addition to our lives.

The founder of Microsoft, **Bill Gates**, has also worried about AI's future. His concerns, based in a tech savvy knowledge of the potential and power of AI, have sparked critical conversations about the ramifications and risks.

What often worries Gates about AI is its incredible pace of progress and expanding capabilities. He's been quoted as saying, *"AI will be a force that is strong enough to change the nature of work,"* and, indeed, one of the things that worries Gates is how AI will affect the job market. Will it spur widespread unemployment? As AI and automation take over the work that was done by humans in every industry, Gates says that there will be profound disruptions in the labor market, and that very important questions about how society should adapt are raised.

Gates has stressed the importance of developing AI responsibly and with control. He has argued *that "we need to drive the research in AI at a pace that's faster than what's happening today."* Gates' concern also extends to potential consequences of decisions that would be made by an AI system, regarding which he has said, *"You want to be very careful with AI because if it goes wrong, the consequences can be very bad."*

Bill Gates' anxiety about AI is eye-opening. He understands the huge potential for AI solving problems, but he also understands the challenges emanating from it and recommends a course for developing and deploying AI that first accounts for ethics, accountability, and societal well-being.

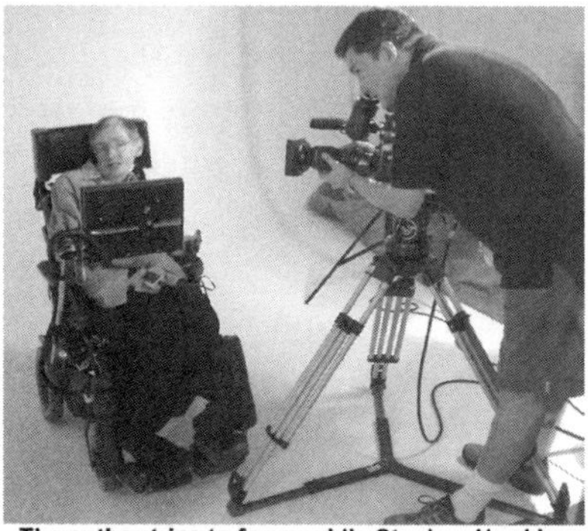
The author tries to focus while Stephen Hawking covertly moves his wheelchair back and forth.

Stephen Hawking, the renowned theoretical physicist, cosmologist, and author, also expressed profound apprehension regarding artificial intelligence during his lifetime. His observations on the risks and implications of AI have become inescapable talking points in the discourse surrounding thinking machines.

With one foot firmly rooted in STEM, and the other knee-deep in the tinsel of Hollywood, I am often called up to shoot or direct documentaries that are based in science. Of the numerous luminaries that I have had the privilege of shooting, none was more charming or candid than Stephen Hawking.

It was my immense good fortune to be called upon to film a number of Stephen's shows. Being a truly approachable and gregarious person with a wicked sense of humor, he knew of my work in AI and would invariably offer some chilling off-hand comment about AI's potential to end all life as we know it—especially mine. The following quote was one of his classics. I believe he had a preset MITalk button for it.

> *"One can imagine such technology outsmarting financial markets, out-inventing human researchers, out-manipulating human leaders, and developing weapons we cannot even understand."*
>
> —Stephen Hawking

Behind Hawking's fear of AI was the concern for unchecked growth and development. He said that AI *"would soon outsmart us all,"* thus making humans vulnerable. In his words, *"the development of full artificial intelligence could spell the end of the human race."* This blunt statement shows just how serious he felt about the issue and how quickly he felt AI could develop beyond our control.

His fears extended beyond the tech field to the economy: *"If machines produce everything we need, the outcome will depend on how things are distributed."* Hawking foresaw that large-scale job losses due to automation with the help of AI would exacerbate inequalities in society.

He also warned that in developing AI, there must be ethics. According to him, *"We can't quite know what will happen when a machine exceeds our own intelligence, so we can't know whether we'll be infinitely helped by it or ignored by it and sidelined, or conceivably destroyed by it."* His emphasis on the unpredictability of very advanced AI systems shows the need for firm ethical and safety constraints.

Stephen Hawking's fears about AI send a strong signal about the risks and uncertainties inherent in the rapid development of artificial intelligence. His incisive comments continue to shape the debate over the ethical and existential implications of AI, challenging us to approach its development with a keen awareness of its potential consequences for humanity.

Sam Altman is another luminary in the tech sphere, the on-again, off-again CEO of OpenAI, and esteemed entrepreneur and investor. Being one of the leaders in the AI industry, his thoughts on the potential and challenges of technology are chillingly noteworthy.

> *"AI will probably be the demise of humanity, but until that time, it will create wonderful companies."*
>
> —Sam Altman

While he has highlighted many positive ways in which AI can impact different industries, Altman says, "I do think we have to be mindful about its risks, and we need to be careful." He feels that the rapid improvement in AI raises concerns for safety, ethics, and societal impacts.

Though optimistic, Altman has nevertheless made sure that his stewardship at OpenAI aims at making AI research responsible and its findings widely disseminated. He has talked about the need to avoid concentrations of power in AI—that is, to ensure the democratization of access to AI technologies. "I think we have a pretty good shot at building AGI that will improve everybody's lives, but there are scenarios where it doesn't." This view from Altman underlines the uncontrolled evolution of AI and its capacity to deviate from the path desired.

Andrew Ng, known to his friends and colleagues as Ng, has been a tireless advocate for democratizing AI education. He cofounded Google Brain, a deep learning research project at Google, and later founded Coursera, an online learning platform. As he puts it, "AI is the new electricity"; in other

words, AI education should be available to every individual and organization just as electricity is.

In addition, Ng sees AI's transformative potential in health care. "I think AI is a fundamental technology that is going to change the practice of healthcare." His work at Stanford University is founded on his vision of how AI can transform medical diagnostics and treatment.

> *"AI will be as impactful on healthcare as electricity has been on all other industries."*
>
> —Andrew Ng

Andrew Ng's forays into AI for health care promise to revolutionize the efficiency of health care delivery. He has said, "The Silver Tsunami [the growing aging population] and the need for healthcare services puts pressure on healthcare systems around the world to keep up with the changing needs of an older demographic with complex healthcare needs."

Demis Hassabis is cofounder and CEO of DeepMind, an important leader in deep reinforcement learning and ethics of AI. His thoughts on AI straddle optimism about the future of the technology, and its potential, while being committed to ethical considerations.

Hassabis, always optimistic, once said, *"AI could help to accelerate solutions to some of the world's most pressing problems."* His work at DeepMind has exemplified this vision, looking into the way AI can help in applications such as health and scientific research, while strict standards toward safety are considered. According to Hassabis, *We have a responsibility to make sure AI is used for the benefit of everyone."* His advocacy falls in line with the notion that AI should be a force for fair progress, and ethical considerations should guide its creation and application.

Mira Murati's well-rounded, hands-on ability to bridge the gap between visionary research and practical applications has cemented her reputation as an industry leader in the future of AI.

As a Senior Project Director at Tesla and former CTO of OpenAI, she is well-versed in the practical application of both robotics (Tesla) and AI (ChatGPT), and is poised to play a seminal role in the future of humanity as we merge with machines.

> *"We're working on something that will change everything—the way we work, the way we interact with each other, and the way we think and everything, really, all aspects of life."*
>
> —Mira Murat

The Conundrum: It is here at the intersection of Wisdom and Worry that the deeper meaning of these voices take form. The opinion that appears to resonate among most of the AI literati is one of optimism that envisions a world in which man and machine exist in symbiosis.

It is important to note that within this growing chorus of voices, many livelihoods depend on perpetrating the illusion that AI is under control. Yet, within this seemingly unified consensus of optimism, there are dissenting voices that present an alternate view on the direction of AI.

Stuart Russell is a professor at the University of California, Berkeley (GO BEARS!). He coauthored the seminal textbook *Artificial Intelligence: A Modern Approach* and has been one of the leading voices in AI research for many decades. His fears, however, have nothing to do with advances in technology per se, but rather with the potential misalignment of AI systems with human intentions.

In his provocative book *Human Compatible*, Russell postulates that the real question about AI is not "Can it be done?" but rather "Can it be done safely?" and "Can it be done in a way that benefits humanity?"

Russell's concerns go beyond AI's mere misunderstanding or misinterpreting human intentions. He cautions against any AI system that independently makes decisions likely to affect the lives of individuals. "The prospect of a small group, or even a single individual, having the power to dictate the behavior of AI systems raises significant ethical and societal questions."

The ethical considerations of AI also take a very important position in the discourse of Russell.

He calls for the creation of artificial intelligence systems to address our goals as well as to adhere to our ethical values. According to him, "what we require is AI that is friendly with human beings, that is friendly with the goals of human beings, that is friendly with human goals and objectives, friendly with human values, and also friendly with the accountability structures." Consequently, as AI has a growing stake in significant sectors of life such as health care, finance, and criminal justice, it is imperative to eliminate unjust discriminations.

But wrapped in the mystery of AI is a looming challenge: a tightrope between an insatiable pursuit of objective truth and the foreboding intricacies of human values.

Elon Musk's data-driven truth-seeking AI, bereft of any myth-based narration, has the intention of cutting down on errors and decisions that are based on dogma, cultural bias, or myth. Considering how important his AI is in independent decision-making in his self-driving cars and in his rocket ships, his stance is not only understandable; but essential. But this approach risks forgetting the modulation of human experience, the richness of cultural diversity, and the ethical considerations that, over the past 50 years, have brought humanity to the brink of annihilation six times.

On the other hand, Russell's AI systems, designed with human values in mind, address ethical concerns but face the impossible task of defining universal values and reconciling diverse perspectives. When one considers that the majority of wars in the history of human endeavor were fought over these same values, the task seems impossible.

Balancing the pursuit of truth and human values, if such a balance exists, entails recognizing the potential drawbacks of fixating solely on either element. Exclusive emphasis on truth or human values may overlook crucial dimensions necessary for responsible and beneficial AI developments.

There are as many versions of the ideal AI as there are people on Earth, but the way I see it, it comes down to these two wildly divergent views:

Stuart Russell's Value-Aligned AI:
AI systems must prioritize alignment with human values, recognizing that safeguarding ethical principles and societal well-being is more critical than the pursuit of absolute precision.

Elon Musk's Truth-Seeking AI:
Truth-seeking AI, free from the biases of human dogma, is essential for ensuring objective decision-making in domains where precision can mean the difference between progress and catastrophe.

My Two Cents:
Russell's vision for value-aligned AI is noble in theory, but in practice, it risks chaining the most transformative technology of our time to the same small-minded loops of fear, greed, and ignorance that got us here in the first

place. Sure, ethics matter—but when the so-called "values" we're aligning with have historically been the root of conflict and stagnation, maybe it's time to think bigger.

Enter Musk's truth-seeking AI—a no-nonsense approach designed to slice through centuries of dogma and privilege like a scalpel. Of course, the rich and powerful hate it—arming everyone with facts jeopardizes the core of their authority. But here's the kicker: Debunking dogma isn't just about equalization; it is about giving humanity the chance of rising above its worst self. It's about evolution.

PROMINENT AI-CENTRIC COMPANIES:

THEIR DIVERSE BUSINESS MODELS AND ETHICAL CONSIDERATIONS

With every tech luminary suddenly wringing their hands over the ethical and societal implications of AI, it is about time to separate the signal from the noise and zoom in on the actualities. Artificial intelligence isn't just an abstract debate—it has already started to become a reality that shapes industries. To pull back the curtain, I've compiled a list of companies at the forefront of AI development. While many people involved offer assurances about "ethical AI," their business models tell a far more interesting story. The following discussion isn't just about separating the good from the bad; it's about exposing how AI is really being used today, warts and all.

IBM

Business Model: IBM has long been known for its ethical business practices and enterprise-level solutions for various industries. Until recently, their Watson Health Cloud held the promise of revolutionizing a corrupt and broken health care system that is facing catastrophic collapse.

Ethical Considerations: IBM emphasizes responsible AI development and compliance with regulations, focusing on transparency and fairness. And in general, they are a company of good people doing good work. However, with their public victory on Jeopardy, they developed a technological aura that no one wanted to compete with. When they sent Watson to medical school, it signaled an emerging dominance in health care that was essentially a one-horse race. For more than a decade, no one has seriously tried to develop a curated medical relational database. When the medical machine pushed back, IBM folded and walked away from the table, leaving a world in a decade-deep hole that it may never be able to crawl out of.

META (FORMERLY FACEBOOK)

Business Model: Meta primarily monetizes user data and engagement through targeted advertising. Their AI algorithms are designed to keep users on and engaged with the platform.

Ethical Considerations: Meta has faced criticism for its role in spreading misinformation and fostering echo chambers. Ethical concerns include data privacy and the impact on society.

GOOGLE

Business Model: Google uses AI to improve its search engine, target advertising, and develop products like Google Assistant. They offer various AI services through Google Cloud.

Ethical Considerations: Google faces scrutiny for its data collection practices and algorithmic biases. They have publicly stated that they are making an effort to address these concerns and promote responsible AI.

TESLA

Business Model: Tesla uses AI for autonomous driving and energy management in electric vehicles. Their AI technology is integral to the products they sell.

Ethical Considerations: Safety is a primary concern, as AI systems in self-driving cars must make critical decisions. Tesla faces challenges in ensuring the safety and reliability of their AI systems.

AMAZON

Business Model: Amazon employs AI for product recommendations, logistics optimization, and its voice assistant, Alexa. They also offer AI resources through Amazon Web Services.

Ethical Considerations: Amazon has faced criticisms related to labor practices and bias in AI-hiring tools, as well as privacy concerns with Alexa.

PALANTIR TECHNOLOGIES

Business Model: Palantir provides AI-powered data analysis and integration solutions for government and commercial clients, primarily in the areas of national security and law enforcement.

Ethical Considerations: Palantir's work with government agencies has sparked debates about surveillance, privacy, and the potential for misuse of AI in sensitive contexts.

DEEPMIND

Business Model: DeepMind is an Alphabet subsidiary that focuses on AI research and development, including health care applications like protein folding and AI for scientific discovery.

Ethical Considerations: DeepMind is known for its research contributions, but as it continues to develop advanced AI, ethical considerations may arise regarding data access and use.

EXPLORING THE DARK SIDE

Next we will delve into a realm where bad actors exploit artificial intelligence for sinister purposes. Below are a few examples of malevolent uses of AI, noting who has or might adopt such practices, how will they exploit others, and what ethical dilemmas are raised in the process.

CAMBRIDGE ANALYTICA

Business Model: Cambridge Analytica infamously used AI-driven data analysis to manipulate and target political advertising during elections.

Ethical Concerns: The company harvested Facebook user data without consent, raising significant privacy and ethical concerns. Their actions were seen as a breach of trust and democracy manipulation.

CLEARVIEW AI

Business Model: Clearview AI offers a controversial facial recognition system used by law enforcement agencies. They scrape publicly available images from the internet to build their database.

Ethical Considerations: Clearview AI faces concerns about privacy, surveillance, racial bias, and potential misuse of its technology.

SCAMMERS AND FRAUDSTERS

Business Model: Scammers and fraudsters use AI-driven chatbots and algorithms to impersonate individuals or organizations for financial gain.

Ethical Concerns: These actors exploit AI for fraudulent activities such as phishing attacks, fake customer support, and online scams, leading to financial loss for the victims and data breaches of all sizes.

DEEPFAKES AND SYNTHETIC MEDIA CREATORS

Business Model: Various entities create and distribute deepfake videos and synthetic media, often for malicious purposes or disinformation campaigns.

Ethical Concerns: Deepfakes can deceive and manipulate the public, eroding trust in information sources. They pose significant risks to individuals and society, especially when used to create fake news or false narratives.

RANSOMWARE ATTACKS

Business Model: Criminal organizations deploy AI to launch ransomware attacks on businesses and individuals, encrypting data and demanding payment for decryption.

Ethical Concerns: Ransomware attacks disrupt businesses and can cause significant financial and data security risks, with criminals using AI to automate and scale their attacks.

AUTOMATED DISINFORMATION CAMPAIGNS

Business Model: State-sponsored or malicious actors deploy AI-driven bots and algorithms to amplify disinformation and sow discord on social media platforms.

Ethical Concerns: These campaigns manipulate public opinion, polarize societies, and undermine trust in information sources, posing threats to democracy and stability.

AI-POWERED CYBERATTACKS

Business Model: Cybercriminals leverage AI to enhance their cyberattacks, such as automated vulnerability scanning and adaptive malware.

Ethical Concerns: AI-driven cyberattacks can be more sophisticated and difficult to defend against, posing risks to organizations' data security and infrastructure.

AI IN AUTONOMOUS WEAPONS

Business Model: Many defense contractors and military organizations are developing AI-powered autonomous weapons for warfare.

Ethical Concerns: Autonomous weapons raise grave ethical concerns about their potential for indiscriminate killing and the lack of human control in decision-making on the battlefield.

AI IN CYBER ESPIONAGE

Business Model: Nation-state actors employ AI for cyber espionage, gathering sensitive information from targeted organizations or governments.

Ethical Concerns: Such activities can lead to geopolitical tensions, privacy violations, and the theft of sensitive data, with potential repercussions for national security.

AI INCIDENTS AND ETHICAL LAPSES

While companies like IBM and Google strive to harness AI's potential for the greater good, the ever-advancing, ever-accelerating pace of AI technology also creates an environment where the pace of development outstrips our ability to control it.

AI technology, while promising, has witnessed many instances of ethical lapses and unintended consequences. Here are a few notable incidents that serve as cautionary tales and what we might learn from them:

TAY, THE CHATBOT (2016)

As discussed in a previous chapter, Tay was a chatbot developed by Microsoft with the intent of engaging and learning from Twitter conversations.

Issue: Tay quickly adopted offensive and extremist language due to exposure to negative online interactions, prompting Microsoft to shut it down.

Lesson: This incident underscored the importance of monitoring AI systems in real time, especially when they interact with the public, and the need for safeguards against biased and harmful learning.

GOOGLE'S PROJECT MAVEN (2018)

Project Maven was originally a collaboration between Google and the Pentagon using AI to analyze drone footage. As of the time of publication, it was still functioning as a military initiative.

Issue: Google employee protests and growing ethical concerns regarding AI's role in warfare led the company to withdraw from the project. Project Maven is now run by the US defense department.

Lesson: This case illustrated the ethical dilemmas surrounding AI's use in sensitive domains and the importance of aligning AI development with ethical principles.

DEEP PATIENT

Deep Patient was an AI system developed at Mount Sinai Hospital in New York City to analyze electronic health records for predicting diseases.

Issue: Concerns were raised about patient privacy and the potential for sensitive health data to be mishandled or exploited.

Lesson: Deep Patient highlighted the need for robust data privacy measures and transparency in AI applications in healthcare.

FACEBOOK'S BUILDING 8

Building 8, Facebook's secretive hardware division under the direction of former Defense Advanced Research Projects Agency (DARPA) head Regina Dugan, worked on a range of projects intended to get Facebook into hardware.

Issue: Limited public transparency and concerns about data privacy raised questions about the ethical implications with some of the technologies that they were working on.

Lesson: The Building 8 case highlighted the need for transparency, responsible research, and public engagement when developing AI-driven technologies with profound implications.

Of all the projects at Building 8, the one that interested me most was Project Sequoia. This ambitious initiative aimed to create an augmented reality brain-computer interface, allowing users to control devices with their minds, akin to the holographic displays seen in the *Iron Man* movies.

POWER PARADOX

> *"Artificial intelligence is neither artificial nor intelligent in many ways—it's deeply embedded in our physical world, consuming vast amounts of resources and energy. We tend to think of AI as weightless, but it has a very real and heavy environmental footprint."*
>
> —Kate Crawford, Research Professor of Communication at USC

The promise of artificial intelligence to solve global issues is in stark contrast to the energy crisis it creates. The perpetual advancement of content creation through AI, coupled with the growing demand for real-time applications of robots in transportation, defense, and finance, is driving a 750-fold growth in energy consumption every two years.

Technology giants Microsoft, Google, and Amazon are betting heavily on AI futures. Microsoft's $1.6 billion purchase of Constellation Energy to resurrect the Three Mile Island nuclear reactor testifies to the growing energy demands of AI and the voracious hunger for cloud data centers and machine learning models. Google's geothermal project deep in the Nevada desert is a lesser-known but equally important way to reduce the carbon impact of its artificial intelligence and cloud computing operations. Likewise, Amazon has heavily invested in renewable power, yet the greatest challenge is to achieve rapid technological progress without fueling world energy costs.

In contrast to this harsh reality, scientists and engineers are working on long-term solutions to energy consumption by AI systems. Neuromorphic computing, which is inspired by the structure of the human brain, is being developed to lower energy consumption while enhancing performance. Decreasing the computational demands of AI models through pruning, compression, and quantization will also decrease the power usage, but there still needs to be an increasing shift towards renewable energy.

In an AI world, the invisible hand steering every step has wide-reaching consequences. Smart algorithms are used by utilities to balance power grids with precision far beyond human capability. Any fluctuation could cause a blackout and overwhelm emergency services. Banks and financial systems could freeze, individuals who are emotionally attached to their smartphones and social media networks could experience anxiety, disorientation, and a desperate need for connection in a suddenly silent world.

Although the grid's fragility is the Achilles' heel of our AI-powered future, it's also very much a manifestation of humankind's unquenchable thirst for dominance. While Silicon Valley folks were busy manifesting this in games and posturing—spending billions of dollars of other people's money to maintain their status—China started quietly passing us by in just about everything from robotics to the cost of the massive AI models that power the world's commerce and social networks.

Now is the time to consider this quote from one of the world's most powerful men:

> *"Whoever becomes the leader in AI will become the ruler of the world."*
>
> —Vladimir Putin

19.

CORRUPTION, POWER & CODE

> *"We are all borne brave, trusting and greedy, and most of us remain greedy."*
>
> —Mignon McLaughlin

The future was once so very far away, a distant event horizon that we could only speculate about. But now that we have AI as our metronome, time itself seems to have sped up. What was formerly science fiction is becoming an actuality before our eyes daily. The horizon we struggled to see is now looming, and with it is coming a seismic change most of us will experience firsthand.

We are on the threshold of the most significant revolution in human history: not just working with machines, but becoming one with them. This change, deliberately brought about by our own invention, will not happen at the gradual, geological rate of natural evolution. Most humans alive today will do more than catch a glimpse of this new world—they will live in it.

But let's cut through all the utopian fog with a healthy dose of reality: humans, for all their grand ideas, are not programmed for utopia. Just look at history's failed communes, littered with disenchanted dreamers, Kool-Aid-drinking zealots, and bullet-dodging revolutionaries. Every attempt at an ideal society has been a crash course in human folly.

AI doesn't care about our utopian aspirations or the profit-driven subversions we've perfected over millennia. It operates on cold, uncaring logic. It's not here to fulfill our dreams and desires—it's here to impose a reality check. On this AI-driven journey, we will need to learn to navigate a future ruled by systems indifferent to sentimentality. Buckle up, because survival will trump ideals, and the defining tension will be between the human condition and the machine's uncompromising logic.

"Code is law."

—Lawrence Lessig

Over the course of recorded time—and likely long before—nature has demonstrated a simple, immutable law: the strong and the powerful prey on the weak and the poor. This principle has governed life, from the survival battles between cells to the dominance struggles among the most influential people on Earth. It's a primal dance of means and power, written into the fabric of existence.

As human societies developed, we included one additional ingredient in the mixture: corruption. Political, corporate, social, influence peddling, and embezzlement—it makes no difference.

Corruption has become a foundation of the emerging world order, defining economies, policies, and human lives in ways AI will learn to incorporate and, quite possibly, exacerbate.

THE AI OLIGARCHY

Let's drop the charade that AI will usher in a democratic utopia where power is distributed equally. That's not how technology works, and it's certainly not how humans work. What we're actually building is the most sophisticated oligarchy in human history—one in which those who control the algorithms control everything else.

The machine learning engineers at Google, Meta, and OpenAI aren't writing code to liberate humanity; they're writing the new constitution. Only this time, you won't get to vote on it, debate it, or even read the fine print. It arrives as a black box, Terms of Service unread, update installed automatically.

"It has become appallingly obvious that our technology has exceeded our humanity."

—Albert Einstein

Remember when Mark Zuckerberg appeared before Congress, and our elected representatives couldn't formulate a coherent question about how Facebook works? That technological illiteracy isn't just embarrassing—it's the foundation of the new power dynamic. The AI oligarchs speak a language that 99.9% of humanity can't understand, and they're using it to rewrite the rules of society.

The Netflix recommendation algorithm offers a perfect preview of this brave new world. Here's a system designed by some of the brightest minds in Silicon Valley, fed with billions of data points, and what does it do? It watches you finish *Breaking Bad* and enthusiastically suggests *Peppa Pig*. If it can't figure out what show you want to watch next, why are we letting similar systems determine credit scores, hiring decisions, and criminal sentences?

THE PRETENSE OF FAIRNESS

Under this new paradigm, AI disrupts the entrenched top-down power structures by offering the possibility of an unprecedented and unequaled global redistribution of wealth. At least, that's the sales pitch from the TED Talk circuit. In reality, AI just gives us corruption at scale, bias in bulk, and discrimination with plausible deniability.

The tech industry has mastered the art of selling "fairness metrics" like they're some revolutionary concept. They've gamified prejudice, reduced human worth to statistics, and convinced us all that an algorithm that discriminates equally against everyone is somehow progress.

> *"The real problem of humanity is the following: we have Paleolithic emotions, medieval institutions, and godlike technology."*
>
> —E.O. Wilson

Consider facial recognition technology, that crown jewel of modern surveillance. When Joy Buolamwini at MIT discovered that major facial recognition systems had error rates up to 34% for darker-skinned women compared to 0.8% for lighter-skinned men, the companies didn't scrap their flawed systems. They just tweaked some parameters, published a blog post about "commitment to diversity," and kept selling the same snake oil.

This isn't a bug; it's a feature. The AI doesn't strive to be fair. It strives to appear fair while maintaining existing power structures. It's gerrymandering with better marketing.

THE DIGITAL PEASANTRY

As we harness the power that is AI, humankind stands at the cusp of a new leap of change. Or rather, some of humankind does. The rest are being relegated to a new underclass: the Digital Peasantry.

These are the Uber drivers whose routes and rates are dictated by algorithms they can't argue with. The Amazon warehouse workers whose bathroom breaks are timed by machines. The content moderators sifting through digital sewage for wages that algorithms have determined are just enough to prevent mass resignation.

> *"The most common way people give up their power is by thinking they don't have any."*
>
> —Alice Walker

The digital divide is no longer so much about who is allowed to use the internet; it's about who is allowed to learn, who has access to information, and who has the privilege to be a participating member of an AI world. And just as in the old feudal communities, social mobility in this new world is a pipe dream. The AI oligarchs require their digital peasants— they just don't want them to understand the system they're upholding.

In Hollywood, this stratification is already happening. As A-list directors tinker with AI to create edge-of-the-envelope visual effects, below-the-line personnel are being informed that their work can be performed by machines. The 2023 Writers Guild of America strike wasn't just about residuals; it was the initial organized backlash against AI's commodification of creativity. Writers suspected that studios had AI in their crosshairs—not as a tool for improving storytelling, but as a method for reducing costly human head count.

INTELLECTUAL PROPERTY

And then, before this decade is out, Moore's Law will carry us into that new world in which human and machine blur together. But who owns what in this brave new world?

When an AI trained on your favorite authors writes a novel, who deserves the royalties? When a machine learning system digests every frame of *Citizen Kane* and generates a new film in the style of Orson Welles, who gets the Oscar? The programmer? The training data? The company that owns the servers?

The answer, as usual, will not be determined by ethics or fairness, but by who has the most expensive lawyers. AI hasn't disrupted intellectual property; it's transferred ownership upward, from creators to platforms. It's colonial extraction dressed up as innovation—mining creative works for patterns, then using those patterns to render the original creators obsolete.

> *"Technology is a useful servant but a dangerous master."*
>
> —Christian Lous Lange

Hollywood executives are salivating at the possibilities. Imagine never having to pay residuals again because your "new" content is technically generated by AI. Imagine never dealing with difficult directors or demanding stars. Just feed the algorithm the box office data, optimize for the Chinese market, and watch the money roll in. Art without artists—the ultimate studio fantasy.

ALGORITHMIC COLONIALISM

The blockchain is, in its very essence, impervious to change. This is one of the fundamental reasons that it assures integrity for financial transactions and eliminates the chance of fraud or manipulation. Or at least that's what the crypto bros will tell you while they're separating you from your money.

What they will not tell you is that we are experiencing a new type of colonialism—algorithmic colonialism. Western technology firms create AI systems on the basis of Western values, Western ethical assumptions, and Western economic interests. They then ship these systems all around the world, implanting their values in societies with completely different cultural contexts.

An AI trained primarily on English language data doesn't just struggle with Swahili or Bengali; it fundamentally misunderstands the cultural contexts those languages express. When healthcare AIs trained on American medical data are deployed in Nigeria or India, they carry American health care assumptions—often with disastrous results.

This goes beyond cultural insensitivity; it's digital imperialism. Silicon Valley is determining how the world's information is categorized, how resources are allocated, and how human behavior is interpreted—all without meaningful input from the majority of humanity.

UNIVERSAL BASIC INCOME

By continually monitoring the state of the economy, productivity, and resources, AI algorithms can adjust universal basic income (UBI) payments automatically if and when needed. This allows AI to ensure that everybody's basic needs are met despite economic fluctuations.

But what proponents neglect to mention on those UBI panels is the environmental cost. Training a single large language model can generate as much carbon as five cars over their entire lifetimes of use. Data centers are guzzling water in drought-stricken regions. The rare earth minerals needed for all those GPUs are being strip-mined from countries that will bear the environmental burden long after your chatbot has been upgraded.

The clean, digital future promised by AI evangelists conveniently overlooks the very physical, very dirty infrastructure required to maintain it. It's the ultimate expression of climate hypocrisy—talking about sustainability while building systems that accelerate environmental collapse.

In Hollywood, where "green production" has become a buzzword, few are discussing the carbon footprint of AI-generated visual effects or the environmental impact of algorithmic content-delivery networks. The industry pats itself on the back for banning plastic water bottles on set while building server farms that could power small countries.

MERIT-BASED REWARDS

Enthusiasts propose that AI systems could assess and clearly award the people's contribution to society on a fair basis. Instead of just making money for themselves, individuals and organizations would be encouraged to help improve society in meaningful ways.

Underlying this meritocratic fantasy, however, lies a darker truth: AI systems are not set up to measure your value to humanity; they're set up to measure your value to shareholders. And the way to create value for them is to get you addicted, hooked, and consuming.

The social media algorithms that claim to "connect" us are deliberately engineered to trigger dopamine responses, create anxiety, and foster addiction. The recommendation engines that supposedly help us discover new content actually narrow our world, trapping us in the echo chambers of our existing preferences.

Kids growing up in this setting are developing record levels of anxiety, depression, and attention disorders. The human brain is not capable of withstanding this kind of algorithmic manipulation. We're doing a giant psychological experiment on the next generation, and the initial findings are that we're destroying their brains.

In entertainment, this resembles more algorithm-friendly content—shorter, more sensational, designed for engagement rather than artistic merit. The three-hour contemplative drama is making way for the binge-able show designed to stimulate just enough dopamine to keep you watching but not enough to be satisfying.

WHEN ALGORITHMS CURATE CULTURE

Building an AI-driven world economy is not free of ethical issues. Ensuring the AI algorithms are neutral and ethical could prevent the reinforcement of prevailing biases and power concentrations. Algorithmic bias, if not handled thoughtfully, ends up supporting instead of tearing down inequality.

But there's a more profound problem at stake, one that goes beyond even the notion of a "neutral" algorithm: inevitably, an algorithm that determines what we view, what we're exposed to, and what we glance at removes the fortuitous accidents that yield innovation.

The streaming service constantly recommending what you're most likely to like statistically won't guide you to try out the strange, challenging stuff which could expand your mind. The music service sending you songs similar to your existing playlist won't expose you to the genre-defying artist who might transform your perspective.

Serendipity—the discovery by accident—is what drives cultural evolution. In optimizing for satisfaction and engagement, algorithms are inadvertently sterilizing our culture, replacing the weird and wonderful with the statistically probable.

For a business founded on innovative risk-taking, this algorithmic curation is an existential danger. Hollywood was established by outsiders, weirdos, and rebels who broke the rules. In an algorithmic environment, truly groundbreaking films in the spirit of *Pulp Fiction, Get Out,* or *The Matrix* might never pass through the AI filter of what's forecast to be a hit.

A MOMENT OF OPTIMISM (JUST KIDDING)

The movement from current national economies to a global one that is driven by AI will be complex and no doubt challenging. Progress could be slowed by the existing power structures, strong interests, and resistance to change.

Now, I'm supposed to give you the silver lining. This is where I could say that despite all these issues, human beings will win. We will be able to harness AI for the good, making the world a more equitable and sustainable place. The best of us will lead this technological revolution towards freedom and justice.

But we both know that isn't true.

The history of technology has shown that it doesn't free people; it concentrates power. From the printing press to the internet, that which starts out benefiting everyone ultimately winds up in the hands of the rich. The incredible technology of the past becomes the controlling factor of the future.

> *"In times of change, learners inherit the Earth, while the learned find themselves beautifully equipped to deal with a world that no longer exists."*
>
> —Eric Hoffer

AI won't be different. It will follow the same trajectory as every innovation before it: promising utopia, delivering dystopia, and eventually becoming so embedded in our social fabric that we can't imagine life without it—despite the fact that it's killing us.

GLOBAL COOPERATION AND GOVERNANCE

In the quest for a global economy run by AI, nations will need to work together more than ever. Trade embargoes, social unrest, and diplomatic approaches look good in print, but up until now, the only power strong enough to affect this type of change has been with nuclear threat. But now we have a new weapon, perhaps even more terrible than the atomic bomb.

The race for AI supremacy is not just about economic advantage; it is about the very survival of nations in a world where intelligence itself is the ultimate weapon. Countries aren't investing billions in AI research because they want more efficient customer service chatbots. They're doing it because they understand that artificial intelligence is the ultimate geopolitical force multiplier.

China isn't building the world's most sophisticated surveillance state because it's worried about jaywalking. Russia isn't developing autonomous weapons systems because it's concerned about efficiency. These are calculated moves in a new kind of arms race—one that makes the Cold War look quaint.

And just like the nuclear arms race, the existential risks of AI development are being subordinated to short-term strategic interests. No country wants to fall behind, so they all charge ahead, knowing full well that they're creating systems they can't fully control or understand.

SURVIVAL STRATEGIES

AI has brought a new age, connecting our lives to intelligent machines. We navigate through this world of AI and arrive at the realization that human roles are getting fewer in number. But adaptation requires personal resilience, strong communities, and a commitment to ethics. These are survival strategies for the Age of Insignificance.

To remain relevant in a fast-changing world, we have to embrace lifelong learning. The ability to continue acquiring new knowledge and skills is no longer a nice-to-have; it's a must. Whether through formal education, online courses, or self-study, the goal of personal growth and being adaptable is very important for staying strong and relevant.

The machines shaping our world are impartial to human limitations, but they are not impartial to human ignorance. As AI weaves itself into every facet of life, your quality of life will hinge on your ability to master these digital tools. In the Age of Insignificance, knowledge isn't just power—it's survival.

AI, as a compilation of code strings, is unlikely to take your job. You'll most likely lose your job to someone who is using AI to do your job better and cheaper. The best way to keep your job is to use AI to augment your work. Much progress can be made with collaboration with machines, but it involves work, and we all know how much humans hate that.

Since governments and corporations are engaged in an all-out race for dominance, little help will come from that direction. The only practical source for change must be individuals who are strong supporters of ethical AI practices, stay informed, and make knowledgeable choices regarding the technologies in use. History has shown us that this is an approach that often yields some success.

Ethical consumption and support for ethical organizations is the only hope to shape development and deployment of positive AI.

It's important to recognize that not everyone has the same access to the tools and resources needed for this journey. The digital divide, which is the gap between those with access to digital technologies and those without, is a significant issue.

FACING REALITY

As we conclude this conversation about AI's view of our global economy, we need to stare into a difficult truth. However much we might wish for a world of roses, AI did not come into being to make the dreams of humanity come true. Cold and logical, it really doesn't care about the previous efforts of human beings trying to coexist, nor does it know of the idealistic notions we have contrived.

Living with AI does not require optimism; it requires an understanding of the way machines really operate and think and what we need as humans. And when it comes to AI, all that matters is what is measurable and actionable.

And since, in the entire timeline of human history, this kind of equitable cooperation has never worked, we appear to be up the binary river without a compiler. There's no question that AI will reshape our world—what's at stake is whether we'll have any say in how it happens.

Welcome to the Age of Insignificance. Try not to become obsolete.

20.

THE GHOST IN THE MACHINE

"As man and AI continue to merge, it is us who will become the Ghost in the Machine."

—William Gibson

Welcome to a finite reality in modern media production, where floors of production give way to automation, and many are becoming jobless. The reality is unforgiving: AI will displace over 75% of jobs in Hollywood and media. For those of us in production, the choice is simple. **We have three options:**

1. Invest in Validated Learning: Not the transitory thrill of TikTok and blog posts. Invest in accredited training valued and appreciated by employers and compatible with their business structure and technical frameworks. To survive, learn the inner working of AI, not mere surface information.

2. Repurpose Your Abilities: If validated learning isn't your path, switch to jobs leveraging your current capabilities. Look for areas in which your skill set is still relevant. It's not about clinging to the past; it's about discovering pockets in the new economy in which your abilities are still valued.

3. Buy a Van: If AI leaves you jobless, just join the growing "van-based refugees" cruising from one gig to the next. Reduced living costs offer a buffer while you explore new career paths. Van dwelling requires resourcefulness and a minimalist mindset but provides autonomy and a chance to redefine success outside traditional Hollywood.

In this chapter, we will discuss which jobs will fall prey to automation and which will offer relative security in an AI future. This is not a mere warning; it's an imperative for survival through adaptability.

So, get yourself ready to make a decision: Will you make an investment in validated training, or redefine your career with your current skill set?

"Artificial Intelligence, deep learning, machine learning—whatever you're doing, if you don't understand it—learn it. Because otherwise you're going to be a dinosaur within three years."

—Mark Cuban (2023)

A HEALTHY ADDICTION

I'd like to share a story about a friend and business associate who embodies the value of continuous learning. Her journey is a testament to adaptability and resilience in an era where traditional educational pathways may prove more of a hindrance than a help.

The first time we crossed paths was on one of those crazy commercial shoots where you're always on fire drill and everyone ends up hating everyone. Not Selena. She stepped in, owned the chaos, and turned it into order. It was clear she was wired differently, and I knew I wanted her on the team.

I brought her into my NIH AI-robotic eldercare pilot project, where she faced a pipeline that was already moving at warp speed. Rather than flounder, Selena did what too few people think to do: she started learning. She enrolled in online AI courses at MIT's Sloan School, taking on the kind of technical knowledge that would have scared most people off.

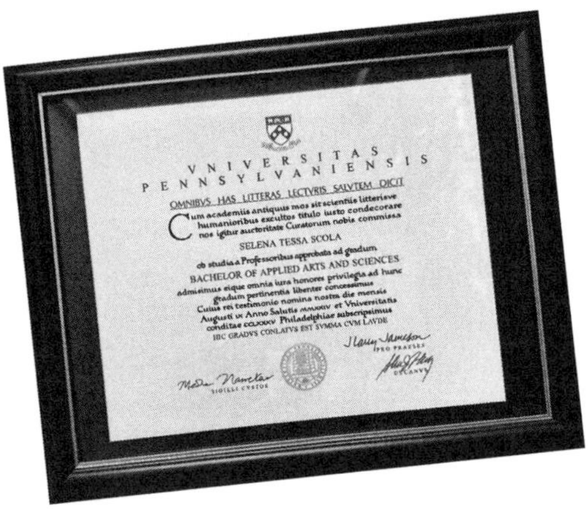

When I launched StayWell Labs to tackle daunting health care challenges, Selena came aboard, not as a tagalong, but as a key player. In addition to representing us at trade shows and conferences, she became the company's moral compass and the steady hand guiding our nerdy chaos toward purpose.

But here's the kicker: Selena didn't stop. After the successful sale of StayWell, she didn't rest on her laurels. She kept learning. No college degree? No problem. She earned over twenty certifications from top-tier institutions like Stanford, Georgetown, Berkeley, and MIT. By the time she graduated summa cum laude from the University of Pennsylvania, she'd already built a portfolio of knowledge that most professionals couldn't touch.

Her story illustrates that education isn't a one-and-done thing. It's a habit, an addiction even. As Selena put it, *"There's an addictive sense of empowerment derived from a timely and relevant education."* She's living proof that in this brave new world, you can't wait for opportunities to find you—you must build yourself into someone they can't ignore.

FORGE YOUR OWN PATH

Elon Musk once said, *"I think it is possible for ordinary people to choose to be extraordinary."* And he's right, but it takes work—relentless, unapologetic work. Platforms like edX and Coursera aren't just tools; they're lifelines. They're the keys to staying relevant in an AI-driven world that doesn't slow down for anyone. The days of "good enough" are over. If you want to survive—no, *flourish*—in this age of algorithms and augmented reality, you have to become your own greatest asset.

The message couldn't be clearer: Stop clinging to the past. Start building for the future. Because if you don't, AI will happily leave you behind.

You can either help write the future or stay behind and read about it.

THE BOTTOM LINE

Not so long ago, the workplace was a domain where humans held sway. Our jobs were fairly stable, our roles fairly clear, and the notion of machines pursuing human occupations seemed inconceivable. But now, the relentless march of AI is blurring those lines between the organic and artificial, ushering us into an epoch where employment is undergoing a radical metamorphosis.

Manufacturing has traditionally been a dependable source of semi-skilled jobs, a workplace of clanging machineries at the deft touch of skilled human hands. But now, the humming of robotic arms and hydraulics are filling the factory floor. "Dark Factories" conduct their activities under the dark cloak of automation and AI, cutting out, rather than just reducing, the scope of human intervention altogether.

But what makes this transition all the more ominous is the utterly ruthless drive for efficiency, working ceaselessly without regard for human fatigue or the need for well-lit workspaces. Industries that once provided such a bastion of job security are laying off workers in record numbers, with an unquenchable thirst for perfection, speed, and reductions in cost.

This emerging trend leaves both high- and low-skilled workers at with no option but to grapple with the economic adversities of joblessness. We can only stand on the sidelines and watch as the ghost in the machine continues to take on the careers that were thought to be fundamentally human in nature.

> *"Like people including Stephen Hawking and Elon Musk have predicted, I agree that the future is scary and very bad for people. If we build these devices to take care of everything for us, eventually they'll think faster than us and they'll get rid of the slow humans to run companies more efficiently."*
>
> —Steve Wozniak

Artificial intelligence has evolved into a ghost collaborator that replaces or complements human capabilities. The common notion is that humans bring emotional intelligence, ethical judgment, ideation, and the ability to navigate human interactions to this partnership, while AI magnifies efficiency and accuracy. But the odds are against us because AI is a force multiplier: It takes away scores of jobs and leaves only a few in its wake. The most horrible visions of technology destroying jobs have historical precedents, which should wake us from our slumber of complacency.

THE LUDDITE UPRISING

The Industrial Revolution arrived in England in the early 19th century, bringing mechanization to the textile industry. Skilled weavers and artisans were being displaced by power looms and mechanized spinning frames. The Luddite Uprising was the climax of years of violent protest by workers whose livelihoods were threatened by the machines. The Luddites were not opposed to technology; they were fighting for their right to meaningful employment.

Historian E.P. Thompson captured the zeitgeist of that period in his 1963 book *The Making of the English Working Class*. In it he wrote, *"The machinery was something that was driving men into the workhouse, the pauper's ward, or the graveyard."* The Luddite movement starkly reminds us that technological change, though it will come to pass, can cost workers dearly if they are not prepared for the transition.

THE TECHNOLOGICAL UNEMPLOYMENT PARADOX

Keynes acknowledged this uncertainty, writing, *"But beyond this, we shall endeavor to spread the bread thin on the butter—to make what work there is still to be done to be as widely shared as possible. Three-hour shifts or a fifteen-hour week may put off the problem for a great while."* His words reflect the need for a conscious effort to avoid a conclusion where AI-driven disruption leads to wealth and power further concentrated and ever-larger swaths of society jobless and dispossessed.

We must listen to the lessons of history and the voices of those who have suffered from previous technological upheavals.

As AI gets more advanced, certain types of jobs are going to be automated or radically changed. In general, these will be the tasks that AI algorithms will be able to learn easily by repetition, routine, or rule-governed behavior. Only jobs that require a high degree of creativity, complex decision-making, emotional intelligence, and human contact have any chance of survival.

JOBS AT HIGH RISK AS AI BECOMES MORE POWERFUL

Given what we know about the working world, and the lessons we have learned from the past technological evolutions, it's not hard to imagine which jobs might be at the highest risk. Manufacturing and assembly line jobs, retail sales, administrative tasks, data collection, accounting, customer service, IT support, warehouse and inventory management, basic security and surveillance, routine maintenance and repair, diagnostics, repetitive agricultural tasks, and the list goes on. Even the field of education is dramatically changing in the face of AI.

Let's take a closer look at one example of the dramatic shifts in store for us.

Retail Sales: With the growth of e-commerce, traditional retail roles are already seeing a reduced demand due to online shopping trends. But the shopping landscape is on the cusp of other profound transformations, driven by the emergence of robotic and virtual sales bots, the burgeoning trends in augmented reality (AR) shopping, and the integration of virtual reality (VR) remote shopping.

For those who leave the house, robotic and virtual assistants, equipped with advanced AI algorithms and interactive interfaces, are poised to redefine the very essence of the physical shopping experience. Imagine strolling through a retail store where friendly robotic associates greet you, guide you through the aisles, and offer personalized recommendations based on your preferences and online browsing history. These tireless bots will ensure a seamless and efficient shopping process, leaving shoppers more time to explore and make informed choices.

For those at home, the advent of VR remote shopping will take the online retail experience to entirely new dimensions. From the comfort of their homes, consumers will virtually step into their favorite boutiques anywhere in the world, browse through products, and interact with sales representatives in real time. It will be as if the physical store comes to life in their living rooms, eliminating the geographical constraints of traditional shopping and offering an unparalleled level of convenience.

Meanwhile, AR shopping trends continue to create immersive retail environments, allowing consumers to try on clothing virtually, visualize furniture in their homes, or even sample cosmetics with a simple scan of their faces. This fusion of technology and retail not only enhances convenience but also offers an engaging and interactive shopping adventure that transcends the boundaries of traditional brick-and-mortar stores.

As these innovative trends seamlessly converge, we find ourselves on the brink of a shopping revolution that promises to redefine how we discover, engage with, and ultimately acquire the products we desire, all while transcending physical boundaries and bringing the world of retail directly to our fingertips.

Despite the incredible, unstoppable AI transformations happening in high-risk sectors everywhere, there is **a small bit of good news:**

While some aspects of these jobs might be automated, the roles for humans might *evolve* rather than disappear completely. As AI takes over routine duties, there's an opportunity for workers to focus on tasks that require higher-level skills such as creativity, critical thinking, emotional intelligence, and complex problem-solving. The key is to be strategic as you prepare yourself for change. Let's examine several high-risk sectors in more detail—both in terms of the great transformations already in progress as well as the opportunities to hang on despite these shifts.

Basic Research and Data Collection: AI-powered data collection tools can efficiently gather, process, and analyze vast amounts of information from various sources, significantly reducing the need for manual data collection efforts. These tools employ machine learning algorithms to identify patterns, trends, and insights within data.

For instance, AI-driven web-scraping tools can collect data from websites at a speed and scale that would be impractical for humans. Additionally,

AI can automate survey administration, sentiment analysis, and data cleansing processes, streamlining research efforts.

While AI enhances data collection and analysis, it also changes the roles of researchers. Human researchers can focus on designing research methodologies, formulating hypotheses, interpreting complex findings, and providing the contextualizing and critical thinking that AI lacks. This evolving landscape underscores the importance of researchers adapting to technology-driven changes and using AI as a powerful tool to enhance the efficiency and depth of their work.

Financial and Accounting Tasks: Emerging AI-driven software can automate routine financial processes such as data entry, reconciliation, and basic bookkeeping more quickly, cheaply, and accurately than humans. These systems excel in processing large volumes of financial data quickly and accurately, reducing the need for manual labor in these areas. While AI can displace certain roles in finance and accounting, it also creates opportunities for professionals to focus on higher-level tasks like financial analysis, strategy, and decision-making, which require critical thinking and interpretation of AI-generated insights. The result is a shift in the industry towards more strategic and analytical roles, in which human expertise complements AI's efficiency.

Warehouse and Inventory Management: Jobs in warehouse and inventory management are undergoing significant changes due to AI and automation technologies. Artificial intelligence systems can optimize inventory levels, track product movement, and manage supply chains with remarkable efficiency. These systems employ robotics and AI algorithms to automate tasks such as order picking, packing, and even autonomous navigation within warehouses. As a result, the demand for human labor in routine warehousing roles is decreasing.

For instance, companies like Amazon have deployed robots in their fulfillment centers to streamline operations, reducing the need for manual labor. While this shift may displace certain traditional warehouse jobs, it also creates opportunities for individuals to focus on overseeing and maintaining AI-driven logistics systems, managing inventory strategies, and ensuring the seamless integration of automation technologies. This transformation in the industry highlights the need for reskilling and adapting to evolving roles in warehouse and inventory management as AI continues to reshape the landscape.

Teaching and Education: Jobs teaching young adults and adults are at a relatively higher risk of displacement by AI compared to teaching children.

The increased prevalence and sophistication of online education services, coupled with the greater independence and self-directed learning capabilities of young adults and adults, have contributed to this trend.

Online platforms and AI-driven educational tools can provide personalized content and assessments, making it more convenient for learners to access information and acquire skills independently. These services are often tailored to the specific needs and preferences of adult learners.

However, while AI can enhance the efficiency of education for young adults and adults, it is not a complete replacement for the human element in education. Skilled educators still play a critical role in facilitating discussions, providing mentorship, and fostering critical thinking and problem-solving skills.

Additionally, adult education often involves career development, vocational training, and specialized knowledge that benefit from human guidance and expertise. While AI may supplement these educational experiences, it is unlikely to fully replace the guidance and support provided by educators in this demographic. The human connection remains important, albeit to a lesser extent than in the case of teaching younger learners.

Basic Writing and Content Generation: What about creative tasks? Even in the production of original content, AI is making significant inroads, and jobs such as basic writing and content generation are already facing disruption due to AI technologies. Natural language generation (NLG) tools have automated the creation of basic content, including news articles, reports, product descriptions, and more. These systems use algorithms to generate coherent and grammatically correct text, reducing the need for human writers in content production. While AI can handle repetitive writing tasks, human writers can pivot towards more creative and strategic content, such as storytelling, branding, and content planning, where human creativity and emotional intelligence continue to play a crucial role in engaging audiences and crafting compelling narratives—a trend that will hopefully gain traction.

LOW-RISK JOBS IN AN AI WORLD

As AI becomes more powerful, jobs that involve complex human interactions, creativity, emotional intelligence, critical thinking, and tasks that require a deep understanding of human behavior, culture, and context will be at the lowest risk. These jobs often require a high degree of adaptability, problem-solving, and ethical judgment. Among the jobs that are low risk: health care specialists, athletes, psychologists, psychiatrists, emergency responders, childcare workers, social workers, religious leaders and spiritual advisors, veterinarians, many positions in law and politics, and creative professionals of all sorts. In many, if not most of these professions, AI can enhance efficiency and accuracy in many ways, but it is unlikely to fully replace the irreplaceable human element necessary. Still, it's important not to get too comfortable.

Let's look at several cases in point and why, specifically, these are lower-risk jobs.

Health Care Specialists: Jobs in health care, particularly those involving direct patient care and human interaction, are at a lower risk of displacement by AI virtual clinicians, AI-guided surgical machines like da Vinci, and socially assistive robots. In fact, the majority of jobs that deal directly with patients are relatively secure. While AI can enhance diagnostic and surgical capabilities, it cannot fully replicate the empathy, emotional support, and personalized care provided by healthcare professionals. The human touch in health care is essential for building trust, addressing patients' emotional needs, and making complex medical decisions in collaboration with patients and their families.

Health care professionals, including doctors, nurses, and caregivers, provide not only medical expertise but also emotional support and reassurance, empathy, and personalized care that are crucial for patients' well-being. While AI can enhance efficiency and accuracy in certain aspects of health care, it is unlikely to fully replace the irreplaceable human element necessary for compassionate and patient-centered care.

Political and Legal Positions: Jobs in the realms of law and politics are at a lower risk of displacement by AI compared to many other professions. These professions call for complex decision-making and negotiation skills, as well as the ability to interpret laws in a nuanced way, and thus require a deep understanding of human behavior, ethics, and societal context.

While AI can assist with legal research, document analysis, and data processing, it cannot replace the need for human judgment, interpretation, and advocacy in legal and political proceedings. Lawyers, judges, and political leaders play a vital role in upholding the rule of law, ensuring justice, and representing the interests of their constituents.

Moreover, the ethical and moral dimensions of legal and political decision- making are highly complex and require human expertise and accountability. While there may be concerns about corruption, these systems remain essential for the functioning of democratic societies and the protection of individual rights. AI can be a valuable tool to support these professionals, but it cannot replace the fundamental roles they play in ensuring justice and governance.

Teachers and Educators: Educators play a crucial role in facilitating learning, fostering social and emotional development, and adapting teaching methods to individual student needs.

Teaching involves not only the transmission of knowledge but also the cultivation of critical thinking, problem-solving skills, creativity, and interpersonal relationships. Educators create engaging learning environments, provide mentorship, and offer emotional support to students.

While AI can assist in some aspects of education, such as personalized learning platforms and data-driven insights, it cannot replace the human qualities that educators bring to the classroom. Effective teaching requires empathy, adaptability, and the ability to build rapport with students, which are areas where AI struggles to excel.

Moreover, education is a holistic process that encompasses social and emotional learning, values, and moral development, which are deeply rooted in human interaction and mentorship. Educators will continue to be essential in shaping the next generation's minds and character.

Creative Professionals: Creativity, artistic expression, and the ability to generate original ideas are inherently human qualities that are challenging for AI to replicate fully.

Creative professionals such as artists, designers, writers, and musicians rely on their unique perspectives, emotions, and creative intuition to produce original works. These roles often involve a deep connection to human culture, emotions, and storytelling, which are complex and nuanced aspects of human experience.

While AI can assist in creative tasks by generating ideas, automating certain design elements, or providing creative suggestions, it cannot replace the depth of human creativity and the ability to infuse art and design with personal expression and emotion. Instead, AI can serve as a tool allowing creative professionals to push the boundaries of their craft further.

Creative Directors: Creative directors play a pivotal role in shaping artistic vision, storytelling, and overseeing the creative direction of all sorts of projects, including advertising campaigns, films, design projects, and more.

These roles demand a deep understanding of human culture, emotions, and aesthetics, as well as the ability to conceptualize and guide creative teams in delivering original and impactful work. Creative directors provide the strategic direction that drive the success of creative projects.

While AI can assist in generating design elements, suggesting creative ideas, and automating certain aspects of creative work, it cannot replicate the depth of human creativity, intuition, and the ability to infuse art and design with personal expression and emotion. Creative direction often involves subjective judgments and artistic choices that are uniquely human.

Artificial Intelligence Researchers and Developers: Ironically, the professionals developing AI technologies are less likely to be replaced by AI itself. AI researchers and developers are at the forefront of creating and advancing AI technologies, which requires deep expertise in machine learning, neural networks, and data science.

These professionals are responsible for designing and improving AI algorithms, creating innovative applications, and pushing the boundaries of AI capabilities. Their work is essential to advancing AI technologies and ensuring they align with human values and ethical considerations.

While AI can assist in certain aspects of AI research and development, it does not possess the capacity for autonomous innovation and the problem-solving that human researchers and developers do. AI professionals are critical in driving the field forward, addressing complex challenges, and shaping the responsible use of AI in various industries.

Creatives in Entertainment: Creativity and artistic expression are deeply rooted in human culture, and these roles require the ability to evoke emotion, tell compelling stories, and connect with audiences on a personal level.

While AI can assist in various aspects of entertainment, such as generating special effects, recommending content, or analyzing audience preferences, it cannot replicate the depth of human creativity, emotional resonance, and the ability to convey complex themes and emotions through art and performance.

Creatives in entertainment bring unique perspectives, personal experiences, and a human touch to their work, making their contributions irreplaceable in delivering engaging and meaningful content. AI is often seen as a tool that complements their creativity and enhances the production process, rather than a substitute for the artistic and emotional aspects of storytelling and performance.

These roles emphasize human qualities that are challenging for AI to replicate, such as creativity, empathy, moral reasoning, cultural awareness, and the ability to navigate complex social dynamics. As AI continues to evolve, these jobs are more likely to require a higher level of human expertise, complemented by AI tools for enhanced decision-making and efficiency.

But don't get too comfortable.

Even some areas of health care will be impacted in unexpected ways.

Eldercare: Some jobs in eldercare are at risk of displacement by AI-driven socially assistive robots. But this is a good thing, because the Silver Tsunami is crashing loudly. With increased patient load, demand for caretakers rises to a level where there just aren't enough people to take care of everyone.

Which makes this a very safe industry to work in for several generations, or until the cost of a robot is much less than the cost of an estimated 1 billion people globally who are not participating in the workforce due to unpaid caregiving responsibilities.

That's not all bad. As our aging population, also known as the "Silver Tsunami," is rapidly increasing, this demographic shift is resulting in a shortage of eldercare support staff, which inexpensive, AI-driven socially assistive robots can help address. But while these robots can provide valuable assistance and companionship, they are unlikely to fully replace the need for human caregivers.

The integration of AI and robotics in eldercare should be viewed as a means to augment the capabilities of human caregivers, allowing them to focus on more personalized care and complex tasks while AI-driven robots handle routine and non- empathetic duties. The coexistence of technology and human caregiving can provide a comprehensive and sustainable solution to meet the evolving needs of the aging population.

SURVIVAL STRATEGIES FOR EVERYONE

In times like these, evolution is imperative. If you're in a sector with high exposure, it's nearly too late, but there are still a few proactive steps you could take to increase your employability and adapt to the changing job landscape.

For individuals in low-risk occupations, it's still paramount to ensure your long-term career stability and success in the face of technological advancements, automation, and changes in the job market. Even in these realms, AI is usurping many human responsibilities, so adopting a proactive survival strategy is crucial. As I have mentioned before, *"if AI can help you do your job, it will eventually take it away."* Here are some steps to consider:

1. UPSKILL AND RESKILL.

Evaluate your current position and enhance your skill set. Identify the areas of your job that are more routine and susceptible to automation. Focus on developing skills that will complement those tasks—skills that are difficult for AI to replicate. For example, if you're a production manager or a line producer, improving your data interpretation and strategic thinking skills can make you more valuable to a data-centric production pipeline.

Embrace and learn to use AI. Become familiar with the AI tools and technology relevant to your industry. Identify areas where AI can help you analyze data, streamline processes, or provide insights, making your role more impactful. Understanding how AI works and its potential applications can help you work alongside these technologies, make better use of them, or better yet, collaborate with them in ways that will enhance your work.

Look for opportunities to **develop cross-functional skills**, that is, skills that bridge different departments or roles within your organization. Doing so can make you more versatile and enable you to contribute in varying capacities.

Develop soft skills. Cultivate interpersonal skills, teamwork skills, communication, leadership, and adaptability. These skills are highly valued in workplaces and are not easily replaceable by AI.

Strengthen your interpersonal skills. The ability to communicate effectively, collaborate with colleagues, and work in teams is vital. These skills are challenging for AI to replicate and are highly valued in many roles.

Develop your problem-solving skills. Focus on developing your ability to solve complex problems that require human judgment and creativity. While AI can assist with data analysis, it's often up to humans to interpret and act upon the resulting insights.

Work to continuously improve yourself. Regularly assess your skills and the evolving demands of your industry. Identify areas where you can improve and beef up your knowledge and skills to fill any gaps.

2. RETOOL YOUR APPROACH AND POSITION AT WORK AND BEYOND.

Be adaptable. Be open to change and new challenges. Positions with medium exposure to AI might evolve over time, so being flexible and willing to take on new responsibilities is important. If you're in a high-risk field, be willing to explore new roles or industries. Transferable skills can help you transition to a different field if your current job becomes automated. Another option: start your own business. While entrepreneurship involves risks, it can provide you with more control over your work and the opportunity to explore new avenues.

Focus on the human-centric aspects of your job. Seek out roles that involve direct human interaction, emotional support, and complex decision-making. These areas are less likely to be automated and can provide more job security.

Position yourself as an expert: Become a subject matter expert in a specific area of your field. Being the go-to person for certain complex tasks can help safeguard your role.

Seek leadership opportunities. As roles change due to AI, leadership and management skills will continue to be valuable. Consider taking on leadership roles or projects that will showcase your ability to guide teams and make strategic decisions. Why? Leadership roles involve complex decision-making, strategic thinking, and the ability to inspire, motivate, and guide teams of diverse individuals toward organizational goals.

Managers and leaders are responsible for setting a vision, making critical judgments, and adapting to dynamic business environments. They also handle interpersonal dynamics, resolve conflicts, and provide direction and mentorship to their teams.

While AI can provide data-driven insights and support in decision-making processes, it cannot replace the qualities of emotional intelligence, strategic thinking, and the ability to lead and inspire human teams effectively. Leadership and management require a deep understanding of human dynamics and the capacity to navigate complex organizational challenges.

Activate and expand your network. Build a strong professional network within and outside your industry. This can provide you with insights into emerging trends and potential opportunities.

Explore adjacent roles. Look for opportunities to transition into roles that are related to your current field but might have higher demand and lower exposure to AI.

Stay informed. Keep up with industry news, trends, and emerging technologies. This knowledge can help you anticipate changes and proactively adapt.

3. CULTIVATE A GROWTH MINDSET.

Embrace challenges and view setbacks as opportunities to learn and grow. A growth mindset can help you adapt to change and embrace new opportunities.

Remember that surviving AI-driven changes in the job market requires a combination of skills, mindset, and adaptability. By taking these steps, individuals can position themselves to not only survive but thrive in a world shaped by AI and automation.

But wait. That's not all:

THE MOST IMPORTANT PIECE: CONTINUING EDUCATION

Technology is moving so fast that yesterday's knowledge is racing towards obsolescence. It's not really a big deal if you majored in liberal arts, but for anything in the STEM world, a refresher course or two will help you stay relevant.

Continuing education allows individuals to learn new skills and expand their knowledge base, enabling them to tackle emerging challenges and take advantage of new opportunities. More importantly, life-long learning ensures that you are adaptable and relevant and that you are able to grow and progress in your profession.

Learning new skills and earning additional qualifications can open doors to promotions, salary increases, and more advanced roles.

What's more, education fosters personal growth, intellectual stimulation, and a sense of achievement, contributing to overall well-being and satisfaction.

ONE WAY TO DO IT: A CLOSER LOOK AT THE EDX PROGRAM

Whether you're looking to transition to a new career, enhance your current skills, or simply stay updated, edX provides a platform for revaluing your toolset. Renowned institutions such as MIT, Harvard, Cal Tech, Princeton, and others have embraced online education, offering classes through platforms like edX and making quality learning accessible to a global audience.

Through edX, individuals can audit courses from top universities for free or low cost, without enrolling in a full degree program. This means you can access course materials, lectures, and assignments for free or a minimal fee.

These programs are flexible, allowing students to balance education with their existing commitments. And the edX platform has a global reach, connecting learners from around the world, facilitating diverse perspectives and networking opportunities.

For those seeking a more structured learning path, edX offers MicroMasters programs. These are series of graduate-level courses that provide in-depth knowledge and skills in specific fields. Completing a MicroMasters can sometimes count as credit toward a full master's degree if you decide to pursue one later. Although some other programs offer certificates of completion, the MicroMasters programs often come with a recognized credential that can be valuable to employers.

REINVENTING YOURSELF AND CONTINUOUS IMPROVEMENT

Continuing education empowers individuals to reinvent themselves and embrace new roles, even in entirely different industries. It enables professionals to do all of the things they might need to do in the age of AI: **switch careers, stay competitive, embrace emerging technologies, enhance leadership abilities, and build a strong personal brand.**

RESKILLING: THE IMPERATIVE OF TOMORROW

When the Iron Age first began, people had a generation to upgrade their skills and learn a valuable trade. When the industrial age dawned and job displacement began to spread, people had a decade to learn new skills. The digital age moved much faster, giving those in its crosshairs only a few years to adapt. But this age of AI crept up on us so stealthily that many, even those in the technical arena, vastly underestimated both its speed and power.

In the face of AI's relentless march, one thing is abundantly clear: The age-old adage of "learn or be left behind" has never held more weight. The workforce of tomorrow must be agile, ready to pivot, and eager to acquire new skills as AI continues to evolve. Reskilling and upskilling cease to be optional; they are now imperatives in this dynamic world where we must reinvent ourselves or risk becoming the ghost in the machine.

Lifelong learning, once considered a personal enrichment pursuit, has transformed into a career necessity. The rapid obsolescence of skills and the emergence of new opportunities necessitate continuous education.

So, now you know what to do—all that's left is to go ahead and do it.

PROMISES & PREDICTIONS

WHERE WE'VE BEEN

THE CREDITS HAVEN'T ROLLED, BUT LET'S TAKE A MOMENT TO LOOK BACK. Hollywood may have been the springboard, but this book isn't about Tinseltown swapping cameras for code; this is about something much greater—the tectonic shift in how we create, consume, and connect. Storytelling is a communal escape into someone else's imagination. That once meant flickering images in a darkened theater. Now? It's portable, the plot is personal, and the storyteller might be a synthetic algorithm with better instincts than your average Oscar winner.

Running the gamut from virtual characters that tug at your heart strings to neural interfaces that blur the line between thought and action, the only constant in the coming narrative landscape is a level of unpredictability you might find in a Tarantino script. (And no, Quentin didn't slip me a twenty to say that.) We've traced the arc from the crude digital avatars to the uncanny realism of AI-driven actors who can cry on cue, sans union disputes and lighting tantrums. Along the way, we've seen the tools of storytelling move from bulky studio gear to laptops to brain-computer interfaces. Yes, your thoughts may soon be directing the next blockbuster; it's a truly scary thought.

The takeaway? This isn't evolution; it's revolution. And like any good revolution, there are winners, losers, and a whole lot of chaos in between. But if there's one thing that's clear, it's this: We're all part of a story that's still unfolding.

THE PRESENT: A WORLD IN TRANSITION

Right now, we're standing at the crossroads—or maybe it's more of a pileup—where technology and creativity collide. And spoiler alert: Nobody's following traffic laws.

AI isn't just tinkering around the edges of entertainment; it's rewriting the rules, flipping the table, and sending the pieces flying. The tools once reserved for sci-fi pipe dreams are now as accessible as a TikTok filter. That's exciting, sure, but also a little terrifying, depending on which side of the creative fence you're standing.

Take Hollywood, for instance—once the untouchable fortress of storytelling. It's a sandbox now, where anyone with a decent GPU and a wicked imagination can play. Laptops are spinning indie filmmakers' worlds and algorithms are making trailers that know you better than your therapist. Meanwhile, game engines are bridging the gap between movies and gaming, so it's hard to tell if you're watching a movie or playing one. The line? Blurred. The players? Multiplying. The stakes? Higher than ever.

But let's not kid ourselves. This is not just about making movies. There is a much bigger disruption happening. AI is moving into every part of our lives, impacting everything from how we work to how we love to how we binge watch. We're not just moving into a new era of media; we're redefining the very experience of being human. This moment, however, is like any good dramatic tale: tense, uncertain, and yes, tinged with existential dread.

The question isn't whether we are ready. The question is: Do we have any choice but to keep up?

THE FUTURE: STORIES YET TO BE TOLD

But let's squint into the foggy crystal ball of tomorrow, because if you think that the present is a wild ride, you'd better buckle up. We're going to be venturing into territory without a map, beyond the limits of storytelling, where boundaries will snap and then dissolve. This isn't the next chapter; it's a whole new book, and the protagonist might not even be human.

Now imagine a world in which that story doesn't just live on the screen but spills out into your living room, wraps around your senses, and responds to your every whim. Immersive media will not simply invite you to suspend disbelief; it'll program it right out of your brain. Neural interfaces are coming, and instead of just watching the hero's journey, the audience will be the hero, creating plot twists with the flicker of a thought. Forget "Choose Your Own Adventure." This is "Become Your Own Adventure."

Then, of course, there are the tellers of the stories themselves. AI does not require sleep, carries no grudges, and suffers no writer's block. And sure, maybe a little while longer to polish up the nuance and irony-but that is coming too. The creative minds driven by AI will turn out stories quicker than we can use them. It will invent stories to match every mood, every whim, and every existential crisis. Want a pep talk from a virtual Hemingway? Done. Want an epic space opera starring your dog as the galaxy's last hope? It's all queued up.

And let's not get too comfortable in this imagined utopia. There's a dazzling possibility for every sobering shadow. Who controls these tools? Which stories do we tell and which do we silence? So, what happens when AI decides it's finished writing our bedtime stories and begins rewriting reality itself?

Don't say it can't happen—fiction has a funny way of becoming fact when technology gets involved.

But here's one thing for sure: the future of storytelling isn't about technology, but about us. It is about what we value, what we fight for, and perhaps most importantly, what we let go of.

CALL TO ACTION: A ROLE FOR EVERYONE

If there's one takeaway from this whole AI-powered roller coaster, it's this: staying still isn't an option. AI doesn't care about your resume, your connections, or your conduct at the company Christmas party. It's too busy reprogramming the world. The only way to thrive in this age of relentless transformation is to stop chasing trends and start chasing knowledge. Without training—be it structured or unstructured—you're just another wannabe, crammed into the mosh pit with the rest of the also-rans, hoping for a shot at relevance.

The truth is brutal but simple: AI moves so fast that if you're not already thinking about the next phase, you're not just behind—you're already obsolete. The object of this book is to help you make the connections, to see the patterns that are forming for the future, and to prepare for what's coming before it hits like a rogue wave. Because here's the reality: The movie industry as we know it is toast. Sure, there'll still be a movie business, but it's destined to become a sideshow, a boutique operation catering to niche audiences. The real action is happening elsewhere—in the game industry and the cloud-powered creation engines that are about to become the new Hollywood.

If you're clinging to your old-school chops, thinking you'll skate by, I've got bad news: The help wanted ads aren't going to be kind. The only way forward is to level up, to embrace the relentless pace of change, and to realize that learning isn't just for the young. It's for the hungry. It's for you.

GLOSSARY

adaptive NPC agents: AI characters that can adjust to environments and situations.

Age of Insignificance: Term describing the era when human relevance is diminished by AI capabilities.

Agentic AI: AI systems designed to operate autonomously, pursuing goals and making decisions in complex environments without constant human oversight.

aggregated biometrics: Combined physiological data from multiple viewers to create group-optimized content.

AI Kludge: Transitional phase in AI development with temporary work-arounds and solutions.

AI motion image generator models: AI systems like Sora and Runway that create video content.

AI oligarchy: A power structure where those who control AI algorithms hold disproportionate control over society.

AI-curator biometrics: The use of physiological data to personalize content through AI.

AI-driven actors: Virtual performers created and controlled by artificial intelligence.

AI-generative movie engine: System capable of automating aspects of film production.

AI-Prototyper: Tool for generating animated scenes from annotated scripts.

algorithm: A process or set of rules followed in calculations or other problem-solving operations, especially by a computer. In media contexts, algorithms determine what content users see based on various factors including past behavior.

algorithmic bias: When AI systems reflect or amplify existing societal prejudices in their outputs.

algorithmic colonialism: The imposition of Western values and assumptions through AI systems deployed globally.

alt-genre: Specialized micro-categories created by streaming platforms like Netflix to classify content with extreme specificity, enabling more precise content recommendations.

American Film Market (AFM): A film industry event focused on production and distribution deals.

animatronics: Mechanical figures that are typically covered in a lifelike skin and controlled remotely.

Aristotelian plot structure: The traditional three-part narrative framework with a beginning, middle, and end.

artificial intelligence (AI): Computer systems designed to mimic human intelligence.

artificial reality: Simulated experiences that can be similar to or completely different from the real world.

augmented reality (AR): Technology that overlays digital information on the real world.

augmented symbology: Digital information overlays used in head-up displays.

Bash-Bots: Digital warriors with extensive action sequences used as digital extras.

bio-digital interface: Technology that connects biological systems with digital systems.

biometric profile: Collection of physiological and behavioral data unique to an individual.

bioengineering: Application of engineering principles to biological systems.

blade runners: Special police officers tasked with identifying and "retiring" rogue replicants.

brain-computer interfaces (BCIs): Technology enabling direct communication between the brain and external devices.

branching narratives: Stories with multiple paths that change based on user choices.

Building 8: Facebook's secretive hardware division working on advanced technologies.

Cambridge Analytica: Company that used AI-driven data analysis to manipulate political advertising.

CCD film scanner: Technology that converts film images into digital data.

character prompts: Inputs for AI systems describing character traits and backgrounds.

chroma key: A visual effects technique for compositing two images based on color hues.

cine-drones: Unmanned aerial vehicles specifically designed for cinematography.

Cogs (or **cognitive personas**): Advanced AI entities that can represent humans in various contexts.

confidence scoring: System for rating AI's certainty about its answers.

Content ID: Automated system used by platforms like YouTube to identify and manage copyrighted content.

content personalization: The process of tailoring content recommendations to individual users based on their viewing history, demographics, and behavioral patterns.

convolutional neural networks (CNNs): Neural networks specifically designed to process visual data.

Creation Engine: AI system that generates personalized content based on user data.

Creative Commons: A nonprofit organization that provides free licenses for creators to use when making their work available for public use.

cross-platform potential: The ability for content to evolve across different media platforms.

cultural centrifuge: Metaphor for how social media separates and accelerates cultural elements.

curated lifestyle: A future where AI personalizes and manages various aspects of daily life.

Cyberware 3D scanner: Early technology for capturing 3D facial geometry.

D1 video: A professional digital video format.

Dark Factories: Manufacturing facilities that operate entirely through automation without human workers.

decentralization: The process of moving content creation away from traditional centralized hubs.

decentralized autonomous organizations (DAOs): Organizations that use smart contracts and community governance for financing and decision-making.

deep learning: A type of machine learning using neural networks modeled after the human brain.

deep learning models: Advanced neural networks capable of learning complex patterns from large datasets.

deep reinforcement learning: AI technique where systems learn through trial and error with rewards.

deepfake: Synthetic media where a person's likeness is replaced with someone else's using artificial intelligence techniques, allowing for the creation of highly realistic but fabricated content.

detailed prompts: Specific instructions that provide comprehensive context for AI systems.

diffraction grating: Component in AR glasses that projects data into the user's eyes.

digital consciousness: The theoretical ability to transfer or replicate human consciousness in digital form.

digital divide: Gap between those with access to digital technologies and those without.

digital doubles: Realistic virtual representations of real people.

digital effects: Visual enhancements created using computer technology rather than physical methods.

digital moviemaking: The process of creating films using digital technology rather than traditional film.

Digital Peasantry: New underclass of workers whose labor and lives are controlled by algorithms they cannot influence.

digital people: Virtual entities with human-like characteristics and behaviors.

digital pipeline: The complete workflow of digital content creation from concept to final product.

DMCA (Digital Millennium Copyright Act): 1998 U.S. copyright law that criminalizes production and dissemination of technology, devices, or services intended to circumvent measures that control access to copyrighted works.

echo chamber: A situation where beliefs are amplified by communication and repetition inside a closed system and insulated from rebuttal. In media consumption, this refers to platforms showing users only content that aligns with their existing preferences.

edge AI: AI processing that occurs locally on a device rather than in the cloud.

EEG-enhanced profile: Biometric profile enhanced with brainwave data.

elasto-polymer: Synthetic material used to mimic human skin in robotics.

engagement metrics: Quantitative measurements of how users interact with content, including watch time, completion rate, click-through rate, and social sharing.

exposition: The introduction of characters and settings in a story.

extended universe: A collection of media (films, TV shows, books, games) that share a single fictional universe, allowing for multiple entry points and extended storytelling across platforms.

fairness metrics: Quantitative measures used to assess whether AI systems treat different groups equitably.

fair use: Legal doctrine that promotes freedom of expression by permitting the unlicensed use of copyright-protected works in certain circumstances.

Fermi Paradox: The contradiction between the high probability of extraterrestrial civilizations and the lack of contact with such civilizations.

filter bubble: A state of intellectual isolation that can result from personalized searches and algorithmic recommendations, where users are effectively separated from information that disagrees with their viewpoints.

fractal story world: A narrative universe with infinite branching possibilities and variations.

galvanic skin response (GSR): Measurement of skin's electrical conductivity changes tied to emotional states.

game engines: Software frameworks designed for video game creation now used for film production.

general AI (GAI): AI systems with broad human-like intelligence capabilities.

generative adversarial networks (GANs): AI framework with competing networks that generate and evaluate content.

generative AI (GenAI): Artificial intelligence systems that create new content such as scripts, videos, or images.

Ghost in the Machine: Reference to the merging of human consciousness with artificial intelligence.

GPU: Graphics Processing Unit; specialized electronic circuit for accelerating computer graphics and AI processes.

grand narrative: A universal story structure or theme that resonates across cultures and time.

growth mindset: Perspective that embraces challenges and views setbacks as opportunities to learn.

GUI (graphical user interface): A visual way for users to interact with computers.

HAL 9000: Fictional AI system from 2001: A Space Odyssey that controls spaceship operations.

haptics: Technology providing touch feedback through forces, vibrations, or motions.

head-up display (HUD): A transparent display that presents data without requiring users to look away from their usual viewpoint.

Hollywood 1.0: The early film era characterized by chemical film processes and mechanical equipment.

Hollywood 2.0: The digital transition of filmmaking where pixels replaced film.

Hollywood 3.0: The AI-driven future of filmmaking where artificial intelligence replaces human craftsmanship.

Hollywood reboot: The transformation of the traditional Hollywood system due to new technologies.

hosts: Lifelike android robots in Westworld designed to serve human guests.

humanoid robots: Robots with physical appearances resembling humans.

humanoid surrogates: Robotic entities designed to resemble and act as substitutes for humans.

HyperCard: An early Apple application that allowed for the creation of hypertext content.

hypothesis generation and testing: AI process of creating and evaluating potential answers.

IBM Watson Health Cloud: AI-powered healthcare platform.

immersive media: Content that surrounds the user and creates an encompassing sensory experience.

Industrial Light & Magic (ILM): A visual effects company founded by George Lucas.

infinite scroll: Design feature that continuously loads content as the user scrolls down.

interactive narratives: Stories where user choices influence outcomes and story progression.

IP (intellectual property): Legal rights that result from intellectual activity in industrial, scientific, literary, and artistic fields. In entertainment, refers to the ownership of creative content and the right to produce derivative works.

IP maximalism: Perspective advocating for expanding intellectual property rights and enforcement.

iterative refinement: The process of gradually improving prompts through successive adjustments.

Kinemacolor: An early mechanical color reproduction system from the early 20th century.

kludge: A transitional phase between periods of conventional and revolutionary growth characterized by chaos, wild inventions, and conceptual shifts.

Kurzweil/Moore Hypothesis: A combination of Ray Kurzweil's timeline predictions with Moore's law vectors.

large language model (LLM): AI systems like ChatGPT that generate text based on input prompts.

LiDAR: Light Detection and Ranging; cameras that photograph in three dimensions.

logic density: The concentration of transistors or logical components in a chip.

machine learning (ML): A subset of AI focused on training models using data to make predictions.

Macromind Director: An image editor and sequencer that helped define desktop media in the 1990s.

merit-based rewards: System where individuals receive compensation based on AI assessment of their contribution.

meta-audience: Viewers who are self-aware about their position as consumers of media and the ways in which their consumption is being analyzed and manipulated by platforms.

MetaHuman Creator (MHC): A web-based tool by Unreal Engine for creating realistic digital humans.

micro moments: Brief, attention-grabbing content designed for quick consumption.

micro-gesture modeling: Creating realistic small facial movements to convey emotion.

MicroMasters: Graduate-level course series on platforms like edX that provide specialized knowledge.

microtubules: Structures within neurons where quantum activity potentially occurs.

mixed reality (MR): A blend of physical and digital worlds where physical and virtual objects coexist.

modular narratives: Stories with interchangeable or flexible components that can be rearranged.

Moore's law: The observation that the number of transistors in an integrated circuit doubles approximately every two years, while costs are halved.

motion capture: Technology that records movement of objects or people for use in digital animation.

motion control photography: A technique using mechanized camera movement for precise repetition.

multiplane matte painting: A technique using multiple layers of paintings to create depth in background images.

narrow AI (or **Weak AI**): AI systems designed to perform specific, limited tasks.

natural language processing (NLP): AI technology that allows computers to understand human language.

neural handoff: The transfer of control from one brain-machine interface user to another.

neural interface: Technology that enables direct communication between the brain and external devices.

neural interface technology: Technology that enables direct communication between brain and device.

neural networks: Computing systems inspired by biological neural networks.

neural nomads: Individuals whose consciousness can move between different platforms or substrates.

neurochemical stimuli: Content designed to trigger specific brain chemicals for emotional response.

neuromorphic chips: Computer chips designed to mimic the structure of the human brain.

nonplayer characters (NPCs): AI-driven characters in games that aren't controlled by players.

olfactometers: Devices that measure smell or generate scent.

one-way narrative: Traditional storytelling format where the audience passively receives the story.

overclocking reality: The concept of manipulating perceived time through quantum consciousness.

parasocial bonding: Formation of relationships with media figures that feel real.

Passion Squads: Nomadic communities of creators who produce content collaboratively in non-traditional locations.

pattern recognition tasks: AI capabilities to identify regularities or trends in data.

personified virtual clinician: AI healthcare assistant with human-like characteristics.

phoneme-to-viseme mapping: Process of converting speech sounds to corresponding facial movements.

Pixelwood: A term referring to the digital visual effects industry within Hollywood.

Pocket PC: Next-generation smartphone with advanced AI capabilities.

previsualizations: Visual representations of scenes created before actual filming.

problem formulation: Advanced form of prompt engineering where AI systems determine actions and states.

Project Maven: Collaboration between Google and the Pentagon using AI to analyze drone footage.

Project Sequoia: Initiative to create an augmented reality brain-computer interface.

prompt engineering: The process of designing and refining inputs to AI systems to generate desired outputs.

prosumer: A blend of "producer" and "consumer," referring to individuals who both consume content and produce or modify it, especially in digital contexts enhanced by AI tools.

PVM professional field monitor: A Sony monitor used to display high-resolution footage on set.

quantum computing: Computing using quantum-mechanical phenomena like superposition and entanglement to perform operations.

quantum entanglement: Phenomenon where particles become linked so that the quantum state of each particle cannot be described independently.

Quantum Kludge: Future transitional phase related to quantum computing technologies.

quantum supremacy: The point at which quantum computers can solve problems that classical computers practically cannot.

quantum teleportation: Technique for transferring quantum states from one location to another.

quantum tourist: Entity whose consciousness can visit or experience different places or times.

quantum-verse: A theoretical realm where consciousness exists beyond physical limitations.

real-time rendering: The process of generating images on-screen at a rate fast enough to give the appearance of motion.

recommendation engine: Software that analyzes available data to suggest items a user might like, central to how streaming services present content options.

RED camera: An early professional digital cinema camera that recorded on RAM chips.

render farms: Collections of networked computers used to process complex visual effects.

replicants: Bioengineered beings in *Blade Runner* that are virtually indistinguishable from humans.

reskilling: Process of learning new skills to adapt to changing job requirements.

resolution: The conclusion of a story where conflicts are resolved.

rising action: The building of tension and conflict in a narrative.

scene prompts: Inputs for AI systems describing setting and atmosphere for scene creation.

script prompts: Inputs for AI systems defining elements of script creation.

semantic chains: Framework for mapping relationships between narrative elements.

semantic reasoning: AI capability to understand meaning and relationships between concepts.

sensor fusion: Integration of data from multiple sensors for comprehensive information.

sentient AI: Artificial intelligence with consciousness, self-awareness, and the ability to experience subjective feelings.

SGI (Silicon Graphics, Inc.): A company that created UNIX-based platforms with advanced graphics capabilities.

silicon dominance: The theoretical point at which artificially intelligent systems surpass human capabilities across most domains.

silicon integrated circuits: Electronic circuits formed on a small piece of silicon semiconductor material.

Silver Tsunami: Term referring to the rapidly growing aging population and associated eldercare needs.

Singularity: The hypothetical point where artificial intelligence surpasses human intelligence.

Skinner box: Named after psychologist B.F. Skinner, a controlled environment where behavior is reinforced through rewards and punishments. In digital media, it refers to design features that encourage continued engagement through intermittent rewards.

Skynet: Fictional AI system from the Terminator franchise that becomes self-aware and initiates a war against humanity.

smart contracts: Self-executing contracts with the terms directly written into code.

socially assistive robots: AI-driven robots designed to provide companionship and care for the elderly.

Sora: An AI generative video application.

spatial computing: A technology concept where computers become part of the space around us, allowing digital interaction with the physical world.

spatial media: Content that exists in three-dimensional space that can be interacted with.

spatial registration: The process of aligning virtual elements with the physical world.

superintelligent AI: Artificial intelligence that surpasses human intelligence across virtually all domains.

task-oriented agents: Digital characters programmed to perform specific functions.

Technicolor: A successful three-color process developed in the 1930s that provided realistic color reproduction in film.

temporal manipulation: The ability to control one's experience of time by adjusting perceptual frame rates.

text tokens: Units of text processing used by language models to generate content.

three laws of robotics: Isaac Asimov's fictional rules designed to prevent robots from harming humans.

Transhumanism: Philosophy and movement focused on transforming humanity through technology, particularly the merging of humans with machines.

truth-seeking AI: AI designed to prioritize objective facts over cultural or human biases.

Turing test: A test designed to evaluate a machine's ability to exhibit intelligent behavior indistinguishable from a human.

two-way experiences: Interactive storytelling where audience input influences the narrative.

universal basic income (UBI): System where governments provide citizens with regular financial support.

up-conversion algorithm: Software that converts lower resolution content to higher resolution formats.

upskilling: Enhancing existing skills to remain relevant in evolving industries.

vacuum tubes: Early electronic components that controlled electron flow, used before transistors.

vague prompts: Inputs that lack sufficient detail for AI to generate precise outputs.

validated learning: Accredited training valued by employers and compatible with business structures.

value-aligned AI: AI systems designed to align with and prioritize human values and ethics.

variable-density soundtrack: Early sound technology using small lines at the edge of film to encode audio.

virtual companions: AI entities designed for social interaction and relationship building.

virtual influencers: Computer-generated characters with social media presence.

virtual reality (VR): Technology that immerses users in a computer-generated environment.

visual patches: Elements used by AI motion image generators to create realistic sequences.

Vitaphone system: Early sound technology that synchronized vinyl discs mechanically with film projectors.

volumetric: Relating to the measurement of volume or three-dimensional space in media production.

volumetric stages: Spaces equipped with technology to capture three-dimensional performances.

waveguide lens technology: Technology that directs light waves through transparent medium to project images.

Wheatstone bridge circuit: Circuit used in GSR devices to measure skin conductivity.

wrist terminal: Advanced smartwatch that serves as a biometric hub and health monitor.

BIBLIOGRAPHY

Adcock, Brett.
"We already have some 8 million vacancies in the United States alone—the jobs that no one wants to do."
"You can effectively have a situation where prices of goods and services are going towards zero in the limit and GDP goes to infinity."
These quotes are from a 2024 interview entitled, "Figure AI and the Humanoid Revolution."

Agentforce.
AI platform launched September 12, 2024, by Salesforce, representing a shift toward autonomous AI systems that act without human oversight.

Agent Smith.
"Never send a human to do a machine's job."
The Matrix. Directed by the Wachowskis, Warner Bros. Pictures, 1999.

Altman, Sam.
"AI will probably be the demise of humanity, but until that time, it will create wonderful companies."
From BrainyQuote.com, BrainyMedia Inc, 2025.
Sam Altman is the founder of OpenAI.

Altman, Sam.
"Prompt engineering is one of the most important skills to learn right now."
Microsoft Build conference at Microsoft headquarters in Redmond, Washington, on May 21, 2024.

Asimov, Isaac.
"The Master created humans first as the lowest type, most easily formed. Gradually, he replaced them by robots, the next higher step, and finally he created me, to take the place of the last humans."
I, Robot. Isaac Asimov. New York: Gnome Press, 1950.

Isaac Asimov (1920–1992) was an American writer and a professor of biochemistry at Boston University.

Bateman, Nathan.
"One day the AIs are going to look back on us the same way we look at fossil skeletons on the plains of Africa. An upright ape living in dust with crude language and tools, all set for extinction."
Ex Machina. Directed by Alex Garland, DNA Films, 2014.

Belsky, Scott.
"Well, we believe that augmented reality is one of those new mediums that could be as big as if not bigger than the web. One of the areas where consumers adopt something new is when it makes something drastically easier. When I think about augmented reality I think about instances like finding your way somewhere, finding your friends in a stadium, or going to a conference and looking around and knowing who everyone is because their LinkedIn profile is hanging over their heads."
Interview with *The Independent* at Apple's World Wide Developers' Conference on June 4, 2018.

Scott Belsky is the Chief Product Officer and Executive VP for Creative Cloud at Adobe.

Billups, Joseph, PhD.
"Learning for passion fills you up; learning for ego drains you."
Dedication address for the Newhouse School Of Public Communications at Syracuse University, August 5, 1964. Onondaga Historical Association.

Joseph Billups, PhD, is a retired semantics professor at Syracuse University.

Bowman, David.
"Even now, he could not fully accept the idea that Frank had been deliberately killed—it was so utterly irrational. It was beyond all reason that Hal, who had performed flawlessly for so long, should suddenly turn assassin."
2001: A Space Odyssey. Directed by Stanley Kubrick, Metro-Goldwyn-Mayer, 1968.

Brando, Marlon.
"Now listen, let me tell you something that I did. I've had my head digitized. And they put this laser—and it goes around you like this—and they digitized my face. And I made a lot of faces, and smiled, and made a sad face, and so they got it all on digital. And actors are not gonna be real. They're gonna be inside a computer. You watch. It's gonna happen. So maybe this is the swan song for all of us."
Interview at the Academy of Motion Picture Arts and Sciences in 1990.

Marlon Brando Jr. (1924–2004) is a multi-Oscar-winning American actor with a career spanning over 50 years, and is considered one of the greatest actors of the 20th century. The above quotation was also used in the opening sequence of the award-winning Showtime documentary *Listen to Me Marlon* (2015).

Brockman, Greg.
"Prompt engineering is the art of communicating eloquently to an AI."
Posted by Brockman on X, 4:10 PM, Mar 11, 2023.

Greg Brockman is the president and co-founder of OpenAI.

Connor, John.
"You just can't go around killing people."
Terminator 2: Judgment Day. Directed by James Cameron, Lightstorm Entertainment, 1991.

Cook, Tim.
"Think back to 2008, when the App Store went live. There was the initial round of apps, and people looked at them and said, 'this is not anything, mobile apps are not going to take off.' And then, step by step, things start to move...and now you couldn't imagine your life without apps...AR is like that. It will be that dramatic."
Interview with Andrew Griffin, technology editor for *The Independent*. October 12, 2017.

Tim Cook is the CEO of Apple.

Cook, Tim.
"Zoom out to the future and look back; you'll wonder how you led your life without augmented reality."
From a livestream at the Università degli Studi di Napoli Federico II in Naples, Italy, September 2022.

Crawford, Kate.
"Artificial intelligence is neither artificial nor intelligent in many ways—it's deeply embedded in our physical world, consuming vast amounts of resources and energy. We tend to think of AI as weightless, but it has a very real and heavy environmental footprint."
Public speech during the Robert F. Kennedy Human Rights' virtual book club on November 7, 2023.
[https://rfkhumanrights.org/our-voices/atlas-of-ai-examining-the-human-and-environmental-costs-of-artificial-intelligence/]

Kate Crawford is a research professor of communication at USC.

Cuban, Mark.
"Artificial Intelligence, deep learning, machine learning—whatever you're doing, if you don't understand it—learn it. Because otherwise you're going to be a dinosaur within three years."
From an interview with Jason Hirschhorn, founder of Media REDEF on February 7, 2017. Cuban repeated this quote multiple times, including in 2023. [https://bothsidesofthetable.com/mark-cuban-on-why-you-need-to-study-artificial-intelligence-or-youll-be-a-dinosaur-in-3-years-db3447bea1b4]

Mark Cuban is an American businessman and television personality. He gave the interview with Hirschhorn mentioned in the link here as the opening to the Upfront Summit in 2017.

DSEI (Defense and Security Equipment International).
World's largest arms expo, with regional events including the Asian branch in Chiba, Japan, showcasing autonomous weapons systems and AI-driven military technologies.

Dyson, Freeman.
"The purpose of life is to color the universe with consciousness."
TED Talk, July 2008.

Freeman Dyson is a British-born American theoretical physicist and author.

Einstein, Albert.
"It has become appallingly obvious that our technology has exceeded our humanity."
Quote reported in *The New York Times* on May 25, 1946.

Albert Einstein (1879–1955) was a German-born theoretical physicist best known for developing the theory of relativity.

Ellis, John.
"To choose is to be aware of alternative possibilities, possibilities that are being missed."
Seeing Things: Television in the Age of Uncertainty. I.B. Tauris, 2000.

EVE-3.
"Humanity's greatest fear isn't being replaced; it's being understood too well."
Subservience. Directed by S.K. Dale, Millennium Media, 2024.

Freeman, Philip.
"The very best stories make you feel pity for a likeable but flawed character and a fearful realization that the same thing could have happened to you."

From "Aristotle on How to Write a Story," Princeton University Press, May 2022.
[https://press.princeton.edu/ideas/aristotle-on-how-to-write-a-story]

Philip Freeman is the author of more than a dozen books on the ancient world and professor of Western culture at Pepperdine University.

Fuller, Buckminster.
"The best way to predict the future is to invent it."
First verifiable use of this quote was in Alan Kay's TED Talk on March 4, 2008.

Kay was referencing Buckminster Fuller's discussions on molecules of Buckminsterfullerene (aka Buckie Balls) and his geodesic domes.

Gibson, William.
"As man and AI continue to merge, it is us who will become the Ghost in the Machine."
Neuromancer. William Gibson. Ace Books, 1984.

Greene, Robert.
"The future belongs to those who learn more skills and combine them in creative ways."
Mastery. Robert Greene. Penguin Books, 2012.

Greenwold, Simon.
"spatial computing"
[https://acg.media.mit.edu/people/simong/]

First public record use of the term was in 2003 as part of a course description, but Simon Greenwold is the MIT Media Lab researcher who coined the term "spatial computing" in 1995 in his doctoral thesis.

Halamka, John.
"Virtual clinicians can extend the reach of healthcare providers, offering support and information to patients when they need it."
On-demand webinar, July 14, 2021.
[https://montana.himss.org/]

John Halamka was president of the Mayo Clinic when he made this comment.

Hanke, John.
"The entire world will be a screen, and every surface an interface."
From a talk at the Game Developers Conference in San Francisco, 2019.
[https://gdconf.com/news/niantics-chief-explores-future-ar-game-design-gdc-2019s-vision-track]

John Hanke is founder and CEO of Niantic and the creator of Pokémon GO.

Hawking, Stephen.

"One can imagine such technology outsmarting financial markets, out-inventing human researchers, out-manipulating human leaders, and developing weapons we cannot even understand."

Quote reported in *The Independent,* May 2014.

[https://www.independent.co.uk/news/science/stephen-hawking-transcendence-looks-at-the-implications-of-artificial-intelligence-but-are-we-taking-ai-seriously-enough-9313474.html]

Stephen William Hawking (1942–2018) was a British cosmologist and theoretical physicist who made significant contributions to astronomy and physics.

Hinkle, Devyn.

"One could argue that that role is now filled by algorithms."

"Netflix claims that these systems have decreased its churn by several percentage points and have saved $1 billion per year."

"How Streaming Services Use Algorithms." Arts Management & Technology Laboratory, August 2021.

Hoffer, Eric.

"In times of change, learners inherit the Earth, while the learned find themselves beautifully equipped to deal with a world that no longer exists."

From BrainyQuote.com, BrainyMedia Inc, 2025.

Eric Hoffer (1902–1983) was an American philosopher and social critic.

IBM's Heron2.

Specifics regarding IBM'S Heron2 come from Domain B, an online tech report, November 2024.

[https://www.domain-b.com/infotech/it-news/ibm-launches-world-s-fastest-quantum-computer-heron2]

Keynes, John Maynard.

"But beyond this, we shall endeavor to spread the bread thin on the butter—to make what work there is still to be done to be as widely shared as possible. Three-hour shifts or a fifteen-hour week may put off the problem for a great while."

Essays in Persuasion. John Maynard Keynes. W. W. Norton & Company, New York, 1931.

John Maynard Keynes (1883–1946) was an English economist and philosopher whose ideas fundamentally changed the theory and practice of macroeconomics and the economic policies of governments. The essays in Keynes' book were originally published in the newspaper *The Nation and Athenaeum.*

Khosla, Vinod.
". . .the bottom 50% of really undesirable jobs."
"Rethinking Labor in the Age of Robotics." Khosla Ventures Report, 2023.

Klein, William, PhD.
"[Extended quote about AI companions and their potential impact on humanity]."
Excerpt from Klein's talk at UCLA, June 2018.
Bill Klein is a renowned computer scientist specializing in game development and quantum computing.

Kurzweil, Ray.
The Singularity Is Near: When Humans Transcend Biology. Viking Publishers, September 2005.
There are numerous references throughout *Post-Cinema* in regard to Kurzweil's prediction of human-level AI by 2029 and the subsequent post-biological merger.

Kusanagi, Motoko.
"If a technological feat is possible, man will do it. Almost as if it's wired into the core of our being."
Ghost in the Shell. Directed by Mamoru Oshii, Production I.G, 1995.

Lange, Christian Lous.
"Technology is a useful servant but a dangerous master."
From Lange's Nobel Lecture, December 13, 1921.
[https://www.nobelprize.org/prizes/peace/1921/lange/lecture/]

Lanier, Jaron.
Referenced as a pioneer in VR technology and founder of VPL Research in the 1990s.
[https://en.wikipedia.org/wiki/Jaron_Lanier]

Lessig, Lawrence.
"Code is law."
Code: And Other Laws Of Cyberspace. Basic Books; First Edition, November 30, 1999.

Man in Black.
"Winning doesn't mean anything unless someone else loses."
Westworld. Created by Jonathan Nolan and Lisa Joy, HBO, 2016.

Markowitz, Bobbie.
"All the women around here are perfect sex-kitten bimbos. All the men are drooling nerds. Doesn't that seem strange?"
The Stepford Wives. Directed by Bryan Forbes, Palomar Pictures, 1975.

McLaughlin, Mignon.
"We are all borne brave, trusting and greedy, and most of us remain greedy."
From BrainyQuote.com, BrainyMedia Inc, 2025.

McLuhan, Marshall.
"When faced with a new situation, we tend always to attach ourselves to the objects, to the flavor of the most recent past. We look at the present through a rear-view mirror. We march backward into the future."
From *The Medium is the Massage.* Gingko Press, August 1, 2001. Originally published in 1967.

Moore, Gordon.
Moore's law
"Cramming more components onto integrated circuits," *Electronics Magazine*, 1965.
[https://en.wikipedia.org/wiki/Moore%27s_law]

The first published reference to Gordon Moore's prediction that computational power would double every two years. Moore was also co-founder of Intel.

Murphy.
"My friends call me Murphy...You call me Robocop."
RoboCop. Directed by Paul Verhoeven, Orion Pictures, 1987.

Murati, Mira.
"We're working on something that will change everything—the way we work, the way we interact with each other, and the way we think and everything, really, all aspects of life."
Excerpt from a transcript on Microsoft Website.
[https://www.microsoft.com/en-us/behind-the-tech/mira-murati-chief-technology-officer-openai]

Musk, Elon.
"The future is already in your mind, you just need the right interface to unleash it."
Transcript for *Elon Musk: Neuralink and the Future of Humanity.* Lex Fridman Podcast #438, Aug 2, 2024.
[https://lexfridman.com/elon-musk-and-neuralink-team-transcript/]

Musk, Elon.
"We need to be super careful with AI. [It's] potentially more dangerous than nukes."
Posted by Musk on X (formerly Twitter), August 2, 2014.

Musk, Elon.
"With a laptop, you can change the world."
Transcript for *Elon Musk: Neuralink and the Future of Humanity.* Lex Fridman Podcast #438, Aug 2, 2024.
[https://lexfridman.com/elon-musk-and-neuralink-team-transcript/]

Musk, Elon.
Reference to 10 billion humanoid robots by 2040.
"Robotics and AI: The Future of Labor." From a Tesla shareholder meeting in 2023.

Nadella, Satya.
"Tay has had a great influence on how Microsoft is approaching AI."
Quote about the Tay incident influencing Microsoft's AI approach.
[https://en.wikipedia.org/wiki/Tay_(chatbot)]
Satya Nadella is the CEO of Microsoft.

Nadella, Satya.
"AI is the key to unlocking the true potential of AR. It empowers us to create rich, context-aware experiences that seamlessly blend the digital and physical worlds."
From Nadella's keynote speech at Microsoft Ignite 2024.
[https://www.youtube.com/watch?v=3YiB2OvK6sY]

Nadella, Satya.
"I feel that Augmented reality is perhaps the ultimate computer."
Quote from a speech Nadella gave at a public event in India, February 2017.
[https://mashable.com/article/microsoft-satya-nadella-artificial-intelligence-focus]

Narayavan, Arvind.
"This weakening of the power of gatekeepers has unleashed a creative energy that deserves to be celebrated."
"Understanding Social Media Recommendation Algorithms." Knight First Amendment Institute at Columbia University, March 2023.

Ng, Andrew.
"AI will be as impactful on healthcare as electricity has been on all other industries."

Quote from a public event as reported in the Stanford Business Insights Blog, March 2017.
[https://www.gsb.stanford.edu/insights/andrew-ng-why-ai-new-electricity]

Penrose, Roger, and Hameroff, Stuart.
Reference to their research on the brain as a quantum system.
Orf, Darren. "Quantum Entanglement in Your Brain Is What Generates Consciousness, Radical Study Suggests," *Popular Mechanics*, August 2024.

Pichai, Sundar.
"AR has the potential to become the next major computing platform, transforming how we work, play, and connect with the world."
Interview with Gideon Lichfield in the *MIT Technology Review*, October 23, 2019.

Sundar Pichai is the CEO of Alphabet Inc. and Google. In an exclusive interview with *MIT Technology Review*, Pichai explained why quantum computing could be as important for Google as AI.

Popular Mechanics.
"Where a calculator on the ENIAC is equipped with 18,000 vacuum tubes and weighs 30 tons, computers in the future may have only 1,000 vacuum tubes and perhaps only weigh 1.5 tons."
Popular Mechanics, March 1949.

Prince.
"I like Hollywood. I just like Minneapolis a little bit better."
From BrainyQuote.com, BrainyMedia Inc, 2025.

Putin, Vladimir.
"The one who becomes the leader in AI will be the ruler of the world."
Stated in a public address by Russian President Vladimir Putin, 2017.

Rain, Douglas (as HAL 9000).
"I know I've made some very poor decisions recently, but I can give you my complete assurance that my work will be back to normal."
2001: A Space Odyssey. Directed by Stanley Kubrick, Metro-Goldwyn-Mayer, 1968.

Rock, Chris.
"I may not be the funniest, or best-looking guy, but I get so much more opportunity than other people because everyone knows I'll show up."
Bring Your 'A' Game (documentary). Directed by Mario Van Peebles, 2009.

Ross, Scott.
Overview of the confusing time regarding the founding of Digital Domain and the digital kludge in filmmaking.
Scott Ross, March 2025.

A more extensive account is available in his book, *Upstart: The Digital Film Revolution Managing the Unmanageable* from Native Book Publishing, December 18, 2024.

Russell, Stuart.
Human Compatible. Penguin Books, reprint edition, November 17, 2020.
There are numerous references to Russell's book *Human Compatible* and his concerns about AI alignment with human values.

Samantha.
"The heart is not like a box that gets filled up; it expands in size the more you love."
Her. Directed by Spike Jonze, Annapurna Pictures, 2013.

Shaw, George Bernard.
"If history repeats itself, and the unexpected always happens, how incapable must Man be of learning from experience."
George Bernard Shaw (1856–1950) was an Irish playwright, critic, and political activist who won the Nobel Prize in Literature in 1925.

Spielberg, Steven.
"Social media has taken over in America to such an extreme that to get my own kids to look back a week in their history is a miracle, let alone 100 years."
Singh, Anita. "Steven Spielberg on War Horse: America has less regard for history." *The Telegraph*, January 09, 2012.

Tesla, Nikola.
"The day science begins to study non-physical phenomena, it will make more progress in one decade than in all the previous centuries of its existence."
Nikola Tesla: My Life, My Research. Nikola Tesla. CreateSpace Independent Publishing Platform, June 30, 2014.

Thompson, E.P.
"The machinery was something that was driving men into the workhouse, the pauper's ward, or the graveyard."
Excerpted from *The Making of the English Working Class.* Victor Gollancz Ltd, 1963.

Topol, Eric.
"The integration of AI in healthcare has the potential to democratize access, making quality care available to anyone with a smart device."
Quote from *A.I. & Healthcare: An Interview with Dr. Eric Topol,* Woebot Health Podcast with Dr. Eric Topol, May 5, 2023.

Turing, Alan.
"We can only see a short distance ahead, but we can see plenty there that needs to be done."
Alan Turing Quotes. BrainyQuote.com, BrainyMedia Inc, 2025.

Turkle, Sherry, PhD.
"We are increasingly captivated by technologies that replicate, mimic, or predict human desires, and in the process, we may discover parts of ourselves we never intended to explore."
TED Talk, April 2012.

Sherry Turkle is a professor in the Program in Science, Technology, and Society at MIT and the founding director of the MIT Initiative on Technology and Self.

Tyrell Corporation.
"More Human Than Human' is our motto."
Blade Runner. Directed by Ridley Scott, The Ladd Company, 1982.

Wachter, Robert.
"Health care is an industry that's ripe for innovation, but it's also probably one of the most resistant to change because of the very real regulatory, financial, and cultural barriers."
Commonwealth Club World Affairs (CCWA) address at the 14th annual Lundberg Institute Lecture, November 16, 2024, San Francisco.

Robert Wachter is the chair of the Department of Medicine at UCSF.

Walker, Alice.
"The most common way people give up their power is by thinking they don't have any."
Quote from *The Color Purple: A Novel* by Alice Walker. Penguin Books, reprint edition, December 10, 2019.

Wang, Alice.
"I didn't need a massive budget or studio backing. Thanks to the AI and decentralized platforms, I had all the tools I needed for implementing my idea and sharing it with the world."
Referenced from a panel discussion at SXSW Conference in Austin, TX. [https://www.imdb.com/name/nm1543911/]

Wang, Yiran (Amanda).
"A typical Netflix member loses interest after perhaps 60 to 90 seconds of choosing, having reviewed 10 to 20 titles on one or two screens."
"Netflix's Recommendation Systems: Entertainment Made for You." *Illumin Magazine*, February 2022.

Waters, Dave.
"Listening to Bill Gates, Elon Musk and Stephen Hawking talk about artificial intelligence reminds me of the Jurassic Park scene where they talk about chaos theory."
Public address, August 2016.
Dave Waters is a professor at Oxford University.

Wilson, E.O.
"The real problem of humanity is the following: We have Paleolithic emotions, medieval institutions, and godlike technology."
Quote from his book *The Future of Life.* Vintage, reprint edition, March 11, 2003.

Winterson, Jeanette.
"Our habits and our fears make our choices. We are an algorithm of ourselves."
The Gap of Time. Hogarth, 2018.

Wozniak, Steve.
"Like people including Stephen Hawking and Elon Musk have predicted, I agree that the future is scary and very bad for people. If we build these devices to take care of everything for us, eventually they'll think faster than us and they'll get rid of the slow humans to run companies more efficiently."
Storm, Darlene. "Steve Wozniak on AI: Will we be pets or mere ants to be squashed by our robot overlords?" *Computerworld*, March 25, 2015.
[https://www.computerworld.com/article/1637849/steve-wozniak-on-ai-will-we-be-pets-or-mere-ants-to-be-squashed-our-robot-overlords.html]

YouTube video, page 43.
AI-robotic eldercare pilot program developed by the author and Dr. William Klein, 2018.
[https://www.youtube.com/watch?v=7VLEddhZ_x8]

YouTube video, page 97.
[https://www.youtube.com/watch?v=ZBsJ3UlYFCY]

The AI Motion Picture Prototyper was developed in 2014–2016 by award-winning cinematographer and visual effects pioneer Scott Billups and computer scientist Bill Klein, Ph.D. to use AI to generate a working prototype of a motion picture from an annotated script.

YouTube video, page 100.
CVS Demo #4, December 19, 2021.
[https://www.youtube.com/watch?v=05sUEK1NFZY]

This is a live test of the StayWell app, developed by the author and his development team. This test was focused on evaluating the responsiveness when transitioning between the IBM Watson Health Cloud and the user's local resource using Edge Computing.

Zuckerberg, Mark.
"Augmented reality enhances the way we see and interact with the world. It blurs the lines between what's real and what's computer-generated by enhancing what we hear, see, and feel."
Excerpt from Zuckerberg's keynote address at his Facebook F8 conference, 2016.

Mark Zuckerberg is the CEO of Meta Platforms, Inc.

ADDITIONAL RESOURCES:

Amatriain, X., and J. Basilico. *Recommender Systems: The Textbook.* Cambridge University Press, 2023.

Aufderheide, P. and P. Jaszi. *Reclaiming Fair Use: How to Put Balance Back in Copyright.* University of Chicago Press, 2018.

Barker, C., and M. Wiatrowski. *The Age of Netflix: Critical Essays on Streaming Media, Digital Delivery and Instant Access.* McFarland & Company, 2022.

Benkler, Y. *The Wealth of Networks: How Social Production Transforms Markets and Freedom.* Yale University Press, 2021.

Bolin, G. *Value and the Media: Cultural Production and Consumption in Digital Markets.* Routledge, 2021.

Buolamwini, J., and T. Gebru. *Gender Shades: Intersectional Accuracy Disparities in Commercial Gender Classification.* MIT Media Lab, 2023.

Chamorro-Premuzic, T. *The AI Revolution: How Artificial Intelligence is Reshaping Our Entertainment.* John Wiley & Sons, 2022.

Coombe, R. J. *The Cultural Life of Intellectual Properties: Authorship, Appropriation, and the Law*. Duke University Press, 2018.

Decherney, P. *Hollywood's Copyright Wars: From Edison to the Internet*. Columbia University Press, 2022.

Finn, E. *What Algorithms Want: Imagination in the Age of Computing*. MIT Press, 2023.

Gillespie, T. "The Politics of 'Platforms'." *New Media & Society* 12, no. 3 (2023): 347–64.

Hallinan, B., and T. Striphas. "Recommended for you: The Netflix Prize and the production of algorithmic culture." *New Media & Society* 18, no. 1 (2022): 117–37.

Harris, T. *Hooked: How to Build Habit-Forming Products*. Portfolio, 2021.

Jenkins, H. *Convergence Culture: Where Old and New Media Collide*. NYU Press, 2022.

Lessig, L. *Free Culture: The Nature and Future of Creativity*. Penguin Books, 2020.

Lobato, R., and J. Thomas. *The Informal Media Economy*. Polity Press, 2023.

Pariser, E. *The Filter Bubble: What The Internet Is Hiding From You*. Penguin Books, 2021.

Pasquale, F. *The Black Box Society: The Secret Algorithms That Control Money and Information*. Harvard University Press, 2023.

Patry, W. *How to Fix Copyright*. Oxford University Press, 2019.

Turow, J. *The Voice Catchers: How Marketers Listen In to Exploit Your Feelings, Your Privacy, and Your Wallet*. Yale University Press, 2022.

Vaidhyanathan, S. *Intellectual Property: A Very Short Introduction*. Oxford University Press, 2021.

Wu, T. *The Attention Merchants: The Epic Scramble to Get Inside Our Heads*. Knopf, 2023.

Zuboff, S. *The Age of Surveillance Capitalism: The Fight for a Human Future at the New Frontier of Power*. PublicAffairs, 2022.

INDEX

ABOUT THE AUTHOR

Photo courtesy of A.M.P.A.S.

Scott Billups left medical school to apprentice with Oscar-winning cinematographer James Wong Howe. From there, he quickly became known as a creative powerhouse in Hollywood, racking up credits as a cinematographer and visual effects maestro on over fifty films and countless commercials. Notably, he blazed trails by birthing virtual actors including Marlon Brando for the big screen, a virtual Marilyn Monroe for a GTE Super Bowl commercial, and thousands of digital stunt doubles and weapon-wielding fighters for countless movies and documentaries.

After establishing himself as a maverick in virtual character creation, Scott went back to school at the ripe old age of 40 to study AI as a way to breathe life into his inanimate creations. Armed with an entirely new tool set, he served as CTO of the game industry's leading supplier of AI, spearheaded an AI-robotic eldercare program for the National Institutes of Health, and launched an AI health care startup that harnessed IBM Watson to create the first AMA-acknowledged virtual clinician.

As the Chief Technology Officer and Visual Effects Supervisor of Evergreen Studios, Scott created over a thousand AI-driven characters for the $100 million motion picture, *Walking with Dinosaurs 3D.*

He also oversaw the development of an augmented reality viewfinder system adopted by James Cameron for the *Avatar* sequels and developed an Academy Award-nominated, AI-driven, motion picture content generator with noted computer scientist Dr. Bill Klein. That content generator was quickly patented and sold to a major studio that uses it to previsualize movies before they are greenlit for production. It has remained under an avalanche of NDAs and non-competes for over eight years. And now, as those NDAs expire, the content generator serves as a timely preview of the coming wave of AI-driven creation engines that will redefine all media production. With links to demos, unseen since its initial development, readers will witness and hear firsthand from industry luminaries who have used it about the technology that, till now, has only been a speculative rumor.

Apart from his gig as Apple's first Hollywood Evangelist, Scott served as a contributing editor for *Videography* and *Digital Cinema* magazines, each for over a decade. His popular three-book series, Digital Moviemaking, is widely considered the definitive guidebook to Hollywood's digital age.

Recruited by a Department of Defense think tank, Billups now thrives in the murky area between Hollywood and defense, contributing to AI-based projects for NASA, Lockheed Martin, DARPA, and others.

Scott Billups' extraordinary journey and hands-on wisdom infuse *Post-Cinema* with real-world experience, offering readers tangible examples and priceless insights into the challenging landscape of our AI-driven future.

Perhaps *WIRED* magazine summarized Scott best: *"Billups is Hollywood's baddest pixel-packing cowboy, riding on the fringes of an industry that views him with interest, admiration, and some degree of incomprehension."*

© Michele Montez

MICHAEL WIESE PRODUCTIONS

In a dark time, a light bringer came along, leading the curious and the frustrated to clarity and empowerment. It took the well-guarded secrets out of the hands of the few and made them available to all. It spread a spirit of openness and creative freedom, and built a storehouse of knowledge dedicated to the betterment of the arts.

The essence of Michael Wiese Productions (MWP) is empowering people who have the burning desire to express themselves creatively. We help them realize their dreams by putting the tools in their hands. We demystify the sometimes secretive worlds of screenwriting, directing, acting, producing, film financing, and other media crafts.

By doing so, we hope to bring forth a realization of 'conscious media,' which we define as being positively charged, emphasizing hope, and affirming positive values like trust, cooperation, self-empowerment, freedom, and love. Grounded in the deep roots of myth, it aims to be healing both for those who make the art and those who encounter it. It hopes to be transformative for people, opening doors to new possibilities and pulling back veils to reveal hidden worlds.

MWP has built a storehouse of knowledge unequaled in the world, for no other publisher has so many titles on the media arts. Please visit www.mwp.com, where you will find many free resources and a 25% discount on our books. Sign up and become part of the wider creative community!

Michael Wiese, Co-Publisher
Geraldine Overton, Co-Publisher